How Does the Constitution Protect Religious Freedom?

American Enterprise Institute for Public Policy Research

A DECADE OF STUDY OF THE CONSTITUTION

How Does the Constitution Protect Religious Freedom?

Robert A. Goldwin
and Art Kaufman
editors

American Enterprise Institute for Public Policy Research
Washington D.C.

This book is the sixth in a series in AEI's project "A Decade of Study of the Constitution," funded in part by grants from the National Endowment for the Humanities. A full list of the titles appears on the series page.

Distributed by arrangement with

UPA, Inc.
4720 Boston Way   3 Henrietta Street
Lanham, MD 20706   London WC2E 8LU England

Library of Congress Cataloging-in-Publication Data

How does the Constitution protect religious freedom?

(AEI studies ; 462)
  1. Freedom of religion—United States.   2. Church and
state—United States.   I. Goldwin, Robert A., 1922–
II. Kaufman, Art.   III. Series.
KF4783.H69   1987   342.73'0852   87-17458
                       347.302852
ISBN 0-8447-3636-8 (alk. paper)
ISBN 0-8447-3635-X (pbk. : alk. paper)

AEI Studies 462   *Printed in the United States of America*

Contents

The Editors and the Authors

ROBERT A. GOLDWIN is resident scholar and codirector of constitutional studies at the American Enterprise Institute. He has served in the White House as special consultant to the president and, concurrently, as adviser to the secretary of defense. He has taught at the University of Chicago and at Kenyon College and was dean of St. John's College in Annapolis. He is the editor of a score of books on American politics, coeditor of the AEI series of volumes on the Constitution, and author of numerous articles, including "Why Blacks, Women, and Jews Are Not Mentioned in the Constitution" and "Of Men and Angels: A Search for Morality in the Constitution."

ART KAUFMAN is a research assistant in the Department of Government at Georgetown University. He has served as acting director of educational programs at the Commission on the Bicentennial of the U.S. Constitution, assistant director of constitutional studies at the American Enterprise Institute, program officer at the Institute for Educational Affairs, and assistant editor of *The Public Interest* magazine. He has taught constitutional law at the Catholic University of America and is coeditor, with Robert A. Goldwin, of *Separation of Powers: Does It Still Work?*, published by AEI.

HENRY J. ABRAHAM is James Hart Professor of Government and Foreign Affairs at the University of Virginia. He has taught and lectured extensively in political science, government, and constitutional law in the United States and abroad. He serves on the advisory committees and editorial boards of numerous organizations and publications, such as the Council of Editors of the *Journal of Church and State*. His many publications include *Freedom and the Court: Civil Rights and Liberties in the United States* (originally published in 1967, now entering its fifth edition), "The Status of the First Amendment's Religion Clauses: Some Reflections on Lines and Limits," and "The Judicial Function under the Constitution: Theory and Practice."

DEAN M. KELLEY, an ordained minister of the United Methodist Church, has been the executive director for religious and civil liberty at the National Council of Churches since 1960. He is the author of *Why Conservative Churches Are Growing* and *Why Churches Should Not Pay Taxes* and editor of *Government Intervention in Religious Affairs*. He was also codirector of the Project on Church, State, and Taxation of the National Conference of Christians and Jews.

LEONARD W. LEVY is Andrew W. Mellon All-Claremont Professor of Humanities and chairman, graduate faculty of history, Claremont Graduate School. He is the author of twenty-seven books on legal and constitutional history. His *Origins of the Fifth Amendment* won the Pulitzer Prize in history in 1969. His most recent book is *The Establishment Clause: Religion and the First Amendment*. He is editor in chief of the recently published four-volume *Encyclopedia of the American Constitution*.

JAMES MCCLELLAN is founder and director of the Center for Judicial Studies and editor of *Benchmark,* a journal on the Constitution and the courts. From 1981 to 1983 he was chief counsel and staff director of the subcommittee on separation of powers of the Judiciary Committee, U.S. Senate. He has served as an aide to Senators John East, Orrin Hatch, and Jesse Helms and has taught political science at several colleges and universities. His publications include *Joseph Story and the American Constitution,* "The Making and the Unmaking of the Establishment Clause," and "Congressional Retraction of Federal Court Jurisdiction to Protect the Reserved Powers of the States." He is also editor of Jonathan Eliot's *Debates on the Adoption of the Constitution* (five volumes, forthcoming).

HARVEY C. MANSFIELD, JR., is professor of government at Harvard University. He is the author of *Statesmanship and Party Government, The Spirit of Liberalism,* and *Selected Letters of Edmund Burke.* He is also editor of *Selected Writings of Thomas Jefferson,* which includes his own essay on Jefferson. His numerous other articles include "Burke on Christianity," "Hobbes and the Science of Indirect Government," and "The Forms and Formalities of Liberty."

JEFFREY JAMES POELVOORDE is assistant professor of political science at Converse College in Spartanburg, South Carolina. He has taught political philosophy, American government, and constitutional law at several colleges and universities, including the College of William and Mary, Hampden-Sidney, Carleton, and Dickinson Colleges and at the University of Virginia. He is the author of *Executive Privilege, Executive Power, and the Constitution* (Ph.D. dissertation) and "Statesmanship and American Foreign Policy."

WILLIAM H. REHNQUIST is chief justice of the United States, appointed by President Reagan and confirmed by the U.S. Senate in 1986. He was associate justice of the Supreme Court of the United States from 1972 to 1986 and served under President Nixon as assistant attorney general, Office of Legal Counsel, Department of Justice. He is the author of many articles on legal subjects in professional journals.

Preface

In 1785, before the Philadelphia Convention met to draft the Constitution of the United States, James Madison wrote and distributed to his fellow Virginians "A Memorial and Remonstrance against Religious Assessments" (reproduced in the appendix to this volume), which included this statement on the relationship between church and state: "The Religion . . . of every man must be left to the conviction and conscience of every man; and it is the right of every man to exercise it as these may dictate."

Few if any Americans today would quarrel with this statement of principle or the sentiment it conveys; yet issues involving government and religion are among the most contentious confronting us as a nation. This book, therefore, examines the origins of the constitutional separation of church and state and the difficulty of achieving both the security of religion in society and its free exercise.

The fact that Madison and others had to argue against what they considered to be establishment of religion in Virginia (and in other states) indicates that the place of religion in a democratic republic was a subject of great debate at the time of the founding. But the number and variety of issues having to do with the relation—or separation—of church and state are even greater today. The specific issues are familiar enough to all of us: prayer in public schools, abortion, tuition tax credits, the teaching of creationism, use of public funds or facilities by parochial schools, and rules regarding tax-exempt status for churches and religious schools, among others.

Religion, it should be noted, was mentioned only once in the original, unamended Constitution—in the provision prohibiting religious tests for government office. Given the alliances between church and state in the old world, however, and the religious tests that were required in most of the states at the time, for many of the framers this crucial prohibition, together with the Constitution's enumeration of limited powers, went a long way to ensure the protection of religious and other civil rights.

The Anti-Federalists, however—those who opposed ratification of the Constitution—thought more explicit provisions were needed, and they were provided. The First Amendment consequently declares that "Congress shall make no law respecting an establishment of religion, or prohibiting the free exercise thereof."

Few constitutional provisions would seem to surpass these in legal clarity. Yet the past forty years have seen the Supreme Court continuously laboring to achieve a consistent interpretation of them, and critics of the Court (including several writers in this volume) have been alleging for just as long that the Court has erred in serious ways, and not only in its inconsistency.

Some authors of the following essays contend that the establishment and the free exercise clauses taken together are designed to guarantee free exercise and that it is in its free exercise that religion itself is protected. From their point of view, government must be neutral, not only among the various religious sects in society, but also between religion and irreligion. Others argue that because religion is essential to the success of a free society, "establishment" should be understood narrowly, so that not every instance of aid to religion is considered to be establishment, just so long as the support does not discriminate in favor of one sect over others. In their view, the framers of the First Amendment had in mind only to answer the states' fears that the new national government would attempt to establish a national religion, or infringe upon their own church-state relations.

Several writers in this book, therefore, also examine the so-called incorporation doctrine, through which the Supreme Court has made the First Amendment religion clauses, explicitly addressed to Congress, applicable to the states by incorporating those clauses into the due process clause of the Fourteenth Amendment. Some contend that no such incorporation was intended by those who wrote and ratified the Fourteenth Amendment; others contend that it is essential to the concept of fundamental liberty.

Much as we may wish to the contrary, however, the question posed by this book—How does the Constitution protect religious freedom?—cannot be answered only by reference to legal doctrines that have emerged during two centuries under the Constitution. It is equally important to examine the origins of the separation of church and state in the political thought that preceded the American founding. The first essay in this volume examines these philosophical origins.

Finally, it is evident that after two centuries under the Constitution the multiplicity of religious sects that James Madison looked to for the protection of religious freedom has, in fact, emerged in our society. Despite this diversity, or perhaps because of it, Americans are committed to peculiarly American principles, institutions, and traditions that unite them. To what extent do these constitute an American civil religion? Does public support for such a civil religion violate the establishment clause of the First Amendment? If not, what, if anything, ought to be done to sustain it? These questions are addressed in the final essay.

The authors in this volume have been deliberately chosen because they disagree with one another about the fundamental issues of church and state under the Constitution. As in the other volumes in AEI's series on the Constitution, each essay is followed by another written from a different point of view. The authors are all authoritatively knowledgeable on the subject, but their analyses lead to different conclusions. Readers are therefore left to ponder the divergent interpretations of the facts and the arguments presented in order to reach their own conclusions. On few subjects is the contemplation of such different views so essential as the protection of religious freedom, especially in the year of the bicentennial of the Constitution.

ROBERT A. GOLDWIN
ART KAUFMAN

1

The Religious Issue and the Origin of Modern Constitutionalism

Harvey C. Mansfield, Jr.

The religious issue was deeply and hotly contested at the origin of modern constitutionalism in the seventeenth century. To see this, one has only to note that the three great founders of constitutionalism to be considered here—Hobbes, Spinoza, and Locke—devoted much of their studies and large portions of their most famous political works to the Bible and its political implications. Two of the four parts of Hobbes's *Leviathan* (1651) concern the Christian theology required for or compatible with his notion of sovereignty. Spinoza's *Theologico-Political Treatise* (1670) is entirely an analysis of Scripture with a view to the consequences for free inquiry and free government. And the first of Locke's *Two Treatises of Government* (1690), together with his *Letter Concerning Toleration* (1690), reveals the same interest in repelling the claims of divine right. For the "religious issue," or the "theologico-political" problem (to use Spinoza's term), is whether men are ruled by God or gods, hence by divine right, or by themselves on principles they discern without necessarily referring to the word of God in Scripture. If rule derives from divinity, all government is theocracy, more or less, since even if priests are not rulers, rulers are required by the principles of divine right to serve, in some sense, as priests. If rule is made by men, government is constituted by human choice out of human nature, and "constitutional government" so understood, though it may seek or accept the support of religion, is not based on—is indeed constituted against—divine right.

To see the continuing importance of the religious issue, however, is not so easy as to recognize its original importance. In our day, the "social issue" appears to be dominant. The social issue dates, perhaps, from the end of the eighteenth century, and, through the nineteenth century, as socialism gained force, it increasingly preoccupied the politics of constitutional governments. Generically, the social issue is the age-old conflict between the rich and the poor, but in constitutional government it has taken a specific form that is reflected in the word *social*. The social issue arose when it was observed or alleged that society, which is private (as we say today, "the private sphere"), was not autonomous because it was not providing for the poor; hence political intervention, either welfare legislation or revolution, was needed to restore the balance of society. This issue now appears paramount because it is the crux both of party conflict within constitutional regimes and of international conflict between constitutional and Communist regimes.

But why should one expect "society" to exist separately, if not altogether independently, from the state, and thus to have its own autonomy or balance? To appreciate the social issue today, one must understand why we assume "society" to exist. This assumption was first put forth in arguments that Hobbes, Spinoza, and Locke used to confront the religious issue; thus to understand the social issue, one must understand the religious issue. One could even suggest that the religious issue *was* the social issue in its first appearance, and that the social issue as it appears today is the consequence of the religious issue. If politics is defined by its issues, the religious issue at the origin of modern constitutionalism is still at the heart of modern constitutionalism.

The State-Society Distinction

Modern constitutional government is limited government, in which the limitation on government is expressed in the distinction between "state" and "society." Invented by Hobbes and developed first by Spinoza and Locke and then by Adam Smith among others, this distinction has become, with the success of liberal constitutionalism, a fundamental belief rarely questioned in our time. We in the liberal democracies do not agree on what government should do or how far it should go, but we do agree that certain things, however we define them, are not the business of the state. The state, which is public, is in the service of society, which is private; and the state is limited to this service as a means is limited by its end. This is not the whole truth, because we do speak of "the public" as having authority over merely private, that is, individual, inclinations, and because constitutional formalities, such as due process of law, cannot be understood merely as means to an end. The subordination of state to society, however, is the main truth of constitutional government, which is shared by liberals, conservatives, and even radicals, despite the various pet projects of intervention in others' liberties cherished by all three parties. That these projects are known as "intervention" indicates the general expectation that government be limited; and their intent, as with the social issue, is to restore the balance of society and enable it to function on its own with only minimum regulation and without being ruled by government.

The basis of the distinction between state and society was stated clearly by John Locke in his *A Letter Concerning Toleration:* it is the further distinction between body and soul. The magistrate, Locke says, has jurisdiction only over "civil interests" such as "life, liberty, health, and indolency of body," together with property, and his power "neither can nor ought in any manner to be extended to the salvation of souls." Society is the realm of the soul, or today what passes for the soul, the self. Thus the distinction between body and soul responsible for the modern constitutional distinction between state and society is stated in the context of the religious issue. But what of private economic activity concerned not with the soul, it would appear, but with material well-being? Constitutional government encourages it, we find, not only because it makes people rich but also because it keeps their souls occupied with harmless, or at least bloodless, acquisition and prompts them to put aside contentious recipes for saving their souls. Today, the economy is said even by economists to be determined by tastes, preferences, or other attitudes of soul in consumers and by enterprise and opportunity seeking in producers: these are affected and regulated, but not prescribed or ruled, by government.

Difficulty arises for the constitutional distinction between state and society when the soul, in its unruly desire to rule itself, tries to rule other souls: that is, when a part of society seeks to use the power of the state to rule the whole of society. For it seems unreasonable not to apply the rule one follows for oneself to others, especially in a matter of importance that is not to be decided by mere idiosyncratic taste. For example, in the abortion debate in America today, the prochoice party is as eager to rule fellow citizens as is the apparently more prescriptive prolife party; one wants a society in which abortion is respectable, and the other wants one in which it is abhorred. These are two very different societies because they would be ruled differently. From such examples it may easily be inferred that the desire to rule others has its root in the desire to rule oneself; thus in societies attempting to maintain a distinction between state and society, in time one hears less of "soul" and more of "self," then less of "self-control" and more of "self-expression."

Our constitutionalist distinction between state and society seems

3

to promote, if not require, a distinction between body and soul in which the soul gradually abdicates its ruling function. This is the apathetic "individualism" that Tocqueville feared, which we see in the wishy-washy liberal and the uncaring conservative or, on the contrary, the rebellious and aggressive self-expression of angry radicals, which equally endangers the constitutional distinction between state and society. How can the state serve society if society craves the state? If government is to remain limited, individuals must be able to rule themselves, at least to some extent, and to do this, religion—which reminds us of the importance of our souls—might seem indispensable.

We have therefore uncovered, in the principle and in the probable history of modern constitutionalism, both a hostility to religion and a positive function for religion. Hostility to religion produces the constitutional distinction between state and society, in order to prevent the state from attempting to save our souls in accordance with the demands of religion. That distinction leaves concern for souls to private individuals in society. But if individuals are not to be responsible for others' souls, why should they be responsible for their own? To enjoin citizens from tyrannizing over their fellows, constitutional government runs the risk of leaving them unconcerned, both for their fellows and for themselves. This risk will appear in the social issue as well as in the religious issue since one can ask, Why be responsible for poverty in property if not for poverty of soul? The answer that religion gives to the question, Why be responsible?, will always be more convincing to more people than any fancy, theoretical calculation of self-interest. But then, if religion is required to maintain responsibility and autonomy in society, so that society does not become dependent on the state, how do we keep religion within constitutional bounds? For religion, as religion, is primarily concerned with saving souls, not with constitutional freedom. With this difficulty in mind, let us see what can be learned from Hobbes, Spinoza, and Locke.

Hobbes: The Question of Sovereignty

Modern constitutionalism, having its origin in Hobbes, was from the first opposed to a rival constitutionalism that began with Plato, was most highly developed by Aristotle, and had its proponents in the seventeenth century (Philip Hunton, George Lawson, Marchamont Nedham, and John Milton among others). This constitutionalism shared the fear of fanatic religious partisanship that animates modern constitutionalism, but instead of finding the solution in limited government, it aimed at a mixed government. Instead of limiting what government might do in response to the demands of *any* party, it attempted to mix what was reasonable and just in the claims of *all* parties. To this end, Aristotelian constitutionalism laid emphasis on the soul and its individual responsibility, because it was only by virtue of some such universal element in all human beings that partisans might be persuaded to do justice to the claims of rival partisans to establish a common or more common good in a mixed constitution. To educate and cultivate just souls was, therefore, so far from prohibited to government as to constitute its main business, and the realm of the "political" was understood to comprehend both state and society as now conceived ("state" meant constitution or regime in the wider sense, and "society" referred to a particular group within the political).

According to Hobbes, this Aristotelian constitutionalism did not work. Rather than moderating, it endorsed and even intensified religious partisanship. The common good, which is intended as the goal to which the parties of a mixed constitution would contribute, becomes in fact an external standard with which to criticize and attack every existing regime. Various parties offer diverse interpretations of the common good, so that the "common good" has no effectual force against their partisanship; tyranny, for example, said to be contrary to the common good, is merely "monarchy misliked." Similarly, the soul, which according to Aristotelian constitutionalism makes men responsible for their actions and capable of justice, according to Hobbes is often captured by vainglorious imagination that makes men strut, boast, and fight one another over senseless issues. Our fears as well as our hopes turn us from the care and perfection of our souls to a more down-to-earth concern for what will happen to us. Under pressure from this concern, yet too lazy to think the problem through, we quickly settle on an invisible cause of our well-being and personify it so that we can assume it is as interested in us as we are in it—calling it "God." Thus, care for the soul's perfection is transformed into anxiety for its salvation, and individual responsibility is handed over to God, or rather to those who claim to speak for God—prophets and priests.

Against this mixed constitution and its disastrously unsuccessful (as Hobbes deemed it) program to moderate religious partisanship, Hobbes raised the question of sovereignty. He raised that question with an extremism never before seen, for he demanded that, to secure government against partisans, not any particular party or combination of parties should win, but someone, *anyone*, should win. The condition necessary to establish sovereignty is that all parties recognize that winning in politics is all-important or that human power (Hobbes was the first political scientist to make a theme of "power") is the sole consideration. All parties based on some (religious) principle that leaves them content to lose or prompts them to fight to the death—indeed, all parties in all politics hitherto—are to be shown by Hobbes's demonstration that their pride is vanity and that their partisans should surrender their otherworldly or utopian goals and put peace foremost. Because men are impelled by religion and vain philosophy to fight over a vision of perfection they never actually see, the establishment of *civil* sovereignty requires the establishment of *human* sovereignty. To seek peace, men must set aside anything supernatural or invisible that might make demands on them and look to their own necessities. The sovereignty of man means the sovereignty of human necessities as opposed to human perfection.

Hobbes's demonstration of this truth is made with the famous "state of nature," a notion he invented that was adopted by Spinoza and Locke and has been fundamental to modern constitutionalism and liberalism (broadly defined) ever since. The state of nature is a prepolitical condition in which men live without conventional restraints or advantages, using only the advantages of their human nature. Though such a state will not ordinarily be before our eyes, we can easily and reasonably imagine it, by contrast to the prophetic dreams of divine revelation. From the fact that we lock our doors and even closets within doors when a government exists, we can infer that without a government, no uncoercive human association could subsist, and men would live miserably in a state of war. And in such a war we can readily imagine that the best or strongest individual would be as vulnerable as the weakest, since cunning would be equal to wisdom and muscle. The state of nature would be a condition of war and equality altogether contrary to that set forth in the Bible in which the first humans, before they sinned, lived in peace and were perhaps equal to one another but, above all, creatures of God, subject to him, and, after they sinned, in need of divine grace. That Hobbes's state of nature is a state of war indicates that men were forced to sin out of necessity, that therefore they did not really sin when scratching or fighting for their lives.

The remedy for "sin," moreover, is not divine grace but a human sovereign with adequate power, that is, human power so plainly visible to men in its execution as to be uncontestable by them. How can such a sovereign be found? Hobbes—this is *his* utopian revolutionism—does not believe that any actual sovereign has ever had the requisite authority. All sovereigns have rested their authority, in the Aristotelian manner, on the claim of a particular political party that has attempted to suppress the claims of rivals. As we have seen, however, the very virtue claimed for such regimes serves first as a standard with which to judge them, then as a lever with which to overturn them. Uncontestable authority can be established only by an appeal to the state of nature, where men are equal and no claim to rule, whether monarchical, aristocratic, or democratic, can reasonably be made. In this state of equality and war, each person has by nature an equal right of self-preservation and, to maintain this right, a further right to be the judge of the means of his preservation. Thus quite precisely, according to Hobbes, nothing is sacred in the state of nature, and each has a right to everything; neither God nor fellow human has property that one must respect. Any claim to sovereignty must be constructed from the ground up, for no conventional claim can be valid in the state of nature, and an examination of that state leads certainly and obviously to the conclusion that no claim of any man to rule another based on a natural superiority can be valid either.

The sovereign authorized by the exercise of men's natural right of self-preservation is wholly artificial and absolute: wholly artificial in order to be absolute, because only natural superiority might be contested by partisans. Since no actual sovereign has ever been absolute, however, Hobbes's doctrine of sovereignty cannot rest on experience but must be expressed in a natural law that calls for the first simply unlimited and undivided sovereign known to history. Although this doctrine has a realistic beginning in the state of nature, it issues in a surprising legalism. Hobbes's natural law consists in what it is reasonable for men in the state of nature to do to seek peace by subjecting themselves to a sovereign; and this reasoning is powerfully supported by fear of violent death should it not be followed. Yet despite this reliance on an unexalted reason and the passion of fear, Hobbes's doctrine of sovereignty teaches, even exhorts, men to act not as they have, nor as they would, but rather as they should. His realism does not simply endorse the world as it is, but seeks to transform it by a novel legalism that requires men to shed their illusions and be their real, as opposed to their actual, selves. This legalism tries to compel us to ignore the actual facts of politics, which always limit the sovereignty even of the most tyrannical governments; for those powers in Hobbes's society that are denied the right to challenge the sovereign will nonetheless have to be respected by him in practice. It is an odd realism that exhorts men to behave as they never have before and an equally odd legalism that defines the law as anything the sovereign wills; but both the one and the other are the essence of Hobbes's sovereign.

Thus Hobbes's doctrine could hardly be more ambivalent in its attitude toward constitutionalism. On the one hand, nothing appears more opposed to constitutionalism than a teaching that every sovereign must be obeyed regardless (almost) of what he does and that there must be no formal constitution of institutions to ensure limited government. On the other hand, Hobbes's doctrine of natural rights establishes a distinction between state and society by removing every duty of the sovereign to educate or compel men to live more virtuously than they would without him, except as virtue is defined as obeying him. As long as men obey the law, they will have considerable liberty in the silences of the law, for Hobbes tells his sovereigns that it is in their interest to require as little as possible from their subjects. Moreover, the natural right to self-preservation has "constitutional" effects in Hobbes's system; he is, for example, the first to allow a right against self-incrimination. And when, far from wanting to abolish Parliament, Hobbes encourages the sovereign to seek counsel from it, he permits a latent constitutionalism to moderate the absolute sovereign in practice.

Hobbes's disposition of religion reflects his ambivalence toward constitutionalism. Religion, according to him, is based on fear of invisible spirits as opposed to fear of the visible sovereign. It causes trouble both by challenging the sovereign, thus disturbing the peace, and by flattering the sovereign, thus tempting him into tyranny. Yet Hobbes does not believe it possible, necessary, or desirable to abolish religion. Even though his doctrine replaces the Bible with the state of nature as the foundation of politics, he expounds in the second half of *Leviathan* a Christianity that serves the purposes of his sovereign while answering human need. There is a "natural seed of religion" in the human propensity to seek an invisible cause of one's well-being. This seed is tirelessly cultivated by the three classes of big talkers to be found in civilized societies—lawyers, priests, and scholars. While attacking them, Hobbes admits religion into society despite the fact that it is based on the principle contrary to that of true sovereignty. Although he tries to prove that Christianity neither needs nor challenges the state, there is no guarantee that his proof will be successful, and in the event, of course, it was not.

As to the soul, Hobbes defines it away. Soul cannot be found in the world of Hobbes's science, which recognizes only bodies in motion. Human beings are moved by necessity—both by reason, which compels them to see how things must be, and by fear and other passions that bring necessity into the next moment of one's life. True choice and true elevation are equally impossible, and so, therefore, is human responsibility. Hobbes's doctrine of authorized sovereignty seems to be a system of human sovereignty by which men for the first time take control of their lives, but in fact it is not. The sovereign is irresponsible because he does not have to answer to anyone, including God; and the people, though formally responsible for every act of the sovereign they have authorized, are actually irresponsible because they must do nothing themselves but accept everything he does.

Spinoza: Natural Right Entire

In Spinoza's works, criticism of revealed religion is even more prominent than in Hobbes's. His *Theologico-Political Treatise* is a criticism of superstition, first by appeal to the Bible and then by appeal from the Bible to reason, the philosopher's reason. Superstition is invented and used by rulers and priests to suppress political freedom in the people and free inquiry among philosophers. In the preface to this book, Spinoza establishes a connection or alliance among religious freedom, democracy, and philosophy in opposition to suppression, hierarchy, and superstition. More precisely, since his philosophy establishes an alliance between religious freedom and political freedom, his politics can be called "constitutionalist." By prudent forbearance, more than by respect for right, Spinoza's state does not attempt to impose itself on society. Although the distinction between state and society is not derived from the natural right of individuals, is not defined legally, and is not protected by constitutional forms and liberties, nonetheless it exists or can be made to exist in effect. Spinoza is known for equating right with might. Let us see how this equation arises from his treatment of the religious issue and how, contrary to our expectation, it results in a practicing constitutionalism.

Spinoza's criticism of the Bible begins with the quite orthodox statement that prophecy or revelation is sure knowledge. But then, by degrees of gradual but relentless insinuation, revelation is revealed to be mere imagination dreamed up to delude a vulgar people. Revelation is temporarily equated with natural knowledge and then, by comparison with it, rejected; next, revelation is relegated to moral truth and then, by comparison with that, again rejected. Spinoza carries this argument to an open denial of the miracles that attest to revelation. He says that since God's power is infinite, we cannot know what is naturally possible, hence cannot know what is supernatural, hence cannot know what is miraculous. Hobbes had said this much, but the bolder Spinoza adds that since God is wise, he would not attempt miracles that would not be convincing as such. Therefore, miracles are impossible as well as unknowable, and it is presumptuous and *impious* to believe in them. Spinoza's premise in this mode of argumentation (which is an elaborate and impudent begging

9

of the question) is that God's will is identical to his intellect, hence perfectly open to human inspection. If it is claimed that God's will is revealed in the Bible, then the Bible can be read as if it were a human book. So read by Spinoza, the founder of historical study of the Bible, it proves to be a very inferior book.

Now, since God's will is infinite, so too is his creation, nature. Nature has no limits defining what is possible; nothing that happens is any more natural than anything else. This means that nothing that happens is any more providential than anything else. The Jews are not God's chosen people; God cares equally for all, that is, for all nature, that is, for no one in particular. It is up to men to govern themselves, and thus Spinoza shares in the premise of modern constitutionalism that government is constituted by humans to answer human needs. Differing from Hobbes, however, Spinoza "keeps natural right entire." Since nothing is unnatural, everything has as much right as it has power; and men have no privileged exemption from this truth.

In consequence, Spinoza's politics lacks the legalism of Hobbes's. He does not agree with Hobbes that the artificial institution of sovereignty establishes the rule of law, supported by the promise to keep one's word as given in the social contract. For him, the sovereign is as natural as the "state of nature" preceding it; the rule of law is rule of the strongest, who made the law; and promises hold only so long as one is compelled to keep them. But if (or because) Spinoza's system lacks the advantages of constitutional legalism and formalism, it has a clearer, more consistent, more revealing realism. In place of Hobbes's authorized sovereign, who may be any form of government, Spinoza says straightforwardly that democracy is the "most natural and most consonant with the liberty, that nature grants to everyone." This is so not because democracy is more just, but because the people will demand their freedom, and not because democracy accords with the equality of rights, but because men will insist on their equality despite the facts. The facts are, according to Spinoza, that men are divided into the rational few and the irrational many. But it is rational for the few, who are weak, to defer to the many, who are strong. Spinoza does not try to maintain that democracy can be seen by the many to be in their interest; so he does not forget that democracy needs to be sustained by republican virtue, that is, martial virtue, and also by charity. Charity, or love of one's neighbor, cannot be supported by reason, since reason teaches men to take and keep what they can; so charity depends on faith. The main work of charity being to counteract religious fanaticism, it is one delusion set against another, worse delusion. After beginning from the standpoint that religion is *the* enemy of human reason and freedom, Spinoza concludes that religion, suitably redefined so that it amounts to charity and nothing more, is a necessary foundation of a free community.

Spinoza's democracy can be considered liberal and constitutionalist because it keeps a place (though not public status) for the wise as distinguished from the ignorant. Together with the "foundations" that qualify simple rule by the ignorant many, the wise will enjoy free inquiry and free speech. Although these are not constitutional "rights," free inquiry cannot be prevented anyway, and free speech is useful because it is inconvenient to priests. The aim of the state is merely bodily perfection (including the low, instrumental virtues mentioned above) as opposed to moral or theoretical perfection. The few who desire theoretical perfection in the life of a philosopher cannot ignore their need for bodily perfection but will not be hindered by demands for moral perfection, nor will the vulgar many who desire merely bodily perfection. In Spinoza the distinction between state and society is constituted by the absence of such demands (except for minimal martial and charitable virtues needed for bodily perfection). Most human souls want vulgar pleasures; some few want contemplation of the whole of nature. The freedom that both want unites them politically, but only in an external sense. The irrational many are irresponsible, and the rational few are responsible to the whole but not to humanity as humanity. The distinction between state and society does not allow—or require—philosophers to become kings.

Locke: Rule of Law

Locke's constitutionalism is close to ours and feels comfortable to us. Either it feels comfortable because it is close, or it is close because it feels comfortable, or both. Locke does not puzzle us with the odd legalism of Hobbes's notion of absolute sovereignty, and he does not frighten us with the unsettling realism of Spinoza's dictum that might makes right. Locke argues his constitutional politics more directly on political grounds. He put the principles of his politics into his *Two Treatises of Government* and left psychology and epistemology for his *Essay Concerning Human Understanding* and biblical criticism for his *Reasonableness of Christianity* and commentaries on St. Paul. Thus he does not force us, nor did he force his contemporaries, to confront the religious issue and to oppose religion with constitutionalism. Rather, he provides two arguments for a liberal constitution, religious and nonreligious, and presents them together, mingled and, it often seems, confused. On inspection, and after disentangling the two arguments, the same unsettling problems that Hobbes and Spinoza bring to the fore may be seen lurking in the shadows of Locke's talkative prose. The confusion, then, is perhaps not his but ours and is intended for our comfort. We should be wary of the fact that Locke is known both for his caution and for his confusion.

The first of Locke's *Two Treatises of Government* is on paternal power, the second on political power. The argument from the inadequacy of paternal power to the adequacy of political power does not seem to raise the religious issue—but in fact it does. Locke's *First Treatise* is devoted to an attack on Sir Robert Filmer's *Patriarcha*, in which Filmer tried to argue that political authority comes from God, hence is passed on, beginning with Adam, from father to father. In this view paternal power is the manifestation of God's rule among men, and true political power resembles paternal power as closely as possible. To refute this conclusion, Locke points out repeatedly that the Bible says "Honor thy father and thy mother," not merely father; so it grants not a single paternal power but a divided parental power. Moreover, Locke asks us to consider the nature of this grant: does it require us to obey our parents no matter what they command, or is the grant to our parents limited by God's other commands? Does the Fifth Commandment stand alone, or is it to be taken with the other commandments? In the latter case, surely the orthodox interpretation, God's grant of power to humans is given with strings attached, and human government is required to put God's commands above human needs. One should obey one's parents, and by extension the political authorities, only when they obey God. Thus Locke's discussion of the absurd doctrine of an obscure polemicist raises the same question of human sovereignty that we saw stated more directly by Hobbes and Spinoza.

Whether Locke answers this question in the same way as Hobbes and Spinoza or follows the Bible has been much disputed, and the doubt that Locke permits, or encourages, on this point is the prime instance of the confusion that has been attributed to him. At the beginning of the *Second Treatise*, Locke brings up the same unbiblical "state of nature" featured by Hobbes and Spinoza and describes it as a "state of perfect freedom . . . within the bounds of the law of nature." A state of perfect freedom is the contrary of a state of obligation toward one's creator, but what are the bounds set by the "law of nature"? Locke does not make it difficult to find them out; they are to preserve himself and the rest of mankind. He does make it difficult, however, to see whether the source of the law of nature is God or human nature regardless of God; so he makes it difficult to see whether following the law of nature is obeying or disobeying God. In any case, one can say, on the one hand, that he does not base his politics on the Bible or on divine right in any sense that overrules merely human needs and, on the other hand, that he expresses his politics not in terms of mere self-interest, but rather in terms of rights conjoined with duties. The duty to preserve others yields to the right to preserve oneself when the two come into competition, but Locke does his best to prevent them from doing so. The duty to preserve mankind in the state of nature is transformed into the duty to obey a constitutional government in civil society.

Constitutional government establishes the rule of law in the modern sense that has best been described by Locke. It is not mere sovereignty, as with Hobbes, or mere power, as with Spinoza; nor is it a mere voluntary association resembling an insurance company to serve as conduit from rights to policies, as with libertarian theorists in our day. The rule of law in its modern sense means not the rule of certain ancient laws or of a higher law of divine origin; nor does it mean the rule of natural law, for Locke says that in civil society, the natural law is simply the preservation of society or of the majority. It means rule by "declared laws" that have been made by the legislative power, which must therefore be both supreme and public. This rule of law is the rule of law making by a "due process" visible to all. On second thought, as it were, Locke admits that "declared laws" have to be complemented by prudence and discretion in the executive and federative (foreign affairs) powers; so the supremacy of the legislature is modified to secure a separation of powers. Thereby, government acquires a formal structure, respect for which is by itself a reassurance (if not a guarantee) that liberty is not endangered. The distinction between state and society, which in Hobbes and Spinoza is merely in the *interest* of both state and society, acquires a formal boundary of procedure to help decide when the state is rightfully intervening, or wrongfully intruding, in society. Whereas with Hobbes the sovereign "represents" the people whatever he does, in Locke's constitution due process in the government, as well as elections to Parliament, give "representation" a more determinate meaning. Though the structure is formal, it bears a convenient resemblance to the constitution of England (with a few alterations), so that Locke does not have to appear to be as revolutionary as do Hobbes and Spinoza. And with England as his model, Locke (in contrast to Hobbes) can forge an alliance with lawyers and allow the common law to specify the rights of citizens when Parliament does not decide. The problem of securing responsible sovereignty still remains, but it is muted and somewhat concealed. Just as today in constitutional democracies, when people elect but constantly denounce politicians, the question of who is responsible gets lost between the people and the government.

With a formal boundary to demarcate state from society, Locke can rely on the voluntary motion of society to secure its own autonomy more than could Hobbes and Spinoza, whose governments had to create their own supports, particularly official religions. The voluntary motion occurs in economics, education, and religion—three great concerns formerly political but treated extrapolitically as private matters in Locke's writings. In regard to religion, he argues against a civil or established religion and for a toleration of religion or sects now to be considered voluntary. Government cannot promise not to interfere with religion because it must ensure that religion does not interfere with government, which it tends, perhaps inevitably, to do. Why does religion tend to be intolerant and to seek, against the very idea of modern constitutionalism, to use government as its instrument? The answer is that religion teaches, inevitably, that men's souls belong to God. Locke says, however, that "the care . . . of every man's soul belongs unto himself." And what if he neglects the care of his soul? Locke answers, What if he neglects his health or his estate? The magistrate cannot force him to be rich or healthy against his consent, so cannot force him to save his soul. This is as much as to say that it is of the essence of the soul to be free to refuse responsibility for itself. It is not of the essence of the soul to cultivate or perfect itself, much less to obey God. The result is a negative freedom or self-satisfaction expressed not so much in gaining what one wants as in the power to refuse. The problem for education (see Locke's *Thoughts on Education*) would be to make something positive of this power and to convince men (or children) who believe they are already independent that they must *learn* to be independent. This is not easy, because to admit one needs to learn is to acknowledge one's dependence.

Modern constitutionalism as we see it in Hobbes, Spinoza, and Locke does not have a solution for the religious issue. A solution would be a society in which the highest human aspiration, the divinity in man, would thrive while human freedom was preserved: the rational society, perhaps, of Hegel, if that could be made to work. Our three constitutionalist philosophers had their hopes for a permanent improvement in human freedom, but they were too sober to believe that this could be done without cost. But did they correctly reckon the cost in human irresponsibility—even to their own project—when men are no longer required or expected to take care of their souls? The measures these philosophers adopted to contain religion by diminishing the soul seem also to endanger freedom.

2

Religion, the Constitution, the Court, and Society: Some Contemporary Reflections on Mandates, Words, Human Beings, and the Art of the Possible

Henry J. Abraham

When I wrote the first edition of my *Freedom and the Court*, now almost two decades ago,[1] my publisher, the Oxford University Press, for the first and only time in what has been an association of more than thirty years, requested that I change a substantive opinion I had penned, on the grounds that it would give needless and unwise offense to readers: My perceived offense was the statement "Like love and war, religion makes no sense except to those who embrace and practice it." Reluctantly, I agreed to remove the offender in favor of an elaborate footnote in which I outlined what I regarded as my own ecumenical experience.[2] Yet the contemporary scene is witness to the patent quotidian fact of life that my observation, however irreverent or flippant it may well be considered, does indeed inform significant aspects of the continuing separationist-accommodationist controversy.

A firm, let alone a permanent, resolution of the controversy, be it on constitutional, legal, political, or, for that matter, pure common sense grounds, is highly dubious at best. That pessimistic assessment is realistic, however, not only because of the long-time uncertainties concerning the meaning of constitutional language, the attendant inconsistencies of judicial interpretation, and the often spotty manifestations of societal compliance with apposite judicial orders and legislative mandates but also because of the absolutist stances of protagonists on both polar wings of the controversy. On the one extreme we find extreme separationists who see impermissible establishment in such symbols as "In God We Trust" on coins and heraldic crosses on official insignias and in the singing of "Silent Night" in a music class. At the other extreme are accommodationists who see no merit in fundamental constitutional opposition to such practices as transforming a religious school classroom into a "public" one by hanging a sign "public school" on the outside of that classroom to circumvent strictures against excessive church-state entanglement or compelling public school children of minority religions to recite prayers from the New Testament.

That we are witnessing a revival of the theory and practice of religion as part and parcel of our sociopolitical dynamics is a truism—whatever its causes. One need not be an expert to recognize that it has at least something to do with the dramatic alteration in mores since the end of the Second World War and particularly since the Vietnam tragedy. It assuredly has something to do with the trauma of the student revolts of the late 1960s, which seared our societal structure and engendered results that are at least questionable for our societal welfare. In any event, that religious and spiritual values do indeed affect political and social dynamics in the United States is axiomatic. They do in all societies that are more or less democratic—and even genuinely in some, though of course not in all, that are not. But the range and extent of their effects differ dramatically, and it would be difficult to quantify the results. One can, however, analyze the presence of the phenomenon and hazard an objective evaluation.

"We are a religious people," wrote William Orville Douglas, the U.S. Supreme Court's libertarian activist and longevity champion—thirty-six and one-half years—in 1952, "whose institutions presuppose a Supreme Being."[3] That free spirit, who would hardly be classified as a very religious person himself, went on to note that there is "no constitutional requirement which makes it necessary for government to be hostile to religion and to throw its weight against efforts to widen the effective scope of religious influence."[4] Justice Douglas was entirely on target, of course, in noting that we are a religious people and that the religious influence is widespread. But that oft-quoted statement requires considerable amplification and explication.

There are some 240 million Americans today (May 1987), of whom about 80 percent acknowledge or profess a formal religious affiliation—although that may well be only skin-deep in numerous circumstances. A total of 239 Christian and Jewish religious organizations or sects now exist officially, all of which play at least some role in public affairs, be it of significant or of nuisance value; and those 239 are augmented by some 1,300 "unconventional" ones. Most numerous among members of the "official" ones are Protestants, totaling some 135 million people, or 56 percent of the population, adhering to diverse subgroups, the largest formally organized among them being the 16 million Southern Baptists. Second in absolute numbers but constituting by far the most numerous single religious unit are the 53 million Roman Catholics (22 percent of the population). In third place are the approximately 6 million Jews (constituting but 2.5 percent of the population). Yet note that more than 40 million Americans, the vast majority of whom come from a Protestant home, refuse to specify any formal religious adherence.

Religious affiliations of that magnitude necessarily play a role in public policy conception and application—although mere size is not necessarily an indicator of influence in political and social dynamics, as the 1984 presidential election campaign bears convincing witness. Not only does much depend on the nature of the issues at hand, but a great deal is bottomed on the organizational skill and prowess of the various denominational groups and their satellites. Much also depends on the concentration of identifiable religious groups in specific geographical locales and their ability to wield influence in the formulation of applied values.

Thus legislation to provide public financial aid to parochial schools will have a far better chance of becoming law in heavily Roman Catholic states, such as Rhode Island and Massachusetts—ranking first and second in Roman Catholic adherents with 63.3 percent and 51.7 percent respectively—than it would in predominantly Protestant states such as Virginia and North Carolina, with but 5.3 percent and 1.4 percent respectively. Yet that by no means gainsays the popularity of the issue of prayer in the public schools in the latter two states. With almost half of America's Jews residing in or near greater New York City, their influence will be infinitely greater there than in the Western mountain states, where the number of Jews is infinitesimal. Yet while Jews are generally "separationist" in church-state philosophy, important segments of their sizable Orthodox wing are ardent supporters of public aid to parochial schools. Public policy in Utah, with its overwhelmingly Mormon persuasion—the Church of Latter-day Saints has some 3.6 million adherents, half of them in Utah—has inevitably reflected that religious and highly moral people. Utah ranks fiftieth among the states in the percentage of children attending parochial and other private schools, a mere 1.6 percent; yet Utah's public schools clearly reflect commitment to the Mormon faith. Evangelical revivalism will find a far more receptive audience in the towns and on the farms of the upper South than it will in the industrial Northeast. And so forth.

Consider also the avowed religious affiliations of Congress. For the Ninety-ninth Congress (1985–1987), these were as follows: Roman Catholic, 142; Methodist, 76; Episcopalian, 67; Presbyterian, 56; "miscellaneous Protestant" or "no affiliation," 52; Baptist, 49; Jewish, 38; Lutheran, 23; United Church of Christ, 14; Mormon, 12; and Unitarian, 9.

Congress is obviously *not* constitutionally designed to be proportionately "representative." The point may well be too obvious to be belabored. But those who advance absolutist responses to the complex problem of the place of religion in society under a written, albeit elastic, Constitution ought at least to recognize that the task of accommodating the vastly different beliefs and professions of so religiously heterogeneous a people is a Herculean one. And it is sobering to recognize the current wide-lensed status of state aid by way of "auxiliary services" to religious elementary and secondary schools throughout the land: whereas a decade ago ten of the fifty states provided *no* such aid, in 1982 only three—Florida, Georgia, and Oklahoma—did not.[5] Services provided in the forty-seven others included textbook loans (twenty-six states), bus services (twenty-seven), health services (twenty-three), released time (twenty-eight), lunch subsidies (*in addition* to federal programs) (seventeen), administrative services (that is, testing and record keeping) (seven), special educational subsidies (fifteen), driver education (four), and tax deductions for educational expenses (two), totaling 149.[6] Other services abound. Of those tabulated thirty-four were probably unconstitutional under contemporary U.S. Supreme Court holdings (of which more below).[7]

Free Exercise

Although Chief Justice Warren E. Burger has severally referred to the two components of the first sentence of the first article of the Bill of Rights simply as "the religion clauses"[8] and although there are seminal links between the concepts of free exercise and nonestablishment, there *are* crucial distinctions, indeed differences. Their existence in language as well as in constitutional law counsels a separate treatment, at least initially, in the context of this essay.[9]

While the constitutional guarantee against "prohibiting the free exercise" of religion has posed fewer problems and spawned less litigation than the ban on "an establishment of religion," the "free exercise" component has hardly been devoid of controversy. It should be clear, however, that the guarantee clearly militates against any governmental action prohibiting that free exercise, the clause having been designed to mean what it says: that neither Congress—nor, by subsequent judicial interpretation and extension, the states—may interfere with the sacred rights of freedom of religious belief and religious exercise. Obviously, however, as Justice Owen J. Roberts took pains to point out in his opinion for a unanimous, 9–0 Court in the crucial 1940 *Cantwell* case,[10] while "freedom of exercise" embraces both the freedom to *believe* and the freedom to *act*, "the first is absolute, but, in the nature of things, the second cannot be. *Conduct* remains subject to [governmental] regulation for the protection of society. The freedom to act must have appropriate definition to preserve the enforcement of that protection." In every case, Roberts continued, "the power to regulate must be so exercised as not, in attaining a permissible end, unduly to infringe the protected freedom."[11]

This, of course, raises as many practical questions as it settles. Yet the four and a half decades since Roberts penned his landmark opinion bear witness to a commendably ascending judicial commitment to a maximum regard for free exercise, even when—as has been true of the practices of such evangelistic sects as the Jehovah's Witnesses, the Seventh-Day Adventists, and the Amish and Mennonites—that exercise does not sit well with a majority of the body politic. Examples are refusal to salute the flag; refusal to mount license plates with patriotic inscriptions; public playing of the offensive gramophone record "Enemies"; objection to the use of an assigned social security number "because numbers are an instrument of the devil";[12] refusal to have a photograph taken for a driver's license (the Court split 4–4 in upholding that);[13] insistence on observing a day of rest other than Sunday under certain (but not all) circumstances; bona fide conscientious objection to any military service generally or, specifically, refusal to bear arms; rejection of compulsory educational requirements beyond the eighth grade; and refusal to put bright orange warning signs on plain black Amish buggies.

There *are* limits, of course, but—with one or two exceptions—they are hardly controversial. Thus few would regard these unsuccessful "free exercise" claims as valid:

- the practice of polygamy (the ban against which was reaffirmed as recently as 1984)
- the alleged right to hold parades on major public highways without obtaining a permit
- the refusal to pay taxes in the absence of a statutory exemption
- the rejection of state certification of teachers and curriculum

• the handling of poisonous snakes in a church
• the claim that prohibitions against growing marijuana in one's garden and growing wheat in excess of federal acreage allotment regulations constitute interference with God's will, as manifested by the fruits of the soil
• the claim that the failure of electrodes to function on an electric chair manifested an act of God superior to otherwise constitutional procedures at the bar of criminal justice
• the claim that for the payment of $25 to be ordained as a minister of the Ecclesiastical Order of the Ism of AM, Inc., one can become tax exempt[14]

The one aspect of free exercise that has continued to be broadly controversial is the realm of conscientious objection to military service; but it has been neutralized, at least for the time being, by the abolition of the draft. Even before that, the Court had so generously interpreted the conscientious objector rule that the only judicial stricture that remained when compulsory military service was abandoned in 1971 was the Court's 8–1 decision two years earlier—to me, entirely rational and fair—against "selective" conscientious objection, that is, the claimed prerogative of personally distinguishing, on free exercise grounds, between "just" and "unjust" wars.[15] Only Justice Douglas, then in his thirty-third year on the Court, dissented, observing wistfully: "I had assumed that the welfare of a single human soul was the ultimate test of the vitality of the First Amendment."[16] (Douglas was no longer on the bench when the Court, in an opinion rejecting bill of attainder and self-incrimination challenges, first upheld, 6–2, in 1984 the statutorily required compliance with the federal 1980 draft registration law in order to receive federal financial aid and also upheld, 7–2, in 1985 against freedom of expression and due process claims, the government's selective prosecution of those who refused to register, regardless of aid. The two dissenters in both cases were Justices William J. Brennan, Jr., and Thurgood Marshall.)[17]

The Douglas dissent not only raises the tantalizing question of what would happen to America's ability to constitute and field armed forces in a "controversial" war (are there any noncontroversial ones?) but also is symptomatic of the already mentioned, sometimes rather generous, claims raised by litigants under the religion clauses. A handful of novel ones advanced during the past few years without success are the following:

• a claim by the National Bible Association and the National Foundation for Fairness in Education that the failure of the Smithsonian

Institution to depict the biblical version of creation in an exhibit, which showed only the evolutionary theory, unconstitutionally established a "religion of secular humanism"[18]

• a contention that the United Methodist church could not be sued for alleged violations of fraud and securities law in connection with seven retirement homes it ran on the West Coast because the church "lacked central management"[19]

• a claim by a "fanatically devout" public elementary school teacher that the school's celebration of Halloween constituted a "pagan observance of every evil and wicked thing in the world" and hence impermissibly violated his religious conscience[20]

• the suit by the always controversial and busy Madalyn Murray O'Hair to remove the phrase "In God We Trust" from U.S. coins and currency[21] (although Mrs. O'Hair garnered considerable support for her also unsuccessful federal lawsuit to restrain the celebration of what she termed a "stupid, archaic" mass by Pope John Paul II on the Mall during his Washington visit on Sunday, October 7, 1979)[22]

• the assertion by a Philadelphian that he was entitled to bring a federal suit against certain public policies because he was "God's Prophet" (the judge accepting the U.S. attorney's contention that his tribunal had no jurisdiction over God)[23]

• the appeal by a Chicago public kindergarten teacher, a Jehovah's Witness, who had been fired by the city's superintendent of schools for "deliberate nonconformity with curriculum" because she frankly refused to carry out the legally required instruction of the Pledge of Allegiance and patriotic songs[24]—her claim being that, under her religious beliefs, the described activities constituted "forms of idolatry, the worship of man-made images, banned by the Bible" and thus violated her First Amendment rights

• the alleged constitutional right of a Christian evangelical group, the Tony and Susan Alamo Foundation, not to pay the minimum wage to its 300 "associate" members, working in such foundation-owned enterprises as construction outfits, retail clothing, candy, and grocery stores, a motel, hog farms, and automobile repair shops and service stations[25]

• Captain S. S. Goldman's contention that the free exercise clause entitled him to wear a yarmulke (skull cap) while in uniform, notwithstanding an air force regulation mandating uniform dress for air force personnel[26]

The mere fact that these intriguing challenges would be litigated and heard by the highest court in our land is living testimony to the high value the American body politic and its governmental organs place on our religious prerogatives. That there are limits violates neither the spirit nor the letter of the religion clauses, for lines must be drawn under the Constitution. Its law cements our society.

Establishment

If, on the whole and on balance, the state of affairs in the "free exercise" segment of the religion guarantees against state interference may be regarded as comfortably satisfactory from the civil libertarian perspective, we come to a rather different situation as we turn to the "establishment" clause, the volatile issue of the *separation of church and state*. For if that clause, "Congress shall make no law respecting an establishment of religion," is commanding in tone and clear in syntax, it is inexorably unclear in its intention. What does it mean? Just what does it forbid? References to history seem only to intensify the riddle. Because the establishment and free exercise clauses are closely related, the complexities of establishment simply cannot be understood if they are treated in isolation from the central problem of religion, of liberty itself. Hence it is hardly astonishing that the establishment clause has proved to be a "riddle within an enigma," a Pandora's box, and an emotion-charged issue of public policy and public law.

At least to a degree this is astonishing, for the intent of the American revolutionary and postrevolutionary leaders—headed by that trio of great Virginians Thomas Jefferson, James Madison, and George Mason—and, during an earlier day and on a somewhat different level, of Rhode Island's Roger Williams seems to be very clear, indeed: that there must never be an established church, such as Virginia's Anglican church before Jefferson's seminal disestablishment statute (the bicentennial of which we observed in 1986), or "the preferred position of a favored Church." Children of the Enlightenment, the Virginians reflected the secular and humanistic view that supported religious liberty and the separation of church and state.

There can be no doubt whatsoever about the intentions of Jefferson's great Disestablishment Bill of 1786. Looking back at the end of a life filled with achievement for his beloved Republic and commonwealth, he regarded his authorship of that bill as second in significance only to that of the Declaration of Independence, and he requested that it be so listed and ranked on his tombstone under the stately trees of the family graveyard at the foot of his beloved Monticello.[27]

Nor is there any doubt about Madison's widely circulated and highly influential "Memorial and Remonstrance" of 1785 against the proposal of the Virginia House of Delegates to provide, through assessments, for teachers of the Christian religion (see appendix to this volume). In fifteen eloquently stated points, that document, supported by Jefferson, argued persuasively through the elegant pen of its author that the state as the secular authority must have jurisdiction over *temporal* matters and that such authority does not extend over *spiritual* matters, "which lie in the domain of private belief and the churches." (It is important to note that the term used is "church*es*," not "church.")

To Jefferson, Madison, and Mason, to other leading Virginians and their devoted followers, the principle of separation was absolutely indispensable to the basic freedoms of belief, conscience, and dissent. They were in no sense hostile to religion—far from it. They simply regarded it as an entirely *private* matter. Overridingly determined to keep religion out of the domain of public affairs—a point made with remarkable consistency on the present Court by its devout Roman Catholic member, Justice Brennan—they were as much concerned with "freedom *from* religion as freedom *of* religion." It is a live concern, as it must be, a concern still reflected in Virginia's constitution and indeed reconfirmed by its revised 1971 model. The latter's tough language (Article I, section 16) thus bars "any appropriation of public funds, or personal property, or any real estate to any church, or sectarian society, association or institution of *any kind whatever*, which is entirely or partly, directly or indirectly, controlled by any church or sectarian society."

As we look about us and reflect on the contemporary status of the relationship between state and church or churches, something obviously must have happened to alter the tenor and the intent of those noble principles. It would not be terribly far from the mark to sum matters up, somewhat cynically perhaps, by concluding that once again that omnipresent and omnipotent alliance of lawyers, politicians, and lawyer-politicians may have done us in. Such a conclusion depends of course on one's point of view; and, be it stipulated at once, that point of view differs dramatically among individual and group observers—and the Supreme Court's last four decisions in the waning days of its 1984–1985 term constituted a pleasant surprise. Indeed, lay as well as professional attitudes run the full gamut:

• an all but utter lack of alarm or even concern, such as the observation by Professor Richard Funston, a sophisticated scholar of the Court and the Constitution, that the establishment clause cases boil down to "much ado about nothing" and that the Court might be well advised to "abandon the field"[28]

• the comment by Leo Pfeffer, the distinguished, long-time separation watchdog and First Amendment attorney, that "compared to the state of law construing other provisions of [the Bill of Rights] such as freedom of the press, or of the right of persons charged with crimes—the Court's interpretation of [the separation clause] is a model of clarity"[29] (I beg to differ)

• the contention by Senator Daniel Patrick Moynihan (Democrat, New York) that "in the years since 1947 . . . [the year of the New Jersey bus case][30] the Court's decisions have become ever more confused and contradictory,"[31] resulting in "an intellectual shambles: one confused and convoluted decision, requiring a yet more confused and convoluted explanation or modification"[32]

• the thoughtful but deceptively facile question by the wise columnist James Reston of the *New York Times* whether the United States, "in this secular and permissive age, is somehow threatened by helping finance the instruction and practice of religion or whether it is in trouble for lack of religion"[33]

• the frank assertion by Antonin Scalia, then a U.S. court of appeals judge, that "Supreme Court jurisprudence concerning the Establishment Clause in general, and the application of that clause to governmental assistance for religiously affiliated education in particular, is in a state of utter chaos and unpredictable change"[34]

• the intriguingly controversial position of a knowledgeable civil rights and liberties scholar and author, Professor Richard Morgan, who is worried not at all by financial aid to "specialized and independent parochial schools" but very much by even "modest prayers in the common public schools"[35]

• the insistence of Dean Jesse C. Choper of the School of Law of the University of California that there is no violation of the separation mandate unless there is "coercion, compromise, or influence" of religious beliefs[36]

• Mrs. O'Hair's continual assaults upon anything she regards as establishment (including her contention, dismissed by the U.S. Supreme Court, that the astronauts' memorable reading of the Bible from outer space violated the separation clause)[37]

• the exasperated dissenting opinion by Justice John Paul Stevens in the troubling 1980 *Regan* ruling, that the "entire enterprise of trying to justify various types of subsidies to non-public schools should be abandoned [and that r]ather than continuing with the Sisyphean task of trying to patch together the 'blurred, indistinct, and variable barrier' described in *Lemon v. Kurtzman*, I would resurrect the 'high and impregnable wall' "[38]

• the resigned observation of constitutional law text authors Victor G. Rosenblum and Didrick Castberg that "determining the constitutional parameters of government aid to parochial schools requires ecumenically the wisdom of Solomon, the love and compassion of John XXIII, and the moral certainty of Billy Graham"[39]

• James J. Kilpatrick's observation at the end of the Burger Court in 1986 that in "recent years the high court has treated the establishment clause . . . as a kind of mulberry bush. The court has gone 'round and round', now approving a municipal crèche in Pawtucket, now disapproving a 'minute of silence' in the classrooms of Alabama. Louisiana's Balanced Treatment for Creation-Science and Evolution-Science Act [heard by the Court in its 1986–1987 term] will take [it] around the bush once more"[40]

Yet it is surely fair to propound the central question of where we stand constitutionally on the separation issue, especially in the face of head shaking over Supreme Court distinctions between, for example, (1) the "lending" of "books" to non–public school pupils, which has consistently been upheld by the Court since it approved it 8–0 on due process grounds in the 1930 *Cochran* case[41] and, more pointedly, 6–3 in 1968 against a potent First Amendment challenge[42] (with Justice Hugo Black, the author of the key ruling approving bus subvention in *Everson*,[43] angrily exclaiming that "a book is not a bus"), and (2) the providing of certain "instructional materials and equipment," which the Court has repeatedly disallowed as violating the separation clause, as it did in the 1973 New York,[44] 1975 Pennsylvania,[45] and 1977 Ohio[46] litigations, in each instance by a 6–3 vote. A cynic might quickly ask what books *are* since they do not seem to be "instructional materials" in the Court's eyes.

Fairness, however, dictates mention of the repeated, however contentious, acknowledgment by the Court that the wall of separation that must unquestionably (or so I would contend) be maintained between church and state is, in its frequently reiterated words, "a blurred, indistinct, and variable barrier depending on all the circumstances of a particular relationship."[47] Few students of the issue would disagree with that wistful observation. There is now arguable justification, however, for questioning the Court's collateral contention, in Justice Harry A. Blackmun's words, that "none the less, the Court's numerous precedents have become firmly rooted, and now provide substantial guidance."[48]

The 1980 *Regan* (New York) 5–4 holding,[49] for one, casts doubt on the Blackmun statement's current applicability. That doubt is reinforced by the Court's 1983 upholding, again by that closest of margins, 5–4, of a Minnesota law permitting state-tax-paying parents of students in all grades in elementary and secondary schools to deduct from their gross income up to $700 annually for "educational expenses" comprising tuition, textbooks, and transportation in Minnesota and in North Dakota, South Dakota, Iowa, and Wisconsin.[50] (Of 815,000 beneficiaries only seventy-nine paid public school tuition—all the others were parochial and private school parents.) That same year saw the 6–3 approval of the practice of employing an ordained Presbyterian minister to open Nebraska's legislative sessions.[51] In 1984 and 1985 the Court upheld, 5–4 and 4–4, respectively, the inclusion of a crèche sponsored by the Rhode Island government as part of a Christmas display in a privately owned park in the heart of Pawtucket's shopping district[52] and a challenge to the refusal of the town of Scarsdale, New York, to permit the erection of a nativity scene by a private group in a public park.[53] And in 1986 it unanimously approved Washington state's financial assistance to a blind person studying at a Christian college and seeking to become a pastor, missionary, or youth director.[54]

Still, on balance, the Court's last few opinion days in 1985 seemed to herald a dramatic halt to what had threatened to become a wholesale flight from basic separation principles. In four dramatic decisions the court in 1985 had struck down as violating the constitutional mandate of the separation of church and state (1) Alabama's 1981 requirement of a daily moment of silent "meditation or prayer" (6–3);[55] (2) Connecticut's law giving workers an *absolute* right to take their Sabbath day off (8–1);[56] (3) the practice of Grand Rapids, Michigan, of sending public school teachers into private religious schools for "remedial and enrichment classes" (5–4);[57] and (4) New York City's use of funds under Title I (Chapter I) of the Federal Aid to Elementary and Secondary Schools Act of 1965 to provide public school teachers on parochial school premises for remedial instruction to disadvantaged youngsters who attend such religious schools (5–4).[58] Razor-thin though two of the decisions were, they constituted a no to more accommodation.

Historical Perspective

Since these reflections endeavor to address themselves to the inherent lines and limits of the religion clauses, fairness dictates at least a brief, if necessarily sketchy, examination of what seems to have happened, or to be happening, to the separation concept since the Virginia statesmen penned their concerns two centuries ago.

What has happened beyond any shadow of a doubt is that Jefferson's concept of the "wall of separation between Church and State" has been eroded—but the Court's June and July 1985 decisions give promise of a significant tempering of that erosion. Only time and the

vagaries of the Court's personnel, present or future, will tell, however. Be that as it may, in responding to the continuing demands for
involvement by the state in financial aid to churches, to church facilities, and, most markedly, to parochial elementary and secondary
schools, the judiciary, as ultimate constitutional interpreter and ar-
biter, has based its sundry decisions on three principal theories of
separation that have come to be advanced as more or less compatible
with the exhortations of the establishment clause of the First Amendment. I have outlined these in considerable detail in my *Freedom and
the Court*.[59]

1. First is the *strict separation* or *no aid* theory, which, presumably
incorporating the Jeffersonian-Madisonian "wall of separation," holds
that its requirements of strict separation forbid any and all governmental support of religion and religious interests. This theory was
judicially applied, for example, by Justice Black in his 8–1 opinion for
the Court in the 1948 case of *McCollum* v. *Board of Education*,[60] striking
down the Champaign, Illinois, practice of "released time," which
featured classes in religious instruction to public school children on
public school premises. Yet that same Justice Black—my judicial
hero—had, alas, found no violation in upholding 5–4 just one year
earlier the New Jersey practice of authorizing treasury subventions for
the busing of parochial and other private as well as public school
children. (Actually, in the locality at issue, Ewing Township, they
were confined to four Roman Catholic schools.) Enunciating the trou-
blesome "child benefit" theory, he could write there:

> The "establishment of religion" clause of the First Amend-
> ment means at least this: Neither a state nor the Federal
> Government can set up a church. Neither can pass laws
> which aid one religion, aid all religions, or prefer one re-
> ligion over another. Neither can force or influence a person
> to go to or remain away from church against his will or force
> him to profess a belief or disbelief in any religion. No person
> can be punished for entertaining or professing religious be-
> liefs or disbeliefs, for church attendance or nonattendance.
> No tax in any amount, large or small, can be levied to
> support any religious activities or institution, whatever they
> may be called, or whatever form they may adopt to teach or
> practice religion. Neither a state nor the Federal Government
> can, openly or secretly, participate in the affairs of any reli-
> gious organizations or groups and vice-versa. In the words
> of Jefferson, the clause against establishment of religion by
> law was intended to erect a "wall of separation between
> Church and State."[61]

In light of this manifesto, Black's concluding passage in his opinion must have come as a bit of a surprise to some of his readers as well as his colleagues: "The First Amendment," he warned, "has erected a wall between church and state. The wall must be kept high and impregnable. We could not approve the slightest breach. New Jersey has not breached it here."[62] Had it not? Four of his colleagues emphatically thought it had; yet the principle of the New Jersey bus case has been, and is to this day (mid-1987), the law of the land, notwithstanding Justice Douglas's 1962 announcement from the bench that he had erred in joining the majority.[63] It was again Justice Black, now invoking the strict separation theory, who spoke for another 8–1 majority in the New York prayer case,[64] striking down New York state's practice of permitting the recitation in its public schools of a twenty-one-word, nondenominational daily prayer drafted by state agency officials, concluding eloquently: "It is neither sacrilegious nor antireligious to say that each separate government in this country should stay out of the business of writing or sanctioning official prayers and *leave that purely religious function to the people themselves and to those the people look to for religious guidance.*"[65]

2. Second is the so-called *government neutrality theory,* which requires the government to be absolutely neutral in matters religious— so neutral, in fact, that government cannot do anything that either aids or hampers religion; that there must be, in the Court's words, *"a secular legislative purpose and a primary effect that neither advances or inhibits religion; that there can be no government action that would either confer a benefit or impose a burden."*[66] Less categorical than the first theory, the neutrality approach leaves us with the delicate need to interpret not only "secular," "burden," and "benefit" but also "religion" itself. In two back-to-back 8–1 decisions totaling 144 pages and featuring five opinions, with a "representative" of each of the three major domestic religious faiths writing a lengthy concurring one, the Court declared unconstitutional a Pennsylvania law requiring the daily reading, without comment, of ten verses from the King James version of the Holy Bible and Baltimore's similar requirement of a Bible chapter or the Lord's Prayer or both. In the controlling opinion Justice Tom Clark, a devout Presbyterian, wrote with feeling:

> The place of religion in our society is an exalted one, achieved through a long tradition of reliance on the home, the church and the inviolable citadel of the individual heart and mind. We have come to recognize through bitter experience that *it is not within the power of government to invade that citadel, whether its purpose or effect be to aid or oppose, to advance*

> *or retard. In the relationship between man and religion, the state is firmly committed to a position of neutrality.*[67]

And he explained:

> To withstand the strictures of the Establishment Clause there must be a *secular legislative purpose and a primary effect that neither advances nor inhibits religion.* . . . [And] the fact [advanced by Pennsylvania and Maryland] that individual students may absent themselves upon parental request . . . furnishes no defense to a claim of constitutionality under the Establishment Clause.[68]

He concluded with the reminder that the Court

> cannot accept that the concept of neutrality, which does not permit a State to require a religious exercise even with the consent of the majority of those affected, collides with the majority's right to free exercise of religion. While the Free Exercise Clause clearly prohibits the use of state action to deny the right of free exercise to *anyone,* it has never meant that a majority could use the machinery of the State to practice its beliefs.[69]

More than two decades later the Supreme Court, now speaking through Justice Stevens, affirmed that position in the Alabama cases.[70]

3. The third theory, I suggest, is very likely the controlling one today, although it is not the sole one used. Quite unoriginally, I term it the *governmental accommodation theory,* for it has featured a sporadic judicial willingness to reconcile the natural clash between the free exercise and separation clauses by accepting some accommodations between the diverse claims of government and religion and thus a fortiori between "state and church." My colleague A. E. Dick Howard, of the University of Virginia School of Law, who argued and won the Grand Rapids case in 1985, said that the term "accommodation" was used almost as much in oral argument as the words "and" and "but." This accommodation is often, but not necessarily always, grounded in the controversial "child benefit" concept, which lends itself to rather ready attack on both logical and constitutional grounds. The genesis of the accommodation theory lies in a 6–3 opinion written by Justice Douglas, of all people, in 1952.[71] It upheld New York's released-time program, which differed from the one struck down in Illinois only in that the New York public school children who were to be given religious instruction were released from classes while the heathens had to stay in class (attendance being taken, covertly and overtly,

respectively). Justice Black, joined by his colleagues Felix Frankfurter and Robert H. Jackson, thundered in dissent:

> State help to religion injects political and party prejudices into a holy field. It too often substitutes force for prayer, hate for love, and persecution for persuasion. Government should not be allowed, under cover of the soft euphemism of "cooperation," to steal into the sacred area of religious choice.[72]

The accommodation theory received further impetus with another 6–3 child benefit ruling in 1968, this one by Justice Byron R. White,[73] upholding the so-called lending of textbooks to students in parochial as well as public schools—a program under which the parochial schools could request the books they wanted, books that might be different from those used by the public school students. Again Justice Black dissented, this time joined by Justices Douglas and Abe Fortas, contending with passion that

> it requires no prophet to foresee that on the argument used to support this law, others could be upheld providing for state or federal government funds to buy property on which to erect religious school buildings or to erect the buildings themselves, to pay the salaries of the religious school teachers, and finally to have the sectarian religious groups cease to rely on voluntary contributions of members of their sects while waiting for the Government to pick up all the bills for the religious schools.[74]

As already pointed out, textbook loans have been repeatedly upheld since that time, falling only once in the instance of a Mississippi law that included as beneficiaries pupils in *all* schools, even in those that practiced racial segregation.[75]

Given the evidently solid, and conceivably increasing, number of votes on the Court in favor of certain kinds of accommodation, it came as no surprise that, using the child benefit loophole, both the Congress and a good many state legislatures began to do their utmost to find ways to provide funds for the activities of parochial schools. A host of statutes was enacted, including the Federal Aid to Elementary and Secondary Education Act of 1965, severally amended and extended since; the Federal Educational Facilities acts of 1963 and 1973; and a plethora of state laws, such as Pennsylvania's, New York's, Rhode Island's, Ohio's, New Jersey's, Michigan's, and Minnesota's in the 1960s, 1970s, and 1980s. All these were designed to provide public funds for direct instructional aid in "nonreligious subjects" to Roman Catholic and other church-related primary and secondary schools;

they included such intriguing devices as the "purchasing" of "secular services" for the teaching of "secular subjects" by parochial school teachers. The cascading number of challenges to the cascading number of laws prompted the Court, through the chief justice, to come up with a collateral umbrella test, namely, that no accommodation may constitute an *"excessive entanglement" between government and religion*—a nonexcessive entanglement evidently being constitutionally acceptable.[76]

That additional element and the earlier requirements of "secular legislative purpose" and "primary effect of neither advancing nor inhibiting religion"—though arguably either qualified or abandoned in the 1984 crèche case[77] but more or less restored in the 1985 separation decisions—now constitute the three-pronged judicial test of the establishment clause. Under it the Court has, since 1971, handed down a series of rulings characterized by accommodation, upholding some and striking down other attempts and devices to fund sundry nonpublic (that is, predominantly parochial) school activities. Table 1 catalogs some of the more important decisions and examples of the past decade and a half of Court decisions on aid to other than public schools.

The four 1977 *Wolman* case opinions, ranging from 8–1 to 3–6, that were billed as lodestar decisions on the accommodation front were hardly models of clarity. They constituted a veritable mishmash of interpretations that were not precisely elucidated. Indeed, they were compounded, if not contradicted, by holdings in the *Cathedral Academy* case in late 1977, the *Regan* case in 1980, and the *Allen* case in 1984—and partly resuscitated in the *Grand Rapids* and *Aguilar* rulings in 1985. The extent to which the Court's three-part test or nexus is still applicable may be a matter of judgment or Russian roulette; but it is evidently more or less res judicata (if that can be "more or less").

Incorporation

Many, indeed most, of the U.S. Supreme Court's rulings discussed or referred to here would probably not have reached the Court had it not been for the much-debated, long-controversial doctrine of "incorporation." Also styled "absorption" or, simply, the application of the Bill of Rights to the states, it was judicially pronounced in the noted opinion by Justice Benjamin N. Cardozo, with only Justice Pierce Butler dissenting, in the landmark decision of *Palko* v. *Connecticut* in 1937[78] and at once recognized as a major doctrinal development.

The Court, speaking through Justice Cardozo, in effect established an "honor roll" of "superior rights", which, by virtue of judicial

TABLE 2-1
SUPREME COURT DECISIONS ON AID TO NONPUBLIC SCHOOLS,
1970–1986

Case	Year	Upheld	Struck Down
Walz	1970	Tax exemption of property used exclusively for religious purposes (7–1)	
Lemon I	1971		Partial payment of salaries of parochial school teachers (0–8)
Early	1971		Purchases of secular services from sectarian schools (1–8)
Tilton	1971	Construction funds for religiously affiliated colleges and universities (5–4)	
Essex	1972		Direct tuition rebates per child of $90 (1–8)
Nyquist	1973	Lending of textbooks (6–3)	Maintenance, repair, tuition, equipment, and record-keeping and tuition reimbursement (3–6 to 1–8)
Meek	1975	Lending of textbooks (6–3)	Counseling, testing, remedial classes, instructional materials and equipment, speech and hearing therapy, psychological services (3–6)
Roemer	1976	Noncategorical financial aid to church-related colleges, if not used for sectarian purposes (first time in history Court approved general-purposes subsidies) (5–4)	
Blanton	1976	Tuition grants to college students, no matter where enrolled (9–0)	
Wolman	1977	Therapeutic, remedial, and guidance counseling on "neutral" sites *off*-grounds (7–2)	

TABLE 2-1 (continued)

Case	Year	Upheld	Struck Down
		Standardized texts and test scoring (provided by public schools) (6–3) Lending of textbooks (6–3) Diagnostic services on grounds (8–1)	
Cathedral	1977		Direct financial aid for testing and record keeping (3–6)
Byrne	1979		Income tax deduction for parents of parochial school students (3–6)
Regan	1980	State-mandated and state-prepared record-keeping and testing requirements (distinguishing Nyquist, where there were no such state requirements or preparations) (5–4)	
Allen	1984	Income tax deductions of up to $700 annually for parents of all school children below college level, distinguishing Byrne, which had confined the deduction to parochial school children (5–4)	
Grand Rapids	1985		"Shared time" program, allowing public school teachers to teach some "remedial and enrichment" courses in nonpublic schools, all but one of which were religious schools (4–5)
Aguilar	1985		Use of federally funded Title I program, state monitored, that provided shared time similar to the Grand Rapids arrangements (4–5)

(Table continues)

33

TABLE 2-1 (continued)

Case	Year	Upheld	Struck Down
Witters	1986	Extension of financial aid under a state vocational rehabilitation assistance program to a blind person studying at a Christian college and seeking to become a pastor, missionary, or youth director (9–0)	

interpretation, applied certain rights enumerated in the federal Bill of Rights—though demonstrably designed to apply only to Congress—to the states as well through the first section of the Fourteenth Amendment. The Cardozo opinion specifically pointed to the free exercise component of the First Amendment as one of those superior rights, which the 1934 *Hamilton* opinion, written by Justice Butler for his unanimous colleagues, had declared applicable to the states as a fundamental right protected by the "due process of law" provision of the Fourteenth Amendment.[79]

Although the separation component was neither mentioned nor viewed as incorporated in either 1934 or 1937, it achieved that constitutional recognition in the 1947 New Jersey bus case,[80] in which Justice Black spoke for a 5–4 majority in upholding state aid for the busing of children to private and parochial as well as to public schools. Just as it had done for free exercise thirteen years earlier, the Court there acknowledged in the instance of the "separation of Church and State" segment that a bona fide violation of that separation would henceforth be constitutionally proscribed by the language and terms of *both* the First and the Fourteenth amendments.

Incorporation was of course not confined to the religion clauses: over a period of forty-four years ending in 1969, the judicial branch, with the Supreme Court at its apex, applied all but five provisions of the federal Bill of Rights to the states, the bulk of the decisions being handed down by the Earl Warren Court between 1961 and 1969. The subject of continuing, lively debate by scholars and laymen alike, the incorporation doctrine has been heavily attacked as a major error of the Supreme Court.

Whatever one's views on the historical and constitutional justification for incorporation—I have devoted an entire, lengthy chapter to it in my *Freedom and the Court*[81]—the doctrine is almost certainly here to stay in its broad compass, if not in every detail. Like the occasionally still engaged issue of the justification for the doctrine of judicial review, it is settled, though not in every nuance; and there is considerable merit in the contention that not every federal practice applied under an incorporated provision need be embraced by the states. Indeed, the Supreme Court has on several occasions supported that disclaimer, especially on the frontiers of jury practices and the administration of criminal justice. Nor does it mean that the policy is indubitably a wise one. Still, in the words of Justice Arthur J. Goldberg's concurring opinion in the 1964 incorporation case of *Pointer* v. *Texas*,

> to deny to the states the power to impair a fundamental constitutional right is not to increase federal power, but, rather, to limit the power of both federal and state governments in favor of safeguarding the fundamental liberties of the individual. . . . [It] promotes rather than undermines the basic policy of avoiding excess concentration of power in government, federal or state, which underlies our concept of federalism.[82]

Of course, that admirable sentiment does not necessarily address satisfactorily the central question of what renders a constitutional right "fundamental" and just to whom it is "fundamental." Moreover, it remains true that under our system of government constitutional rights—and, one hopes, obligations as well—are declared to be such by the vote of nine members of the highest tribunal in the land. These nine, appointed rather than elected, are, to be sure, jurists; but they are also human beings affected by, in Justice Cardozo's hauntingly beautiful words, "the cardiac promptings of the moment."[83] They, to paraphrase another superb jurist and stylist, Judge Learned Hand, are warmed by the same sun, exposed to the same winters, and washed by the same waters as ordinary men and women.

The Burger Court

How have the members of the Supreme Court (that is, of the last Burger Court, July 1986) lined up on the religious clauses, in particular on their church-state component? That component has once again become so controversially lively that the Court saw fit to grant review and schedule oral argument in seven major cases for its 1985–1986 term. It was a closely divided Court that set about the task at hand—closely divided because it was philosophically and jurisprudentially a trichotomous body on these issues:

- three safely predictable "accommodationists": Justice White, Chief Justice–designate William H. Rehnquist, and retiring Chief Justice Burger (listed in descending order of their commitment to the principle)
- four just as safely predictable "separationists": Justices Brennan, Marshall, Stevens, and Blackmun (again listed in descending order of commitment)
- two far more difficult to predict "swing" votes: Justices Lewis F. Powell, Jr., and Sandra Day O'Connor

Justice O'Connor more often than not initially leaned toward the accommodationists, especially when the issue came down to the so-called entanglement component; yet her 1985–1986 term votes evinced a less accommodative stance. She clearly disapproves of the three-pronged test.

Justice Powell, however, maintained a genuine centrist, separation-conscious, case-by-case stance. Indeed, it is Justice Powell who has been and who—it may safely be hazarded—will continue to be, assuming his presence on the Court, the key vote in church-state cases (as he has often been on other major constitutionally touchy issues, such as affirmative action and reverse discrimination).[84] Frequently referred to as "the Court's conscience," he not only has been the key swing vote but was on the winning side in each of the twenty-nine major church-state cases in which he participated from the day he took his judicial oath (January 7, 1972) to September 1986. Ten of the twenty-nine favored the accommodationist side,[85] nineteen the separationist view,[86] and many were decided 5–4. In at least two cases in which Powell did not participate, the Court was evenly divided. Thus, while each wing of the Court on church-state matters could lay claim to a number of victories and each sustained a number of defeats, Justice Powell batted 1,000.

In brief, a solid group of four separationists continued to take a hard line. (Justice Blackmun's conversion to this group from a former more or less centrist posture was a byproduct of his general move to the Court's "liberal" wing in the early to middle 1970s.) The four have been firmly committed to a close reading of the First Amendment, in which they perceive the purpose-effect-entanglement requirements to mean that every legislative or executive attempt to be accommodationist *must,* to meet constitutional mandates, (1) have a bona fide secular purpose; (2) have a primary effect that neither hinders nor benefits, neither inhibits nor advances, religion; and (3) entail not only no "*excessive* entanglement" but *no* "entanglement" at all.

The retiring chief justice, Justice White, and Chief Justice–designate Rehnquist appeared to be firmly on record as finding constitutional support for almost any kind of accommodation, provided they could detect *some* kind of secular purpose—and, arguably, one is almost always findable. For Chief Justice Burger this commitment was tempered by his view of entanglement: he was not opposed to it per se, but he insisted that it not be "excessive." But White and Rehnquist, especially White, have not been concerned with either the primary effect or the entanglement component. If they saw any secular purpose in the public policy in question, no matter how sectarian or quasi-sectarian it might be in its effect, they voted, and undoubtedly will continue to vote, to uphold it. For them, in fine, not only has the three-pronged test of constitutionality in effect been reduced to a single one of the presence of a secular purpose as readily recognized by them, but they view the establishment clause as demanding little more than no preference of any religion. For Chief Justice Burger the test had one and one-half dimensions.

The crucial significance of the two centrist justices is thus obvious—and the outcome will very likely continue to rest on the shoulders of the now seventy-nine-year-old Powell, who has demonstrated such an outstanding, and so far unfailing, success in fashioning winning combinations. The incoming junior justice, Scalia—if his public statements on the issue are a guide to his likely voting pattern on the Court—may be expected to side with the White-Rehnquist position, but there is no certainty on the Court.

Conclusion

Where, then, do we stand as we continue our public life in 1986–1987? In my judgment, there is little doubt that a degree of erosion has taken place in the separationist commitment of the Court, notwithstanding the consistent presence of the bloc of four devotees of that point of view—just one short of a majority. This relaxed and evidently continuing commitment to a more sympathetic hearing for accommodationist claims seemed to have become majoritarian, or at least plurality, Court policy in a host of church-state areas: at least indirect financial support for auxiliary services in parochial schools and the sanctioning of symbolic or patriotic practices, perhaps one day to include formal moments of silence in public schools for meditation, albeit not for prayer, as the *Wallace* v. *Jaffree* decision in June 1985 made clear.[87] And the two defeats for the accommodationists on the last day of court in July 1985 on shared-time practices, albeit by razor-thin 5–4 margins, promised distinct limits to any broadening of the cracks in the wall of separation.[88] The implications of those most recent developments point to some tentative conclusions:

- A separationist majority, though a delicate one, still exists on the Court.
- The three-part secular purpose–primary effect–excessive entanglement test does live, by and large, but, depending on the commitments of new appointees to the Court, may well be in some trouble.
- Fears of political divisiveness, especially vis-à-vis primary and secondary education, play an important part in the Court's attitude to the religion cases.
- A majority of the justices are at least leery of direct financial aid to nonpublic schools.
- The justices do have their ears to the ground: there are limits to their willingness to be persuaded by history and precedent.[89]

The separationist-accommodationist controversy defies facile analysis or resolution—as this discussion has endeavored to demonstrate. Propounded answers are as numerous and diverse as their range—from the absolutist "no" to any accommodation of a Leo Pfeffer or a Leonard W. Levy, through the "yes but only to a degree" of a Jesse Choper or a Richard E. Morgan, to the "yes" to accommodation or accommodation "plus" of a James O'Neill or a Robert L. Cord.[90] History, presumably worth more than logic—in Tocquevillian and Holmesian terms—is not inevitably the guide one might wish or presume, as the incorporation controversy, for example, also manifests (another highly controversial issue that does not readily lend itself to authoritativeness).[91] Documental language is sometimes happily clear, but all too frequently it is not. "I only want to know what the words mean," Justice Oliver Wendell Holmes would observe on many an occasion; yet, as E. M. Forster was fond of noting, it is quite feasible "to find wine in words"—and to find other, less consumable liquids.

While an absolutist posture on either side of the controversy might theoretically simplify matters, any embrace of such a position by the Court would engender serious public policy problems. It is at best doubtful that the American public would sanction it. No consistent Court majority now or in the future is likely to embrace it. Hence, for better or for worse and however imperfectly, the three-pronged test of constitutionality developed in *Lemon* will probably serve as a general guide for the justices, not perhaps in every instance but in a good many and certainly in the most controversial ones. A measure of accommodation, arguably even an increased one, is certain to continue. Thus it is entirely possible that the Court would uphold a simple requirement for a period of "silent meditation," without more, for public schools while continuing to reject "prayer," even if that be nondenominational. Symbolism, chaplains, religiously tinged patriotic observances will surely continue to be sanctioned; pervasively intrusive activities with heavy religious overtones will not. The large majority of America's citizenry will go along. The battle will be joined, however, at the all but certain attempts to broaden and indeed to generalize financial assistance to nonpublic primary and secondary schools, that is, parochial schools, going well beyond the already extant, often indirect, financial aid. Whether in the form of vouchers, tax relief, aid to students, or aid to their parents, it will engender a firestorm of controversy. On that issue many who, like me, consider themselves quasi-centrist or "reasonable" on the church-state imbroglio will draw the line: whatever the future may hold, as a supporter of the spirit of the basic Jeffersonian-Madisonian imperative of separation, I prefer to take my stand with Justice Wiley B. Rutledge's ardent dissenting opinion in the 1947 New Jersey bus case, in which he warned: "Like St. Paul's freedom, religious liberty with a great price must be bought. And for those who exercise it most fully, by insisting upon religious education for their children mixed with secular, by the terms of our Constitution the price is greater than for others."[92] It is, I submit, a price tag well worth paying for the hallowed imperative of liberty.

Notes

1. Henry J. Abraham, *Freedom and the Court: Civil Rights and Liberties in the United States* (New York: Oxford University Press, 1967); now entering its 5th edition.

2. Ibid., fn. 1, p. 172 (fn. 1, p. 220, in 4th ed.).

3. Zorach v. Clauson, 343 U.S. 306, at 313.

4. Ibid., at 314.

5. Albert R. Papa, *Auxiliary Services to Religious Elementary and Secondary Schools: The State of State Aid* (Washington, D.C.: Americans United for the Separation of Church and State, 1982), pp. 10–11.

6. Ibid.

7. Ibid., p. 12.

8. For example, National Labor Relations Board v. City of Chicago, 440 U.S. 490. (It ought to be noted that the Court ducked the constitutional issue here, however.)

9. See Henry J. Abraham, "The Status of the First Amendment's Religious Clauses: Some Reflections on Lines and Limits," *Journal of Church and State*, vol. 22, no. 2 (1980), on which some aspects of this essay rely heavily.

10. Cantwell v. Connecticut, 310 U.S. 196.

11. Ibid., at 306.

12. Bowen v. Roy, 54 LW 4603 (1986).

13. Jensen v. Quaring, 53 LW 4787 (1985). But cf. the 1979 holding in Johnson v. Motor Vehicles Division, 444 U.S. 885.

14. The Ecclesiastical Order of the Ism of AM, Inc. v. I.R.S., 53 LW 3739 (1985).

15. Gillette v. United States and Negre v. Larsen, 401 U.S. 437.

16. Ibid., at 469. For a discussion of the problem, see Abraham, *Freedom and the Court*, 4th ed., pp. 226–35.

17. Selective Service System v. Minnesota Public Ordered Research Group, 104 S.Ct. 3348 and Wayte v. United States, 105s S.Ct. 1524, respectively.

18. Crowley v. Smithsonian Institution, 462 F. Supp. 725 (1978).

19. Milhouse v. District Court, United Methodist Church v. Barr, 444 U.S. 973 (1979), certiorari denied.

20. See the Associated Press wire accounts of December 21 and 22, 1979, date-marked Fairfax, Virginia (*Charlottesville Daily Progress*, December 22, 1979, p. C-5).

21. O'Hair v. Blumenthal, 588 F. 2d 1144 (1979).

22. *Charlottesville Daily Progress*, September 18, 1979, p. A-2.

23. *Philadelphia Bulletin*, August 30, 1978, p. 9.

24. Palmer v. Board, 444 U.S. 1026 (1980).

25. Tony and Susan Alamo Foundation v. Secretary of Labor, 53 LW 4389 (1985).

26. Goldman v. Weinberger, 54 LW 4298 (1986).

27. "And not a word more," were his instructions for the epitaph he composed: "Here was buried Thomas Jefferson . . . author of the Declaration of Independence . . . of the Statute of Virginia for Religious Freedom and the Father of the University of Virginia."

28. Richard Y. Funston, *Constitutional Counterrevolution?* (Cambridge, Mass.: Schenkman, 1977), p. 235.

29. Leo Pfeffer, "The Current State of the Law in the United States and the Separationist Agenda," *The Annals*, vol. 446 (November 1979), p. 5.

30. Everson v. Board of Education of Ewing Township, 330 U.S. 1.

31. As quoted by James Reston in "Moynihan and the Court," *New York Times*, June 3, 1979, p. E-19, from a speech Senator Moynihan had delivered in Staten Island a few days earlier.

32. "What Do You Do When the Supreme Court Is Wrong?" *Public Interest*, vol. 57, no. 11 (Fall 1979).

33. Reston, "Moynihan and the Court."

34. As reported by Ruth Marcus, *Washington Post*, June 23, 1986, p. 17.

35. Richard E. Morgan, *The Supreme Court and Religion* (New York: Free Press, 1972), p. 207.

36. Jesse C. Choper, "Defining 'Religion' in the First Amendment," *University of Illinois Law Review*, no. 3 (1982); and letter to me, August 27, 1984.

37. O'Hair v. Payne, 397 U.S. 531 (1970), appeal dismissed.

38. Committee for Public Education and Religious Liberty v. Regan, 44 U.S. 646 (1980), dissenting opinion, at 671.

39. Victor G. Rosenblum and A. Didrick Castberg, eds., *Cases on Constitutional Law* (Homewood, Ill.: Dorsey Press, 1973), p. 73.

40. James J. Kilpatrick, "Questions about Religion Send Court 'Round Again," *Charlottesville Daily Progress*, May 17, 1986, p. A-4.

41. Cochran v. Louisiana State Board of Education, 281 U.S. 370.

42. Board of Education v. Allen, 392 U.S. 236.

43. Everson v. Board of Education of Ewing Township.

44. Committee for Public Education and Religious Liberty v. Nyquist, 413 U.S. 476.

45. Meek v. Pittenger, 421 U.S. 349.

46. Wolman v. Walter, 433 U.S. 229.

47. For example, Chief Justice Burger's opinion for the Court in Lemon v. Kurtzman, 403 U.S. 602 (1971), at 614; and Justice Harry Blackmun's in Wolman v. Walter, at 233.

48. Wolman v. Walter, opinion for the Court, at 236.

49. Committee for Public Education and Religious Liberty v. Regan.

50. Mueller v. Allen, 463 U.S. 388 (1983).

51. Marsh v. Chambers, 463 U.S. 783 (1983).

52. Lynch v. Donnelly, 465 U.S. 668 (1984).

53. Village of Scarsdale v. McCreary, 471 U.S. 83 (1985).

54. Witters v. Washington Department of Services to the Blind, 106 S.Ct. 748 (1986).

55. Wallace v. Jaffree, 53 LW 4665.

56. Thornton v. Caldor, 105 S. Ct. 2914.

57. Grand Rapids v. Ball, 105 S. Ct. 3316.

58. Aguilar v. Felton, 105 S. Ct. 3232.

59. Abraham, *Freedom and the Court*, 4th ed., chap. 6, "Religion," pp. 264–94.

60. McCollum v. Board of Education, 333 U.S. 203.

61. Everson v. Board of Education of Ewing Township, at 15–16.

62. Ibid., at 16.

63. Engel v. Vitale, 370 U.S. 421, concurring opinion, at 443.

64. Ibid., majority opinion.

65. Ibid., at 435 (emphasis added).

66. Abington School District v. Schempp and Murray v. Curlett, 374 U.S. 203 (1963) at 222, 224 (emphasis added).

67. Ibid., at 226 (emphasis added).

68. Ibid., at 222, 224 (emphasis added).

69. Ibid., at 225–26 (emphasis added).

70. For example, Wallace v. Jaffree, 53 LW 4665 (1985).

71. Zorach v. Clauson.

72. Ibid., at 32.

73. Board of Education v. Allen.

74. Ibid., at 253.

75. Norwood v. Harrison, 413 U.S. 455 (1973).

76. Articulated by him in Walz v. Tax Commission of the City of New York, 397 U.S. 664 (1970), although the Court found no such "entanglement" there.

77. Lynch v. Donnelly.

78. Palko v. Connecticut, 302 U.S. 319.

79. Hamilton v. Board of Regents of the University of California, 293 U.S. 245.

80. Everson v. Board of Education of Ewing Township.

81. Abraham, *Freedom and the Court*, 4th ed., "The Bill of Rights and Its Applicability to the States," pp. 28–91.

82. Pointer v. Texas, 380 U.S. 400 (1964), at 414.

83. Benjamin N. Cardozo, *The Nature of the Judicial Process* (New Haven, Conn.: Yale University Press, 1921).

84. See, for example, his two majority opinions in the two prongs of the seminal case of Regents of the University of California v. Bakke, 438 U.S. 265 (1978).

85. Hunt v. McNair, 413 U.S. 734 (1963); Meek v. Pittenger (1975), in part only; Roemer v. Maryland Public Works Board, 425 U.S. 736 (1976); Wolman v. Walter (1977), in part only; Committee for Public Education and Religious Liberty v. Regan, in part only; Bob Jones University and Goldsboro Christian School v. United States, 461 U.S. 574 (1983); Mueller v. Allen; Marsh v. Chambers, 51 LW 5162 (1983); Lynch v. Donnelly; and Witters v. Washington Department of Services to the Blind, 54 LW 4135 (1986).

86. Essex v. Wolman, 409 U.S. 808 (1972); Committee for Public Education and Religious Liberty v. Nyquist, 413 U.S. 756 (1973); Marburger and Griggs v. Public Funds for Public Schools, 417 U.S. 961 (1974); Meek v. Pittenger (1975), in part only; Wolman v. Walter (1977), in part only; New York v. Cathedral Academy, 434 U.S. 125 (1977); National Labor Relations Board v. Bishop of Chicago, 440 U.S. 490 (1979); Byrne v. Public Funds for Public Schools, 442 U.S. 907 (1979); Stone v. Graham, 449 U.S 39 (1980); Bradshaw v. Hall, 450 U.S. 965 (1981); St. Martin's Lutheran Church v. South Dakota, 451 U.S. 772 (1981); Larkin v. Grendel's Den, 454 U.S. 116 (1982); Larsen v. Valente, 456 U.S. 228 (1982); Wallace v. Jaffree, 52 LW 3719 (1984); ibid., 53 LW 4665 (1985); Tony and Susan Alamo Foundation v. Secretary of Labor; Thornton v. Caldor, Inc. (1985); Grand Rapids v. Ball, 105 S. Ct. 3216 (1985); and Aguilar v. Felton (1985).

87. Wallace v. Jaffree.

88. Grand Rapids v. Ball and Aguilar v. Felton.

89. See A. E. Dick Howard, "The Supreme Court and the Serpentine Wall" (Paper prepared for Symposium on Virginia Statute for Religious Freedom, Charlottesville, Va., September 19–21, 1985).

90. See, for example, Leo Pfeffer, *Religion, State, and the Burger Court* (New York: Prometheus Books, 1984); Leonard W. Levy, "The Establishment Clause," in this volume; Jesse C. Choper, "The Religion Clauses," *University of Pittsburgh Law Review*, vol. 41, no. 4 (Summer 1980); Richard E. Morgan, *The Supreme Court and Religion* (New York: Free Press, 1972), chap. 3ff.; James O'Neill, *Religion and Education under the Constitution* (New York: Da Capo Press, 1972); and Robert L. Cord, "Church-State Separation: Restoring the 'No Preference' Doctrine of the First Amendment," *Harvard Journal of Law and Public Policy*, vol. 9, no. 1 (Winter 1986).

91. See Abraham, *Freedom and the Court*, 4th ed., chap. 3, "The Bill of Rights."

92. Everson v. Board of Education of Ewing Township, dissenting opinion, at 59.

3

Hand's Writing on the Wall of Separation: The Significance of *Jaffree* in Future Cases on Religious Establishment

James McClellan

If, in the opinion of the People, the distribution or modification of the Constitutional powers be in any particular wrong, let it be corrected by an amendment in the way in which the Constitution designates. But let there be no change by usurpation; for though this, in one instance, may be the instrument of good, it is the customary weapon by which free governments are destroyed. The precedent must always greatly overbalance in permanent evil any partial or transient benefit which the use can at any time yield.

Thus spoke George Washington in his famous farewell address to the nation when he left office in 1796, urging his countrymen to be eternally vigilant against usurpations of authority.

Inspired by that passage, a federal judge recently delivered one of the most extraordinary opinions ever written by a member of the federal judiciary. He is Judge W. Brevard Hand of the United States District Court for the Southern District of Alabama in Mobile. The opinion was rendered on January 14, 1983, in the case of *Jaffree* v. *The Board of School Commissioners of Mobile County*, otherwise known as the Alabama prayer case.[1]

In a carefully reasoned opinion that is sure to haunt the Supreme Court for years to come, Judge Hand repudiated the entire body of case law that has been erected around the establishment clause of the First Amendment. Holding that federal courts do not even have jurisdiction over cases involving prayer in the public schools of Alabama, Hand offered impressive historical evidence—much of it over-looked or ignored in previous establishment cases—to demonstrate inherent flaws in the original prayer decision of 1962[2] and to show further that the Court has completely misunderstood and mis-construed the meaning of the establishment clause for more than thirty-five years.

The power and originality of Judge Hand's scholarly opinion do not stem from new documentary material uncovered by the judge himself, although many of the published sources that appear in his opinion have never before been included or seriously discussed in a judicial dialogue on religious establishment.[3] Rather, the significance of the case lies in Hand's assault on the doctrine of incorporation, his repudiation of the wall of separation doctrine, and his claims to judicial independence. He is apparently not only the first member of the entire federal judiciary in more than fifty years to question the Supreme Court's jurisdictional claims over church-state relations in the several states but also the first to challenge the application of the Bill of Rights to the states.[4] He is also the first federal judge since the Supreme Court assumed jurisdiction over state establishment ques-tions to argue that the religious prohibitions of the establishment clause were never intended to include school prayers or any other form of government aid to religion short of "the outright establish-ment of a national religion."[5]

Federalism and the Establishment Clause

To appreciate the significance of the *Jaffree* case, it is essential to begin where Judge Hand begins—with Justice Hugo Black's opinion for the Court in *Everson* v. *Board of Education*, decided in 1947.[6] *Everson* is the key to an understanding of the issues involved and the foundation for every establishment clause case decided by the Supreme Court.

In *Everson* Black promulgated two revolutionary principles of constitutional construction. First, he held, *without supporting argu-ment*, that the establishment clause applied to the states.[7] By this radical innovation the Court overturned more than one hundred and fifty years of constitutional law that had regularly permitted the states to determine their own church-state relationships in accordance with their own state laws and constitutions.

Second—and equally novel—Black announced that the establish-ment clause erected a "wall of separation" between church and state that prohibited the states from giving any aid of any kind not merely to specific religious sects or denominations but to religion generally. "Neither a state nor the Federal Government," said Justice Black, "can set up a church. Neither can pass laws which aid one religion, *aid all religions,* or prefer one religion over another. . . . No tax in *any* amount, large or small, can be levied to support *any* religious activities or institutions."[8] On the basis of these absolutist pronouncements in *Everson,* the Court subsequently ruled in *Engel* v. *Vitale*[9] that the voluntary recitation of a state-composed prayer, though non-denominational, constituted an aid to, and thus an establishment of, religion.

As Judge Hand demonstrates rather convincingly in the *Jaffree* case, neither of the principles embraced by the Court in *Everson* is supported by the language or intent of the Constitution or by historical experience. Throughout most of this century, it would seem, the Supreme Court has been misreading the meaning and purpose of the Bill of Rights in general and the establishment clause in particular, to the extent that the first nine amendments of our Constitution are being used by the Court to establish total federal control over all civil and criminal rights disputes in the nation. This is the very result that the Bill of Rights was designed to prevent.

The Bill of Rights, according to Judge Hand, originally had a dual purpose. It was designed not merely to assure each individual that the federal government would not abridge the freedoms enumerated but also to assure each *state* that the federal government would not encroach upon the jurisdiction of the states over such matters. With regard to this second purpose, therefore, the Bill of Rights was conceived as a states' rights document. Each amendment was a guarantee to the individual *and* to the states.[10]

A survey of constitutional development leading to the creation and adoption of the Bill of Rights during the formative era of American history lends considerable weight to Judge Hand's thesis. In the Federal Convention of 1787, one of the leading spokesmen for states' rights was George Mason of Virginia, who doggedly resisted the Nationalist plan at every turn.[11] Shortly before the convention completed its work on September 17, Mason remarked that he "wished the plan had been prefaced with a Bill of Rights," adding that he "would second a motion if made for the purpose."[12] Elbridge Gerry of Massachusetts, who had been fighting at Mason's side throughout the summer against the Nationalists, quickly obliged and moved the establishment of a committee to prepare the document.

Only one member of the convention, Roger Sherman of Connecticut, spoke against the motion, but his response ended the debate as abruptly as it had begun. A Bill of Rights would be redundant, Sherman explained, because "the State Declarations of Rights are not repealed by this Constitution; and being in force are sufficient."[13]

Mason feared that "the laws of the U.S. are to be paramount to State Bills of Rights,"[14] but the delegates agreed with Sherman that Mason's apprehensions were unfounded, and the motion was voted down unanimously.[15]

This brief exchange on the need for a bill of rights is the only mention of the subject during the entire Federal Convention. The reasons for the lack of interest are rather obvious: First, the delegates were already agreed that the states would retain jurisdiction over most civil rights disputes between a state and its citizens under the new Constitution, and there had been no serious attempt to establish federal control in this area at any time during the convention. Second, it was generally assumed, as Sherman explained, that state bills of rights would remain the supreme law of each state; the new system of government did not call for uniformity of civil rights but preserved intact the diversity that existed under the Articles of Confederation. Third, the delegated and enumerated powers of the central government did not include the power to prescribe national standards or rules for the states in the field of civil liberties.[16]

This also explains why the Federalists "bowed to the wishes of the Antifederalists in the ratification fight and, without much of a struggle, agreed to the adoption of a bill of rights. . . . The Bill of Rights changed nothing as far as the Constitutional structure was concerned and neither reduced federal power nor increased state power. It simply declared what was already understood."[17] The issue, in other words, was not who would establish civil rights policies within the states but the proper wording of the Constitution that would ensure *state* enforcement of civil liberties in disputes between a state and its citizens. Judge Hand correctly observes in his opinion that

> the federalists . . . acceded to the demands of the Anti-Federalists for a Bill of Rights since, in the opinion of all, nothing in the Bill of Rights changed the terms of the original understanding of the federal convention. It was thought by all that the Bill of Rights simply made express what was already understood by the Convention: namely, the federal government was a government of limited authority and that authority did not include matters of civil liberty such as freedom of speech, freedom of the press, and freedom of religion.[18]

Likewise, the dominant theme of the Antifederalist critique of the Constitution was not civil rights but states' rights. During the ratification struggle Antifederalists placed far greater emphasis on the federalism of the Bill of Rights than on the substantive content or meaning of the liberties themselves. Six states proposed long lists of amendments before the Constitution was adopted. A distinguished political scientist remarked back in 1931:

> It has frequently been stated that the motive behind these amendments was a desire to secure greater protection for the natural rights of the people. This is true only in part. An examination of the proposals of the first three states to make them, Massachusetts, South Carolina, and New Hampshire, will afford sufficient evidence of the fact that the members of these conventions were much more perturbed about the rights and powers of the states than about the rights of the people.[19]

Massachusetts offered nine amendments for consideration, but only the sixth, referring to grand juries, dealt with an individual liberty. At one point the brief list of proposed amendments offered by South Carolina mentions "freedom of the people," but otherwise it addresses the issue of the "sovereignty of the states." Of the twelve amendments submitted by New Hampshire, only the last three bear on personal liberty. Only two states, Virginia and North Carolina, proposed a true bill of rights.[20]

The debates in the First Congress, which drafted the Bill of Rights, also support Judge Hand's reading of the First Amendment. Most scholars, Michael Malbin rightly complains, "underestimate the importance of the [federalism] issue for the members of the First Congress. But, according to the only comprehensive study of that Congress written by a historian who used the First Congress Project's materials, federalism was *the* overriding issue throughout the Congress."[21] No event in that historic Congress better illustrates this point or better illuminates the intent of the framers than the debate on the drafting of the First Amendment.

The task of sorting through the various constitutional amendments proposed by the states and reducing them to a coherent whole was given to James Madison. On June 7, 1789, Madison introduced two amendments dealing with the subject of religion. The first provided that "the Civil Rights of none shall be abridged on account of religious belief or worship, nor shall any *national* religion be established, nor shall the full and equal rights of conscience be in any manner, nor on any pretext infringed."[22]

The wording of the amendment clearly indicated that the prohibition against religious establishment applied only to the federal government and that the states would retain exclusive control over church-state relations within their spheres of authority. This understanding prevailed in subsequent drafts and became a permanent feature of the First Amendment. The language finally approved exempted the states and declared only that "Congress shall make no law respecting an establishment of religion."

Madison's second amendment (his fifth resolution), which would have reversed the consensus of the convention and revolutionized the relationship between the federal and state governments, met a different fate. It provided—and no state had even hinted at the idea—that "no *State* shall violate the equal rights of conscience, or the freedom of the press, or trial by jury in criminal cases."[23] Here, then, was the first and only attempt to apply any portion of what was to become the Bill of Rights to the states. The measure was referred to a select committee, whose membership included Madison, which recommended the part to limit the powers of the states respecting the equal rights of conscience. It passed the House after little debate but was defeated in the Senate.[24] As Tucker of South Carolina wisely observed,

> This [proposal] is offered as an amendment to the Constitution of the United States. It will be much better, I apprehend, to leave the State governments to themselves, and not to interfere with them more than we already do; and that is thought by many to be rather too much.[25]

As finally approved, the relevant portions of the First Amendment provide that "Congress shall make no law respecting an establishment of religion, or prohibiting the free exercise thereof." It may thus be seen that the First Amendment to the Constitution that evolved out of these congressional proceedings was a stunning victory for states' rights. The amendment was framed, considered, and adopted with federalism in mind, and it applied only to the federal government. Not even Madison wished to apply the establishment clause to the states, and his attempt to restrict the state power under an early version of both the free exercise and the freedom of the press clauses was nipped in the bud.

In his *Jaffree* opinion, Judge Hand summarized the intent of the framers accordingly:

> The prohibition in the first amendment against the establishment of religion gave the states, by implication, full authority to determine church-state relations within their respective jurisdictions. "Thus the establishment clause actually had a dual purpose: to guarantee to each *individual* that Congress would not impose a national religion, and to each *state* that it was free to define the meaning of religious establishment under its own state constitution and laws. The Federal gov-

ernment, in other words, simply had no authority over the states respecting the matter of church-state relations."[26]

Addressing the members of the U.S. Senate in 1800, Charles Pinckney, who served as a delegate to the Federal Convention, expressed the common understanding of the framers and the purpose and effect of the Bill of Rights in these striking words:

When those amendments became a part of the Constitution, it is astonishing how much it reconciled the States to that measure; they considered themselves as secure in those points on which they were the most jealous; they supposed they had placed the hand of their own authority on the rights of religion and the press, and . . . that they could with safety say to themselves: "On these subjects we are in future secure; we know what they mean and are at present; and such as they now are, such are they to remain, until altered by the authority of the people themselves; no inferior power can touch them."[27]

For more than a century the Supreme Court, with only a few scattered dissents, interpreted the Bill of Rights in conformity with this understanding. Speaking for a unanimous Court in *Barron* v. *Baltimore*, Chief Justice John Marshall declared in 1833 that the first eight amendments "contain no expression indicating an intention to apply them to the state governments."[28] The Court held firmly to this position in later decisions between 1833 and 1868 involving the First, Fifth, Sixth, Seventh, and Eighth amendments. In *Permoli* v. *New Orleans*, for example, Justice Catron upheld for a unanimous Court a city ordinance challenged by the Catholic church, asserting, "The Constitution makes no provision for protecting the citizens of the respective States in their religious liberties; this is left to the State Constitutions and laws."[29]

Even after the adoption in 1868 of the Fourteenth Amendment, which prohibited the *states* from denying a person life, liberty, or property without due process of law, an undivided Supreme Court continued to follow the *Barron* principle. Throughout the latter half of the nineteenth century and well into the twentieth, state and federal courts summarily dismissed the notion that the Bill of Rights applied to the states. "In at least twenty cases between 1877 and 1907," noted Charles Warren, "the Court was required to rule upon this point and to reaffirm Marshall's decision of 1833."[30] As late as 1922, in *Prudential Insurance Co.* v. *Cheek*, the Court was reassuring the bar that "neither the Fourteenth Amendment nor any provision of the Constitution imposes restrictions upon the states about freedom of speech."[31]

Three years later, however, the Court arbitrarily announced in a dictum:

> For present purposes *we may and do assume* that freedom of speech and of the press—which are protected by the First Amendment from abridgement by Congress—are among the fundamental personal rights and "liberties" protected by the due process clause of the Fourteenth Amendment from impairment by the states.[32]

By these words the Supreme Court launched a major constitutional revolution. Thus was born the Court's so-called doctrine of incorporation, a new rule of interpretation whereby the various liberties enumerated in the Bill of Rights may be "incorporated" into the word "liberty" of the due process clause of the Fourteenth Amendment and made applicable to the states.

Surely the most revolutionary decision handed down by the Supreme Court in its history, *Gitlow* v. *New York*[33] prepared the way for a massive shift of power from the states to the federal judiciary. The ultimate power to define—and therefore to expand or restrict—civil liberties had silently slipped from the hands of the states to those of the central government, or more particularly the Supreme Court. A staggering blow had thus been inflicted at the very heart of federalism. Such a drastic and swift rupture with the past could only have succeeded through a profound misunderstanding of the constitutional structure by the members of the American legal profession.

So casual and matter-of-fact was the Court that one is tempted to believe the justices themselves did not fully grasp the implications of their own rhetoric. So easily, so fortuitously, was the very purpose of the Bill of Rights thus defeated. Charles Warren, the distinguished constitutional historian, was apparently the only scholar who realized at the time what had happened to the Constitution and Bill of Rights in the *Gitlow* case. Writing in the *Harvard Law Review* in 1926, Warren observed apprehensively that the Supreme Court had followed *Barron* v. *Baltimore* even after the adoption of the Fourteenth Amendment.

> Yet, in this *Gitlow* case, *without even mentioning* [any] *previous cases, the Court assumes, without argument,* that this right of free speech is so protected by the Fourteenth Amendment. Thus, by one short sentence, rights, the protection of which have hitherto been supposed to be within the scope of the State Courts alone, are now brought within the scope of Federal protection and of the United States Supreme Court.[34]

Warren's premonition that the Court had expanded the meaning of the word "liberty" "in a manner which is likely to have important consequences, the extent of which has received little attention as yet,"[35] received little more notice than the assumptions of the Court in the *Gitlow* decision that had prompted it. In 1931, in *Near* v. *Minnesota*,[36] the Court embarked on the revolutionary trail blazed by *Gitlow* by incorporating the freedom of speech and the press of the First Amendment into the word "liberty" of the due process clause of the Fourteenth. In subsequent cases the Court added freedom of assembly[37] and freedom of religion.[38] With the extension of the incorporation doctrine to the establishment clause in *Everson* v. *Board of Education*,[39] decided in 1947, the nationalization of the First Amendment was complete.

Since 1961 the Supreme Court has successfully nationalized state criminal procedure by incorporating the Fourth,[40] Fifth,[41] Sixth, [42] and Eighth amendments[43] and more recently has gone beyond the specific guarantees of the Bill of Rights to create new rights. By incorporating the Ninth Amendment and combining it with other amendments to form a "penumbra" of rights, the Court was able in *Griswold* v. *Connecticut*[44] to devise a new right of privacy, a right further amplified by the Court in *Roe* v. *Wade*[45] to include a right of abortion. The possibilities for the judicial creation of more rights and, in effect, an entirely new Bill of Rights are endless under the Court's incorporation doctrine.

Through this rule of interpretation, it may now be seen, the Supreme Court has been engaged in a wholesale usurpation of state power for more than fifty years. As a result, nine individuals sitting on the Supreme Court for life now have virtually unlimited power to determine the scope and meaning of nearly every freedom that the American people possess. That the Court has met so little resistance in achieving this remarkable result demonstrates rather convincingly that few Americans, particularly in this century, have fully understood the meaning and purpose of the Bill of Rights or appreciated that it has been transformed into an instrument of minority rule by a handful of federal judges—the very essence of tyrannical government.

The engimatic response of the American legal profession to the Court's incorporation of the establishment clause is a case in point. *Everson,* as noted earlier, was the first instance in which the Court interpreted the establishment clause as a restriction on the states. The state law in question sought to reimburse the parents of parochial school children for school transportation costs and was challenged on the ground that it constituted an "establishment of religion." A majority of the justices found the law valid under the theory that it was a welfare measure benefiting the children rather than religion, but not one member of the Court challenged Justice Black's unsupported assumption of jurisdiction. To this day no member of the Supreme Court has ever questioned the application of the establishment clause to the states.

Even more astonishing is the fact that, until *Jaffree*, not a single attorney appearing before the Supreme Court during the past four decades ever challenged the incorporation of the establishment clause. During the course of their research, the intervenors in the *Jaffree* case examined all the oral arguments and all the briefs in the leading establishment and free exericse cases argued before the Court since 1940. To their surprise and confoundment, they discovered that

> a jurisdictional challenge has heretofore not been made to federal jurisdiction asserted over state religious matters left beyond the reach of federal intervention by the first amendment and unaffected by the fourteenth amendment. To our dismay, a thorough review of all the available briefs, *including those of amici curiae*, and oral arguments in major United States Supreme Court establishment clause cases reveals that no one challenged federal usurpation of exclusive state jurisdiction over state religious matters as prohibited by the first amendment and unchanged by the fourteenth amendment.[46]

Such is the level of understanding about the federalism of the Bill of Rights among the rising generation of American lawyers. The Constitution has largely been entrusted to their care. Their failure to explore the origins of the Constitution concerning so important a matter as the Bill of Rights, their resulting inability, it would seem, to grasp the theory and purpose of the system, and their proclivity to accept the Supreme Court's interpretation of the Constitution as gospel constitute a serious indictment of the profession. The problem is surely attributable in part to the case method of study in modern legal education, which emphasizes judicial interpretations of the Constitution rather than original sources and encourages lawyers to structure their arguments within the narrow framework of current case law and the crabbed learning of the judges. Nothing illustrates these points better than the fact that Judge Hand's landmark opinion in *Jaffree* is based almost exclusively on the accumulated research and writing of political scientists. Indeed, it is they and not the lawyers who have led the assault on the doctrine of incorporation and exposed its inherent fallacies, particularly as it applies to the establishment clause.

If it could be demonstrated satisfactorily that the framers of the Fourteenth Amendment deliberately sought to apply the Bill of Rights to the states and to reverse both *Barron* v. *Baltimore* and *Permoli* v. *New Orleans,* then, of course, the original purpose of the establishment clause would not be paramount; for the intent of the framers of 1868 would have superseded that of the framers of 1789–1791. But a paucity of evidence supports this proposition, and an abundance of documentary material drawn from the debates of the Thirty-ninth Congress and contemporaneous newspapers, owing to the exhaustive research of Charles Fairman, points to the conclusion that the Fourteenth Amendment was not intended to overturn *Barron.*[47]

In 1947, the same year that Justice Black wrote his opinion for the Court in *Everson,* he delivered an important dissent in the case of *Adamson* v. *California,*[48] purporting to demonstrate that the authors of the Fourteenth Amendment intended to apply the entire Bill of Rights to the states. Rejecting the Court's practice of "selective incorporation" of the First Amendment only, Black maintained:

> My study of the historical events that culminated in the Fourteenth Amendment, and the expressions of those who sponsored and favored, as well as those who opposed its submission and passage, persuades me that one of the chief objects that the provisions of the Amendment's first section, separately and as a whole, were intended to accomplish was to make the Bill of Rights applicable to the states. With full knowledge of the import of the Barron decision, the framers and backers of the Fourteenth Amendment proclaimed its purpose to be to overturn the Constitutional rule that case had announced.[49]

Issued in dissent, Black's sweeping hypothesis was rejected by his fellow justices at the time. Since 1961, however, the doctrine of incorporation has been extended beyond the First Amendment to most other provisions of the Bill of Rights, and Black's position is essentially that of the Court today.

According to Fairman, whose lengthy analysis of legislative history and original documents compares favorably with Justice Black's brief recital of timeworn secondary sources,[50] in Black's contention that section 1 of the Fourteenth Amendment "was intended and understood to impose Amendments I to VIII upon the states, the record of history is overwhelmingly against him."[51] "In the absence of any adequate support for the incorporation theory," adds Professor Stanley Morrison, "the effort of the dissenting judges in *Adamson* v. *California* to read the Bill of Rights into the Fourteenth amounts simply to an effort to put into the Constitution what the framers failed to put there."[52] Speaking for most constitutional scholars who have studied the issue, the late Alexander M. Bickel concluded that Fairman "conclusively disproved Justice Black's contention; at least such is the weight of opinion among disinterested observers."[53]

Alert to the significance of this debate and its bearing on the issues raised in *Jaffree*, Judge Hand devoted a substantial portion of his opinion to a reexamination of events leading up to the adoption of the Fourteenth Amendment, relying not only on Fairman but also on the more recent studies of Raoul Berger.[54] Their analyses, concluded Hand,

> show that Mr. Justice Black misread the Congressional debate surrounding the passage of the fourteenth amendment. . . . So far as Congress was concerned, after the passage of the fourteenth amendment the states were free to establish one Christian religion over another in the exercise of their prerogative to control the establishment of religions.[55]

The Blaine Amendment

These views are strengthened and confirmed, at least as regards the establishment clause, by circumstances surrounding the consideration and defeat of the Blaine amendment. In 1875 President Ulysses S. Grant delivered an address to the Army of the Tennessee in which he expressed opposition to government support of sectarian schools and concern about the intrusion into public schools of "sectarian, pagan or atheistical dogmas."[56] That same year in his annual message to Congress, Grant called for a constitutional amendment to correct the problem,[57] and the Blaine amendment was introduced in the House of Representatives.

As originally proposed, Representative James Blaine's amendment provided that

> no *State* shall make any law respecting an establishment of religion or prohibiting the free exercise thereof; and no money raised by taxation in any State for the support of public schools, or derived from any public fund therefor, nor any public lands devoted thereto, shall ever be under the control of any religious sect, nor shall any money so raised or lands so devoted be divided between religious sects or denominations.[58]

In this form the amendment gained the necessary two-thirds vote to secure passage in the House. It then went to the Senate.

Attentive to detail and intent on extending the reach of the amendment, the Senate Committee on the Judiciary lengthened the proposal and sent it to the floor for consideration. In its new and revised form, the amendment read as follows:

> No State shall make any law respecting an establishment of religion, or prohibiting the free exercise thereof; and no religious test shall ever be required as a qualification to any office or public trust under any State. No public property and no public revenue of, nor any loan of credit by or under the authority of, the United States, or any State, Territory, District, or municipal corporation, shall be appropriated to or made or used for the support of any school, educational or other institution under the control of any religious or anti-religious sect, organization, or denomination, or wherein the particular creed or tenets of any religious or anti-religious sect, organization, or denomination shall be taught. And no such particular creed or tenets shall be read or taught in any school or institution supported in whole or in part by such revenue or loan of credit, and no such appropriation or loan of credit shall be made to any religious or anti-religious sect, organization, or denomination, or to promote its interests or tenets. *This article shall not be construed to prohibit the reading of the Bible in any school or institution;* and it shall not have the effect to impair rights or property already vested.
>
> Sec. 2. Congress shall have power, by appropriate legislation, to provide for the prevention and punishment of violations of this article.[59]

The Blaine amendment was subsequently defeated in the Senate, only to reappear in the Republican party platform of 1876. Between 1876 and 1929 the amendment was introduced twenty times in Congress. It never passed, and it was never referred to the states for ratification.[60] Significantly, the Congress that considered the Blaine amendment included twenty-three members of the Thirty-ninth Congress, which passed the Fourteenth Amendment. "Not one of the several Representatives and Senators who spoke on the proposal," notes one scholar, "even suggested that its provisions were implicit in the amendment ratified just seven years earlier."[61]

Representative Nathaniel Banks of Massachusetts, a member of the Thirty-ninth Congress, observed: "If the Constitution is amended so as to secure the object embraced in the principal part of this proposed amendment, it prohibits the States from exercising a power they now exercise."[62] Senator Frederick Theodore Frelinghuysen of New Jersey urged his colleagues to support the "House article," which "prohibits the States *for the first time,* from the establishment of religion, from prohibiting its free exercise."[63] In opposition to the amendment Senator John Stevenson, a Kentucky Democrat, argued from the position of states' rights, citing Thomas Jefferson as authority:

> Friend as he [Jefferson] was of religious freedom, *he would never have consented that the States . . . should be degraded and that the Government of the United States, a Government of limited authority, a mere agent of the States with prescribed powers, should undertake to take possession of their schools and of their religion.*[64]

The remarks of other senators—William Eaton of Connecticut, Oliver Morton of Indiana, William Whyte of Maryland, Isaac Christiancy of Michigan, Lewis Bogey of Missouri, Theodore Randolph of New Jersey, and Francis Kernan of New York—"give confirmation to the belief that none of the legislators in 1875 thought the Fourteenth Amendment incorporated the religious provisions of the First."[65]

Blaine himself, who also had taken an active part in the debates on the framing of the Fourteenth Amendment in the Thirty-ninth Congress, reiterated the common understanding of the time that the Fourteenth Amendment did not apply the establishment clause to the states. In a letter to a political figure in Ohio, published in the *New York Times* two weeks before he introduced his amendment, Blaine wrote:

> The Public School agitation in your late campaign is liable to break out elsewhere. . . . The only settlement that can be final is the complete victory for non-sectarian schools. . . . The First Amendment of the Constitution, the joint product of Jefferson and Madison, proposed in 1789, declared that "Congress shall make no law respecting an establishment of religion, nor prohibiting the free exercise thereof." At that time when the powers of the federal government were untried and undeveloped, the fear was that Congress might be a source of danger to perfect religious liberty, and hence all power was taken from it. At the same time, states were left free to do as they pleased in regard to "an establishment of religion," for the Tenth Amendment, proposed by that eminent jurist, Theophilus Parsons, and adopted contemporaneously with the First, declared that "All powers not delegated to the national government . . . are reserved to the States. . . ."
>
> A majority of people in any state in this Union can, therefore, if they desire it, have an established church—under which the minority can be taxed for the erection of church edifices which they never enter and for the support of creeds which they do not believe. This power was actually exercised

in many states long after the adoption of the federal constitution, and although there may be no danger of its revival in the future, the possibility of it should not be permitted. . . .

And in curing this constitutional defect, all possibility of hurtful agitation on the school question shall also be ended. Just let the old Jefferson-Madison amendment be added to the inhibitory clause in Section 10, Article 1 of the federal Constitution, viz: "No State shall make any law respecting an establishment of religion, nor prohibiting the free exercise thereof; and no money raised by taxation for the support of the public schools, or derived from any public fund therefor, shall ever be under the control of any religious sect, nor shall any money so raised ever be divided between religious sects or denominations."

This, you will observe, does not interfere with any state from having just such a school system as the citizens may prefer, subject to the one single and simple restriction that the schools shall not be made the arena for sectarian controversy or theological disputation. This, it seems to me, would be comprehensive and conclusive, and would be fair alike to Protestant and Catholic, to Jew and Gentile, leaving the religious conscience of every man free and unmolested.[66]

It is difficult, if not intellectually dishonest, to avoid the conclusion that the fifty-year struggle to apply the establishment and free exercise clauses to the states through the abortive Blaine amendment settles the issue of the intent of the Fourteenth Amendment. Francis O'Brien, one of the first constitutional scholars to explain the significance of the Blaine amendment in the current debate, noted more than a quarter-century ago that "a *conclusive* argument against the incorporation theory, at least as respects the religious provisions of the First Amendment, is the 'Blaine Amendment' proposed in 1875."[67] Charles Rice has rightly insisted that "from the history of the Blaine Amendment, one can only conclude that the Establishment Clause was not applied against the States by the Fourteenth Amendment. That history confirms the other and overwhelming indications that none of the provisions of the Bill of Rights was so applied."[68]

To these observations we may add those of Judge Hand, whose opinion reflects a careful reading of Fairman as well as the debate on the Blaine amendment. That amendment, he concludes,

is stark testimony to the fact that the adoptors of the fourteenth amendment never intended to incorporate the establishment clause of the first amendment against the states, a fact which [Justice] Black ignored. This was understood by nearly all involved with the Thirty-ninth Congress to be the effect of the fourteenth amendment.[69]

As Edward S. Corwin has amply demonstrated, the application of the establishment clause to the states also requires a rather bizarre juggling of words and an artful manipulation of legal and historical precedents. In the first place, the establishment clause is not the embodiment of a personal liberty that one may exercise but a general principle of interpretation that, like the Tenth Amendment, delineates in principle the spheres of power between two levels of authority. The key word in the incorporation process, it should be kept in mind, is the word "liberty" in the due process clause of the Fourteenth Amendment, a word or condition or right that can theoretically be inflated to include a personal freedom such as freedom of speech but can hardly be used to accommodate a political principle for limiting the powers of government. The establishment clause of the First Amendment does not confer a right to nonestablishment any more than it allows an individual freedom of nonestablishment; otherwise the free exercise clause would be redundant, and we would be driven to the erroneous conclusion that the framers knew not what they were doing. At best the establishment clause was clearly understood as a *means* to religious freedom, distinguishable from the condition of liberty itself.

In the second place, notes Corwin, "the principal importance of the [First] Amendment lay in the separation which it effected between the respective jurisdictions of state and nation regarding religion, rather than its bearing on the question of the separation of Church and State."[70] In other words, the federalism of the First Amendment and the desire of Congress in 1791 to assure the states that the new central government would have no authority over local church-state relations explain the underlying purpose of the establishment clause of the First Amendment. The refusal of the Court to recognize this fundamental truth has, in the view of Mark de Wolfe Howe, led the Court "to disregard—even to distort—the intellectual background of the First Amendment."[71] The justices of the Supreme Court, Howe has suggested, have arbitrarily embraced the erroneous idea

> that the policies of freedom and equality enunciated in 1868 in the Fourteenth Amendment must be read back into the prohibitions of the First Amendment—the familiar process of incorporation carried out, as it were, in reverse. The consequence may be admirable law, but it is . . . distorted history.[72]

Against this backdrop the real significance of Judge Hand's contribution comes into sharper focus. His opinion invites a reexamination of the doctrine of incorporation, the great wellspring of judicial activism in our time that has given nine individuals—and often just five—the awesome power of setting public policy over the entire range of individual freedom for a nation of some 240 million souls. It thus transcends the immediate issue of religious establishment and calls into question the whole course of constitutional development under the broad heading of civil liberties during the past half-century. "The historical record," he concludes,

> shows without equivocation that none of the states envisioned the fourteenth amendment as applying the federal Bill of Rights against them through the fourteenth amendment. It is sufficient for purposes of this case for the Court to recognize, and the Court do so recognize, that the fourteenth amendment did not incorporate the establishment clause of the first amendment against the states.[73]

These are fighting words that threaten to topple the house of incorporation cards the Court has built on the flimsy foundation of *Gitlow*.

Faults and Fissures in the Wall of Separation Doctrine

Even if the Fourteenth Amendment were intended to apply the establishment clause against the states, it is clear that the Court's view of religious establishment has little basis in American history. In almost every establishment case the Supreme Court has been at pains to justify its absolutist interpretation of the establishment clause on historical grounds. From Justice Black's opinion in *Everson* down to the present there are lengthy discourses on religious liberty purporting to demonstrate the universal acceptance throughout the American past of the Jeffersonian proposition that the First Amendment "erected a wall of separation between church and state," prohibiting the federal and state governments from giving aid of any kind not only to particular religious sects but to all religions or for general religious and moral purposes.

> What strikes the critical student of the Constitution as peculiar is the fact the historical material dredged up by the Court, much of which relates to religious conflict in England in the seventeenth century, is totally irrelevant to the absolutist position the Court is attempting to substantiate, and invariably refers to the consequences and dangers of political aid to one religious sect rather than religion generally.[74]

Moreover, when the Court turns to the American experience, it has usually limited its inquiry to the Virginia struggle against the Anglican establishment in the eighteenth century and has interpreted the Virginia experience as that of the Congress of 1791 and of the American republic generally. Narrowing its focus yet further, the Court has relied almost exclusively on the writings of two Virginians—Madison and Jefferson—to buttress its claims. Both the majority and the dissenting members of the Court were unanimously agreed in *Everson* that the establishment clause should be interpreted as an absolute restriction on governmental aid to religion. "In the words of Jefferson," concluded the Court, "the clause against the establishment of religion by law was intended to erect 'a wall of separation' between church and state."[75]

The facts show, however, that no such wall was ever intended. Indeed, it never existed. A bare catalogue of church-state relations in all the states before and after the adoption of the Constitution would require many volumes. Suffice it to say that the overwhelming majority of states had clearly rejected the principle that there should be an absolute separation of church and state at the time they ratified the Bill of Rights. In 1791 there were three patterns of church-state relations in the United States: (1) quasi-establishment of Congregationalism in New England, where the church enjoyed direct and indirect benefits through state constitutions and statutes; (2) quasi-establishment of the Protestant religion in ten states; and (3) disestablishment of all religious sects in Rhode Island and Virginia.[76]

The establishment clause preserved intact these various relationships and served two purposes. First, it served as a guarantee to the states that the federal government had no authority either to disestablish a sect or religion enjoying a preferred status or to pass a law *respecting* (that is, dealing with the subject of) the establishment of a religion.[77] To suggest that any of the states ratified the First Amendment with the understanding that their assent cleared the way for federal interference in their internal religious affairs is to misunderstand the basic purpose of the establishment clause. The second purpose, as Justice Joseph Story explained in his *Commentaries on the Constitution*, was "to prevent any national ecclesiastical establishment that would give to an hierarchy the exclusive patronage of the *national* government."[78]

The debates in the First Congress, which drafted the Bill of Rights, also reflect strong opposition to the view that the federal government should be prohibited from giving "any aid of any kind" to religion. In his analysis of documentary sources on the First Congress, including the notes of the reporter Thomas Lloyd, Michael Malbin has noted "that the members of the First Congress did not intend the establishment clause to mean anything remotely resembling what the Supreme Court has been saying it means, at least since

1947."[79] Summarizing the debates, the various drafts of the amendment leading up to the final version, and the events surrounding the parliamentary struggle, Malbin concludes, "The legislative history of the establishment clause shows that the framers accepted non-discriminatory aid to religion."[80]

Turning finally to legislative proposals offered contemporaneously with the debate and adoption of the First Amendment and in the early years of the Republic, we again discern widespread acceptance of the principle that nondiscriminatory aid to religion generally and to Christianity in particular is consistent with the purposes of the First Amendment. One of the earliest acts of the House of Representatives, for example, was the election of a chaplain and an appropriation of $500 to pay his salary. Madison was a member of the committee that recommended the chaplain system.

While a member of the House, Madison endorsed Washington's presidential proclamations dealing with thanksgiving, fasting, and prayer. Later, while serving as president, Madison himself issued four prayer proclamations.[81] Of the first four presidents of the United States, only Jefferson declined to issue executive religious proclamations; but his refusal derived not from the belief that such exercises constituted an establishment of religion but from his conviction as a states' rightist that the federal government had no authority to enter the field.[82]

The historical record, concludes Judge Hand in his survey of these activities, shows that

> the framers never intended the establishment clause to erect an absolute wall of separation between the Federal government and religion. . . . From the beginning of our country, the high and impregnable wall which Mr. Justice Black referred to . . . was not as high and impregnable as Justice Black's revisionary literary flourish would lead one to believe. . . . Enough is enough. Figurative illustrations should not serve as a basis for deciding constitutional issues.[83]

Madison and Jefferson would surely agree. Madison, as we have seen, supported various practices that are incompatible with the Supreme Court's reading of the establishment clause. Jefferson's "wall of separation" rhetoric, lifted out of context from a private letter and annexed by the Supreme Court to the First Amendment, has been employed willy-nilly by the justices in such a way as to misrepresent both the meaning of the First Amendment and the political principles of Jefferson, the champion of states' rights and one of its principal architects. Jefferson fully understood that one of the purposes of the establishment clause was to grant exclusive jurisdiction over state establishment issues to the states themselves. As he remarked in a letter to a Presbyterian clergyman in 1808:

> I consider the government of the United States as interdicted by the Constitution from intermeddling with religious institutions, their doctrines, discipline or exercises. This results not only from the provision that no law shall be made respecting the establishment or free exercise of religion, but from that also which reserves to the States the powers not delegated to the United States.[84]

In sum, "it should be clear that the traditional interpretation of Madison and Jefferson is historically faulty if not virtually unfounded."[85]

Circling the Walls of Jericho: *Everson* under Siege

The long-range consequences of Judge Hand's constitutional challenges to the Supreme Court are yet to be seen. Implicit in his opinion was the hope, if not the expectation, that his stunning disclosure of new facts about the origin, purpose, and early history of the establishment clause and his revelation of its spurious relationship to the Fourteenth Amendment would force the Court to reexamine its position or at least produce a rebuttal.

The Court has eluded Judge Hand's net, however, and the crucial questions he raised will have to simmer in the reports until another judge rekindles the debate. On May 12, 1983, the U.S. court of appeals in Atlanta overturned Judge Hand's ruling.[86] Not surprisingly, the Court made no attempt to respond to Hand's arguments, relying exclusively on Supreme Court precedents. Notwithstanding the "case" and "controversy" requirement, the Supreme Court then narrowed the issues of the case and avoided the real basis of the dispute.[87] At its inception *Jaffree* involved a challenge to vocal classroom prayer led by teachers without benefit of statute. As redefined by the Supreme Court, the question became the constitutionality of a state law authorizing a "moment of silence" for meditation and prayer. The Court also refused to consider the incorporation question, and the state of Alabama therefore did not argue the point.[88] Despite Alabama's right of appeal, the Court arbitrarily reframed the issues to get the kind of case it wanted. Such are the ways in which the justices expand their jurisdiction and manipulate the Constitution nowadays as self-appointed guardians of public policy.

Affirming the court of appeals decision, a divided Court ruled in *Wallace v. Jaffree*[89] that the Alabama "moment of silence" statute violated the establishment clause. The majority not only turned a deaf ear to Judge Hand's exposition of the incorporation doctrine but ignored as well his arguments disproving the separationist theory of construction. Like an incantation, the Court summarily recited its own decisions in reply to Hand's opinion, barely acknowledging the documentary evidence of original intent the judge had amassed to support his position. These are telltale signs of raw judicial power; and they reveal an uneasiness and uncertainty in that high tribunal, intimating self-doubt, not self-confidence.

We would be shortsighted, however, if we concluded from the holding in *Jaffree* that Hand's effort was an exercise in futility; for Hand has stirred a national debate of no small importance. He has found a convert on the Supreme Court—then-Justice William H. Rehnquist, who asserted for the first time in his judicial career that on the subject of religious establishment the Supreme Court has been laboring under a "mistaken understanding of constitutional history" during the past forty years.[90] In a lengthy dissent that includes original source material cited by Hand, Rehnquist argued that the Court should promptly abandon the erroneous "wall of separation" theory (see chapter 5 of this volume). "There is simply no historical foundation for the proposition that the Framers intended to build the 'wall of separation' that was constitutionalized in *Everson*." It is a "mischievous diversion of judges from the actual intentions of the drafters of the Bill of Rights," he observed, and "has no basis in the history of the [First] amendment."[91] Justice Byron R. White also dissented, asserting that he "would support a basic reconsideration of our precedents." On the basis of Rehnquist's persuasive analysis of the religion clauses, said White, "it would be quite understandable if we undertook to reassess our cases dealing with these clauses, particularly those dealing with the Establishment Clause."[92] But for Hand's challenge to the Court, these dissents would surely not have been written.

The influence of Judge Hand's opinion does not end in the pages of the Supreme Court reports. The incorporation doctrine, for example, has percolated to the surface of public debate since *Jaffree* and is now a common topic of discussion; and for the first time its legitimacy has been questioned by the attorney general of the United States. In a major address before the American Bar Association, Edwin Meese III spoke critically of the "bewildering" logic and "tangled case law" exhibited by the Supreme Court in establishment cases, pointing to *Jaffree* in particular.[93] "Most Americans forget," he reminded the legal profession, "that it was not until 1925, in *Gitlow* v. *New York*, that *any* provision of the First Amendment was applied to the States. Nor was it until 1947 that the Establishment Clause was made applicable to the States through the Fourteenth Amendment."[94] Noting further that the doctrine of incorporation was imposed "without any substantive argument" and that it rests on an "intellectually shaky foundation," the attorney general surmised that "nowhere else has the principle of federalism been dealt so politically violent and constitutionally suspect a blow as by the theory of incorporation."[95] Without mentioning Brevard Hand by name, the attorney general endorsed his view that the wall of separation notion contravened the meaning and purpose of the establishment clause, concluding that there is "much merit in Justice Rehnquist's dissent in *Jaffree*."[96]

In the final analysis, it seems clear that Judge Hand's opinion has left a deep and permanent scar on the face of the Supreme Court; for he has rather successfully challenged the Court's self-proclaimed infallibility, at least on the question of religious establishment, eliciting thereby a favorable response from two of its members. Moreover, he has laid bare the utter falsity of the incorporation and wall of separation theories. The study and practice of constitutional law in this country, notwithstanding Leonard Levy's chimerical writings on the establishment clause, will never be quite the same. Taken together, the Hand and Rehnquist opinions invigorate the legitimacy of a great body of scholarship that has been ignored by the Court, creating a haven for dissenters that will strengthen their position as never before. In these respects *Jaffree* may well mark an important turning point in American constitutional history. Truth is a stubborn adversary and has a way of haunting men—even those on the high court.

Notes

1. 553 Fed. Supp. 1104 (S.D. Ala., 1983).
2. Engel v. Vitale, 370 U.S. 421 (1962).
3. See 553 Fed. Supp. at 1113, n. 5, citing the works of James McClellan and Robert Cord, and n. 26, citing those of Raoul Berger.
4. The debate within the Supreme Court on the doctrine of incorporation has centered primarily on the application of specific amendments dealing with criminal procedure rather than the First Amendment or the Bill of Rights as such. See, for example, Justice John Harlan's dissent in Duncan v. Louisiana, 391 U.S. 145 (1968), but also Justice Hugo Black's dissent in Adamson v. California, 332 U.S. 46 (1947).
5. 553 Fed. Supp. at 1115.
6. 330 U.S. 1 (1947).
7. Ibid. at 8.
8. Ibid. at 15, 16 (emphasis added).
9. 370 U.S. 421 (1962).
10. 553 Fed. Supp. at 1114.

11. See A. Koch, ed., *Notes of Debates in the Federal Convention of 1787* (reported by James Madison) (Athens: Ohio University Press, 1966), pp. 87, 190, 366, 491, 549.

12. Ibid., p. 630.

13. Ibid.

14. Ibid. Mason's position is clear enough. Although he has been depicted as a liberal champion of civil rights at the convention, a reading of the debates shows that Mason's primary concern was states' rights. In this respect he was part of the emerging consensus favoring retention of state bills of rights.

15. Ibid. The votes were taken by delegation and not individually.

16. The exception is Article I, section 10, whereby the states were prohibited from passing bills of attainder, ex post facto laws, or laws impairing the obligation of contracts.

17. James McClellan, *Joseph Story and the American Constitution* (Norman: University of Oklahoma Press, 1971), p. 145.

18. 554 Fed. Supp. at 1114. See McClellan, *Joseph Story*, p. 146.

19. B. Wright, *American Interpretations of Natural Law* (Cambridge, Mass.: Harvard University Press, 1938), p. 146.

20. Ibid., p. 147.

21. Michael J. Malbin, *Religion and Politics: The Intentions of the Authors of the First Amendment* (Washington, D.C.: American Enterprise Institute, 1978), pp. 15–16.

22. Ibid., p. 4 (emphasis supplied).

23. Ibid. (emphasis supplied).

24. Ibid., pp. 5–12.

25. McClellan, *Joseph Story*, pp. 147–48.

26. 554 Fed. Supp. at 1114, quoting James McClellan, "The Making and Unmaking of the Establishment Clause," in P. McGuigan and R. Rader, eds., *Blueprint for Judicial Reform* (Washington, D.C.: Free Congress Research and Education Foundation, 1981), p. 300.

27. McClellan, *Joseph Story*, p. 148.

28. 7 Peters (32 U.S.) 243 (1833).

29. 3 Howard (44 U.S.) 589 (1845).

30. Charles Warren, "The New 'Liberty' under the Fourteenth Amendment," *Harvard Law Review*, vol. 39 (1926), p. 436.

31. 259 U.S. 530 (1922).

32. Gitlow v. New York, 268 U.S. 666 (1925).

33. Ibid.

34. Warren, "The New 'Liberty,' " p. 433 (emphasis supplied).

35. Ibid., p. 432.

36. 283 U.S. 697 (1931).

37. De Jonge v. Oregon, 299 U.S. 353 (1937).

38. Cantwell v. Connecticut, 310 U.S. 296 (1940).

39. 330 U.S. 1 (1947).

40. Mapp v. Ohio, 367 U.S. 643 (1961).

41. Malloy v. Hogan, 378 U.S. 1 (1964).

42. Gideon v. Wainwright, 372 U.S. 335 (1963); Pointer v. Texas, 380 U.S.

400 (1965); Parker v. Gladden, 385 U.S. 363 (1966); Klopfer v. North Carolina, 386 U.S. 213 (1967); Washington v. Texas, 388 U.S. 14 (1967); and Duncan v. Louisiana, 391 U.S. 145 (1968).

43. Robinson v. California, 370 U.S. 660 (1962).

44. 381 U.S. 479 (1965).

45. 410 U.S. 113 (1973).

46. Reply brief for appellants Douglas T. Smith et al., at 16, Wallace v. Jaffree and Smith v. Jaffree, 705 F.2d 1526 (11th Cir. 1983), on appeals to the Supreme Court, nos. 83-812 and 83-929.

47. See Charles Fairman, "Does the Fourteenth Amendment Incorporate the Bill of Rights? The Original Understanding," *Stanford Law Review,* vol. 2 (1949), p. 5.

48. 332 U.S. 46 (1947).

49. Ibid. at 71.

50. Justice Black relied substantially on Horace Flack, *The Adoption of the Fourteenth Amendment* (Baltimore: Johns Hopkins University Press, 1908).

51. Fairman, "Does the Fourteenth Amendment," p. 139.

52. Stanley Morrison, "Does the Fourteenth Amendment Incorporate the Bill of Rights? The Judicial Interpretation," *Stanford Law Review,* vol. 2 (1949), p. 173.

53. Alexander M. Bickel, *The Least Dangerous Branch* (Indianapolis, Ind.: Bobbs-Merrill Co., 1962), p. 102.

54. 554 Fed. Supp. at 1119–1120, citing Raoul Berger, *Government by Judiciary: The Transformation of the Fourteenth Amendment* (Cambridge, Mass.: Harvard University Press, 1977).

55. 554 Fed. Supp. at 1122.

56. As quoted by Charles Rice in brief amicus curiae of the Center for Judicial Studies in support of appellants at 15, Wallace v. Jaffree and Smith v. Jaffree, 705 F.2d 526 (11th Cir., 1983), on appeals to the Supreme Court, nos. 83-812 and 83-929.

57. Ibid.

58. Ibid. at 15–16.

59. Ibid. at 16.

60. Ibid. at 17.

61. Francis O'Brien, *Justice Reed and the First Amendment* (Washington, D.C.: Georgetown University Press, 1958), p. 116.

62. Ibid.

63. Ibid.

64. Ibid., pp. 116–17.

65. Ibid.

66. Rice, amicus brief, at 18–19.

67. O'Brien, *Justice Reed,* p. 116.

68. Rice, amicus brief, at 19. See also C. Rice, "The Jaffree Case," *Benchmark,* vol. 1 (May–June 1984), p. 15.

69. 554 Fed. Supp. at 1126.

70. Edward S. Corwin, "The Supreme Court as a National School Board,"

reprinted in *A Constitution of Powers in a Secular State* (Charlottesville, Va.: Michie Co., 1951), p. 106.

71. Mark de Wolfe Howe, *The Garden and the Wilderness: Religion and Government in American Constitutional History* (Chicago: University of Chicago Press, 1965), p. 31.

72. Ibid.

73. 554 Fed. Supp. at 1124.

74. McClellan, *Joseph Story*, p. 135.

75. 330 U.S. at 15. See McClellan, *Joseph Story*, p. 296, n. 7.

76. McClellan, *Joseph Story*, pp. 300–308.

77. Ibid., p. 146, n. 97.

78. Joseph Story, *Commentaries on the Constitution* (Boston: Little, Brown and Co., 1833), vol. 3, section 1871.

79. Malbin, *Religion and Politics*, p. 2.

80. Ibid., p. 16.

81. Robert Cord, *Separation of Church and State* (New York: Lambeth Press, 1982), pp. 16–36.

82. Ibid., p. 40. See also McClellan, *Joseph Story*, p. 156.

83. 554 Fed. Supp. at 1117–1118.

84. As quoted in Cord, *Separation of Church and State*, p. 40. "In matters of religion," said Jefferson in his second inaugural address, "I have considered that its free exercise is placed by the constitution independent of the powers of the general government. I have therefore undertaken, on no occasion, to prescribe the religious exercises suited to it; but have left them, as the constitution found them, under the direction and discipline of State or Church authorities acknowledged by the several religious societies." Adrienne Koch and William Peden, eds., *The Life and Selected Writings of Thomas Jefferson* (New York: Modern Library, 1944), p. 341.

85. Cord, *Separation of Church and State*, p. 47.

86. 705 F.2d 1526 (11th Cir. 1983).

87. American practice has traditionally recognized that the parties are entitled to a judicial resolution of the issue raised. The framers never intended federal judges to roam at large in construing the Constitution and laws of the United States and were agreed, as the language of section 2 indicates, that disputes should be resolved in a "judicial manner." Proposals for associating the judges in a Council of Revision to pass on laws generally were voted down four times in the Federal Convention; and when William Samuel Johnson of Connecticut proposed to extend the judicial power to cases arising under the Constitution as well as under federal laws and treaties, Madison rose in opposition, stating that he "doubted whether it was not going too far to extend the jurisdiction of the Court generally to cases arising under the Constitution, and whether it ought not be limited to cases of a Judiciary Nature." Johnson's motion was roundly defeated. Max Farrand, ed., *The Records of the Federal Convention of 1787*, rev. ed. (New Haven, Conn.: Yale University Press, 1937), p. 430.

88. Professor Levy creates the erroneous impression that the Supreme

Court actually reconsidered the incorporation doctrine in *Jaffree* when it treated Judge Hand's opinion with "the contemptuous disdain it deserved." See Leonard Levy, *The Establishment Clause: Religion and the First Amendment* (New York: Macmillan, 1986), pp. 171–72.

89. 472 U.S. ———, 86 L.Ed. 2d 29 (1985).

90. Ibid. at ———, 86 L.Ed. 2d at 66.

91. Ibid. at ———, 86 L.Ed. 2d at 75, 76, 79.

92. Ibid. at ———, 86 L.Ed. 2d at 66.

93. Edwin Meese III, "The Jurisprudence of Original Intention," *Benchmark*, vol. 2 (1986), p. 4.

94. Ibid., p. 5.

95. Ibid.

96. Ibid.

4

The Establishment Clause

Leonard W. Levy

What does history show about the meaning of the establishment clause at the time of its framing and adoption? What did an establishment of religion mean to the generation that adopted the First Amendment? In Europe an establishment of religion meant a state church: one church exclusively enjoying the benefits of a formal, legal union with the state. It was the church of the state; attendance at its services was compulsory unless the state indulged the existence of open religious services by dissenters; all subjects, even the dissenters, paid for its support; its doctrine and rites alone could be publicly taught in schools; and its clergy alone had civil sanction to perform sacraments. An establishment of religion denoted a legal alliance of government and religion if by "religion" is meant the religion of a church or of a single denomination, such as Roman Catholicism in Spain, Anglicanism in England, Presbyterianism in Scotland, or Lutheranism in Sweden.

A book by James O'Neill in 1949 advocated the thesis that aid to religion generally or to all churches without discrimination did not constitute an establishment of religion and therefore could not violate the First Amendment.[1] O'Neill's thesis has enjoyed a revival in recent years; works by Chester J. Antieau, Michael Malbin, Walter Berns, James McClellan, and Robert L. Cord, among others, recognizing the pluralistic and religious nature of American society, have refurbished the thesis by arguing that government assistance to religion generally—to all religions and their institutions—does not constitutionally breach the wall of separation between church and state.[2] Like O'Neill, all see an establishment of religion as a state church. All agree with Edward S. Corwin, who contended that the Supreme Court's *Everson*

This essay, originally composed in 1984, became the basis of my book *The Establishment Clause: Religion and the First Amendment* (New York: Macmillan Publishing Co., 1986).

doctrine on the unconstitutionality of government aid to "all religions" is "untrue historically."[3]

In the eighteenth century, however, America broke with the precedents of Europe by providing legal recognition and tax support to more than one church within a single colony and, later, within a state. Indeed, at the time of the framing and ratification of the First Amendment, the establishments of religion that still existed in the United States were plural or multiple establishments of churches; they authorized the taxation of all for the support of religion but allowed each person's tax to be remitted to the church of his choice. Without doubt, an establishment of religion still conveyed the basic idea of exclusivity or preference, but that was not the only idea that it conveyed. To the generation that adopted the First Amendment it had also come to mean the support of religion generally.

Granted, religion was then virtually synonymous with Christianity, indeed, in most of America, with Protestantism. In Europe a state church meant exactly that: the church of one denomination, not Christianity or Protestantism. Christianity or Protestantism may signify one religion in contrast with Judaism, Islam, or Hinduism; Protestantism may, more dubiously, be one religion in contrast with Roman Catholicism. But nowhere after the sixteenth century had Christianity or Protestantism been the solely established religion except in America. An establishment of Christianity or of Protestantism in the American states that permitted an establishment in about 1790 would have been, for practical purposes, a comprehensive or nonpreferential establishment. No American state at the time maintained an establishment in the European sense of having an exclusive state church designated by law. Europe had never provided government aid to all churches or religion generally, as did the American states whose law still permitted establishments when the First Amendment was framed.[4]

The Nonpreferential Interpretation

A formidable school of nonpreferentialists (accommodationists) has developed a plausible but fundamentally defective interpretation of the legislative history of the establishment clause, to prove that its framers had no intention of prohibiting government aid to all religions or to religion on a nonpreferential basis. Antieau, following in the tradition of O'Neill and Corwin, is the unrecognized maven of the nonpreferentialists, who include his former associates Downey and Roberts, as well as Berns, Malbin, McClellan, and Cord.[5] Their view is that the legislative history of the clause and its final phrasing prove an intent to impose on the national government merely a ban against aiding an exclusive or preferential establishment, which results in their conclusion that government aid to religion generally without a hint of discrimination would not violate the establishment clause.[6]

The nonpreferential interpretation is persuasive if one can ignore or forget that the First Amendment, no matter how parsed or logically analyzed, was framed to deny power, not to vest it. The fundamental defect of the nonpreferential interpretation is that it results in the unhistorical contention that the First Amendment augmented a non-existent congressional power to legislate in the field of religion. The nonpreferential interpretation is persuasive if one can also ignore or forget that neither Christianity nor Protestantism was ever a state church. The nonpreferentialists, having a tin ear for history, called Christianity or Protestantism one religion as if one religion were the equivalent of one church in the term "state church."

Thus Antieau managed to employ the term "multiple establishment" without marring his argument that any establishment preferred one religion over another. He defined multiple establishment in various ways, including the admission of dissenting churches to the same privileges and protections as the colonial established church had enjoyed. But a multiple establishment, he said, always "failed to extend legal equality to all religions."[7] If Virginia's general assessment bill had passed, he declared, it would have singled out Christianity, as Maryland had, thus preferring Christian sects over Jews, a fact that "roused the opposition of many other Virginians, including Baptists, Quakers, Presbyterians, the few Catholics, and many Methodists."[8]

Cord, who invariably ended up with "state church" as the definition of an establishment of religion,[9] claimed that the establishment clause was

> designed to establish a separation of Church and the national State. This separation was to be ensured by denying to Congress the constitutional authority to pass legislation providing the formal and legal union of any single church, religion, or sect with the Federal Government. Thus the preferential status of one church, religion, or sect—elevating it to an exclusive governmental position of power and favor over all other churches or religious denominations—would be prevented.[10]

The nonpreferentialist effort resulted in the proposition that government aid to religion without hint of discrimination would not violate the establishment clause. For Antieau and company the legislative history of the establishment clause provided elaborate proof of their thesis.

71

Although James Madison initially proposed "nor shall any national religion be established," in the debate that followed he explained himself by saying that his proposal meant "that Congress shall not establish a religion." The word "a" became significant to the nonpreferentialists. Antieau and his followers emphasized the fact that in the debate Madison wished to proscribe "*a* national religion," that is, a single or exclusive religion preferred over all others, said Antieau, "and nothing else." Similarly, Antieau observed that the term used in the final version of the amendment is "an establishment of religion." He noted that the "use of the singular noun, 'an establishment,' had the effect of narrowing the intended prohibition."[11] Malbin, who had the eccentric notion that no one before him had ever analyzed the debates of the First Congress on the framing of the establishment clause,[12] contended that Madison merely wanted to prohibit "discriminatory religious assistance" and "a national church." Malbin summed up this view as follows:

> At the same time, the phrase "an establishment" seems to ensure the legality of nondiscriminatory religious aid. Had the framers prohibited "*the* establishment of religion," which would have emphasized the generic word "religion," there might have been some reason for thinking they wanted to prohibit all official preferences of religion over irreligion. But by choosing "an establishment" over "the establishment," they were showing that they wanted to prohibit only those official activities that tended to promote the interests of one or another particular sect.[13]

Preferring "religion over irreligion" is a red herring; the question of such a preference was not at issue except to one congressman.

What shall we say, however, about the interpretation based on the use of the indefinite rather than the definite article? First, we are not interpreting a verbatim record of the debate. The record we have derives from unreliable newspaper reports. It is incomplete and does not purport to be a literal transcription of the words of the speakers. Reporters took notes that they later rephrased and expanded for publication. Any interpretation of the debate that turns on single words or precise nuances of phrasing must be suspect. And any interpretation that turns on the use of the indefinite article rather than the definite article must be utterly rejected, for the simple reason that the reporter who took shorthand notes of the debates on the Bill of Rights omitted articles, definite and indefinite, and reconstructed speeches from his memory. Second, "the" is not generic; it is specific. Third, "the" can be as singular as "a" or "an." But those are quibbles. The more important fact is that the article made no difference for any practical purpose. President Thomas Jefferson, for example, when refusing to proclaim a day of national thanksgiving, thought the establishment clause did use "the" instead of "a," for he misquoted it, stating that it said "no law shall be made respecting *the* establishment or free exercise of religion."[14] What is significant is not the misquotation by Jefferson but his belief that the ban on an establishment extended to presidentially proclaimed fast and thanksgiving days.

The Views of James Madison

Similarly, President Madison misquoted the establishment clause but also had an extremely broad view of it. He usually quoted it as if it outlawed "religious establishments," showing, it seems, that he understood the clause to mean that Congress had no power over religious institutions or religion. A "religious establishment" is a church or some religious institution and carries no such implication of government aid to religion or involvement with religion as does an "establishment of religion." In 1808, when vetoing a land grant bill intended to remedy the peculiar situation of a Baptist church that, by a surveying error, had been built on federal land, Madison saw a dangerous precedent in the appropriation of federal funds to support a religious society, contrary to the provision in the Constitution "which declares that 'Congress shall make no law respecting a religious establishment.' "[15] He had earlier misquoted the establishment clause the same way in another veto message against a bill that would have incorporated a church in the District of Columbia, showing that he regarded even simple recognition without financial support as within the ban.[16]

Similarly, in his Detached Memoranda, written sometime after he retired from public office in 1817, he warned against evil "lurking under plausible disguises, and growing up from small beginnings. Obsta principiis" (Resist the beginnings).[17] The Constitution, he said, misquoting again, "forbids everything like an establishment of a national religion."[18] He included chaplains for Congress, military and naval chaplains, and presidential proclamations "recommending fasts & thanksgivings" as examples "of a *national* religion."[19] Rather than let these examples that went beyond "the landmarks of power" have the effect of legitimate precedents, he said, it was better to apply to them "the legal aphorism of de minimus non curat lex" (the law does not bother with trifles). Thus the proposition that Madison meant merely a national church or no preference in the support of religion is groundless, as foolish perhaps as his proposition that the provision of military chaplains was like a national religion. The point, however, is that to Madison "a national religion" broadly comprehended even the most trifling matters.

Among the evidence that Cord warped to prove that Madison "took the word 'establishment' to mean a governmental religion such as a state church"[20] is Madison's statement at the Virginia ratifying convention of 1788. The emphasis is Cord's:

> Fortunately for this Commonwealth, a majority of the people are decidedly against *any exclusive establishment*—I believe it to be so in other states. *There is not a shadow of right in the general government to intermeddle with religion.* . . . The United States abound in such a variety of sects, that it is a strong security against religious persecution, and it is sufficient to authorize a conclusion, that no one sect will ever be able to outnumber or depress the rest.[21]

I do not know why Cord thought that the second set of words he italicized helped his thesis; to me those words prove that Madison opposed all government support of religion, because government had no power to legislate on the subject. But Cord concluded from the quotation that Madison simply opposed "raising one religion above the others."[22] The fact that Madison undoubtedly opposed an exclusive establishment does not prove that he equated every establishment with exclusivity. Cord yanked his statement out of context, altering its implication.

The immediately preceding speaker, Patrick Henry, had opposed ratification of the Constitution because, in part, it had no bill of rights to protect religious liberty. Madison reminded the delegates of some recent Virginia history to make the standard Federalist point that a bill of rights was not necessary and would not protect the people. Virginia's constitution of 1776 had a bill of rights that guaranteed the free exercise of religion, but it was no security for religious liberty because it would not have prevented an exclusive establishment if one sect dominated. Having a national bill of rights, he argued, would not defend liberty if a majority of the people were of one sect. The country enjoyed religious liberty because of "that multiplicity of sects which pervades America, and which is the best and only security for religious liberty in any society"; the existence of many prevented one from oppressing the others. "Fortunately for this commonwealth," he continued—and here Cord picked up Madison's remarks. Thus Madison was not saying that he or the people of Virginia opposed *only* an exclusive establishment. He was saying, rather, that the worst fear would not materialize even if the proposed Constitution had no bill of rights.

Cord, however, transmogrified Madison, turning that principled opponent of all financial assistance by government to religion into an advocate of such aid on condition that it be nonpreferential. Cord argued that Madison opposed Virginia's general assessment bill only because it "placed Christianity in a preferred religious position."[23] Cord disagreed with the conventional interpretation of Madison's Memorial and Remonstrance, which Walter Berns endorsed when he wrote that "this famous statement of Madison's own views calls for the separation not only of church and state but of religion and the state."[24]

The conventional interpretation is the right one because Madison opposed all establishments on grounds of principle. The first of his fifteen arguments against the general assessment bill declared that the duty man owes his creator and the manner of discharging it must be voluntary, not coerced, and that religion is "wholly exempt" from the cognizance of government. Cord's rhetorical questions about whether Madison was really an absolutist—would he have opposed a civil act against human sacrifice or polygamy?—were absurdly out of context. A negative answer to the questions does not alter the fact that Madison opposed all establishments, not just an establishment that favored Christianity over other religions: "Because if Religion be exempt from the authority of the Society at large [religion being a natural right], still less can it be subject to that of the Legislative Body" was Madison's second argument. The third was "take alarm at the first experiment on our liberties" and avoid the consequences of usurped power as well as entangling precedents "by denying the principle." Cord, however, distorted one Madisonian argument after another and arbitrarily concluded: "In sum, only Madison's arguments against exclusive religious aid—in which he assailed the religious [sic] discriminatory Assessment Bill and the evils it was likely to produce— are germane in appraising Madison's attitude about the appropriate relationship between Church and State."[25]

Cord denied us the wonder of seeing how he could distort the meaning of the Virginia Statute for Religious Freedom, which Jefferson had drafted and whose passage Madison guided through the state legislature. That document, like Madison's Memorial, described freedom of religion as a natural right exempt from civil governance, contended that forcing a person to support even the religion of his own persuasion was tyrannical, and made the support of religion private and voluntary. It too expressed Madison's views. If he had opposed the general assessment bill simply because it preferred Christianity over other religions, he would have directed his argu-

75

ment to the reasons for broadening the act to include Zoroastrianism, Hinduism, Judaism, and Islam. Madison made no such argument because he opposed any government tax for religion on the principle that it constituted a threat to religious liberty deriving from an unwarranted exercise of power in a domain forbidden to government. As John Courtney Murray wrote, the theme of the Remonstrance is that religion "must be absolutely free from governmental restriction and likewise absolutely free from governmental aid . . . for the essential theological reason that religion is of its nature a personal, private, interior matter of the individual conscience, having no relevance to the public concerns of the state."[26]

In the same year as the Remonstrance, 1785, Madison opposed a plan of the Continental Congress to set aside public land in each township in the western territories for the support of religion. To James Monroe he wrote: "How a regulation, so unjust in itself, so foreign to the Authority of Congress . . . and smelling so strongly of an antiquated Bigotry, could have received the countenance of a Committee is truly matter of astonishment."[27] In 1790, before the adoption of the First Amendment, Madison in Congress gave this reason for omitting ministers from enumerated occupations in a census bill:

> As to those who are employed in teaching and inculcating the duties of religion, there may be some indelicacy in singling them out, as the general government is proscribed from interfering, in any manner whatsoever, in matters respecting religion; and it may be thought to do this, in ascertaining who, and who are not ministers of the gospels.[28]

Surely one who opposed nonpreferential land grants for religious purposes and who objected to a federal census report of ministers cannot be regarded as an opponent of only such public aid to religion as failed to provide for non-Christians.

Madison served on the joint committee that created congressional chaplains. We have no record showing that he then objected to such chaplaincies or that he favored them, but we do have his letter of 1822 to Edward Livingston in which he declared that he had not approved in 1789 or later:

> I observe with particular pleasure the view you have taken of the immunity of religion from civil jurisdiction. . . . This had always been a favorite principle with me; and it was not with my approbation, that the deviation from it took place in Congress, when they appointed chaplains, to be paid by the National Treasury.[29]

Cord and Antieau made much of the supposed fact that Madison did not oppose the chaplaincy bill in 1789, but they ignored his later statement that he disapproved of it.[30]

In the First Congress Madison did not say that his proposed amendment should be construed as banning just preferential aid or exclusive establishments. He was saying that despite Anti-Federalist warnings the government under the Constitution would not adopt an exclusive establishment, because it had no power whatsoever over the subject of religion. Cord, however, maintained that Madison in 1789 "believed Congress was being denied the power to 'establish a national religion' *not religion*."[31] Cord seems to say that Madison believed that Congress could establish religions but not religion.

This peculiarly fatuous view locks into the nonpreferential thesis that because the ban on establishments reached only preferential supports, the government could constitutionally support all religions. Thus, when Walter Berns examined the Senate's recommended draft of the establishment clause before the joint conference committee altered it, he said that its language would have "permitted federal aid to religion on a nondiscriminatory basis."[32] Because Madison made the remark about a ban on "a national religion," Berns, following Malbin, took note of Madison's willingness to accommodate those who wanted "nondiscriminatory assistance to religion."[33] But no one in the debate on the proposal that became the First Amendment recommended any language that would empower the government to take any positive action favoring religion. Madison sought to accommodate only one group, those who wanted reassurance that the government would not legislate on religious matters.

The Need for an Amendment

During the debate Madison expressly disclaimed taking any position on the question whether an amendment on the matter was needed. When Roger Sherman declared that an amendment was "altogether unnecessary" because Congress had no power "to make religious establishments," David Carroll replied that an amendment on the subject would "conciliate the minds of the people to the Government," and Madison agreed with Carroll. Although he would not say whether an amendment was necessary, Madison reminded the House that some state conventions had expressed the fear that Congress might establish a national religion by the exercise of a power under the necessary and proper clause. In his great speech of June 8, when he urged the House to consider amendments to protect "the great rights of mankind,"[34] he repeated seven times that amendments, whether needed or not, would allay public fears. People feared that Congress would establish a national religion, and he had introduced an amendment calculated to appease them.

Madison mentioned that some people feared the dominance of one sect or the possibility that two might combine to establish a religion to which others might have to conform.[35] Anti-Federalists had persistently expressed exaggerated fears about the way the new government would abuse its powers if the Constitution were ratified. In North Carolina, for example, Henry Abbott frenetically predicted, at his state's ratifying convention, that the treaty power would be used "to adopt the Roman Catholic religion in the United States,"[36] and Major Lusk warned the Massachusetts ratifying convention that "Popery and the Inquisition may be established in America."[37] In his own ratifying convention, Madison had heard Patrick Henry prophesy that the United States would "extort confession by torture," perpetrate "the most tyrannical and oppressive deeds," and send tax gatherers into everybody's homes to "ransack, and measure, every thing you eat, drink, and wear."[38]

Madison and the Federalists could not swing sufficient votes to secure Virginia's ratification of the Constitution without first accepting recommendations for amendments submitted by Henry. His amendments included a proposed bill of rights, one provision of which declared that "no particular religious sect or society ought to be favored or established, by law, in preference to others." After perfunctory endorsement by a committee on amendments, the convention accepted all Henry's proposals. That was the price of ratification by Virginia.[39]

Madison, therefore, did not express his personal opinion on how best to frame an amendment. His record on the point was clear: Congress had no power to meddle with religion, and there was no need to limit a nonexistent power. But he felt obligated to make an effort, to satisfy popular demand for something explicit on the subject of establishments of religion, as well as on religious freedom. His motives were more political than we like to recognize. Understandably, we exalt the Bill of Rights, which gives constitutional recognition to precious freedoms, and we assume that its framers were wise statesmen who pondered just the right phraseology to make every provision possess a resonance and rightness for the ages. In fact they were more interested in discussing tonnage duties, and their debate was brief, apathetic, and ambiguous.

Moreover, the Anti-Federalists, knowing that the adoption of a bill of rights would sink their movement for a second convention and make unlikely the amendments they really wanted, amendments that would cripple the powers of the national government, sought to scuttle Madison's proposals. Failing that, they tried delaying tactics, depreciated the importance of the very protections of individual liberty that they had formerly demanded as a guarantee against impending tyranny, and then tried to weaken the provisions.[40] Madison understood and would not be put off. Privately he said he was engaged in "the nauseous project of amendments," but among the reasons he gave for persisting in a policy that even some members of his own party opposed was his belief that the Anti-Federalists would make political capital out of a failure by Congress to propose amendments in the nature of a bill of rights. Moreover, he declared, the amendments "will kill the opposition everywhere, and by putting an end to disaffection to the Government itself, enable the administration to venture on measures not otherwise safe."[41]

From a constitutional standpoint, Madison believed that the entire enterprise was unnecessary; from a political standpoint, however, the stakes were high. He meant to give the people what they seemed to want, guarantees that nightmares pictured by demagogues would not become real. Politics had demanded that the ratificationist forces swallow Henry's recommended amendments in Virginia in return for crucial votes. Those amendments included some that Federalists vehemently opposed, such as the requirement of a two-thirds majority by Congress for the enactment of laws regulating commerce. Conversely, George Mason, who made much, publicly, of the absence of a bill of rights in the Constitution, had said at the Constitutional Convention that he would rather cut off his right hand than sign the Constitution without that two-thirds provision.[42] Henry's phrasing for the Virginia convention's recommendation against preferred sects ignored the language of Virginia's Statute for Religious Freedom, which went much further; Madison and the ratificationists did not take the no-preference language seriously as a reflection of Virginia's opinion, but it was harmless: who, after all, any longer favored a preferential establishment?

In any case, Madison, when making the proposal that became the establishment clause, went further than the Virginia recommendation. New York, conditioned by its aversion to admitting that the Anglican church had ever been established, had also recommended an amendment in no-preference language. Maryland, contrary to Cord,[43] proposed no amendment on the subject, although as Antieau pointed out, some prominent men had favored the proposal that "there shall be no national religion," which is close to what Madison initially urged. New Hampshire had recommended that "Congress shall make no laws touching religion," which concisely expressed Madison's personal view of the matter but did not address the issue of an establishment. North Carolina at its 1788 convention had refused to ratify the Constitution but recommended amendments that followed Virginia in using the language of no preference; Rhode Island would also use that language but did not hold its convention until after Congress had already recommended the Bill of Rights; North Carolina also belatedly ratified.[44]

Evidence from the States

Antieau, having rigorously analyzed the phrasing of the establishment clause as it proceeded through both houses, rejected "a dogmatic" interpretation of the finished version, a reason perhaps that those who have stolen his thunder have given him so little credit. After all his parsing and deducing, he concluded that it was impossible to state the framers' intention with accuracy and added that all interpretations "seem clothed with reasonableness. All are conjectural."[45]

Yet he managed to maintain his thesis that the establishment clause prohibited only preferential aid to religion by arguing that the way to find out what "establishment of religion" meant is to look at the use of that term immediately before the first session of Congress.[46] He meant, oddly, that we should look at the state recommendations for amendments to the Constitution. He mentioned the recommendations of Maryland, which took no action, New York, Virginia, and New Hampshire. Of these four only two used the language of nonpreference, one used the broadest possible language, and Maryland, which made no recommendation, considered language that Madison found acceptable. From these few recommendations Antieau drew an astonishing conclusion: "Thus it can be seen that the proposal which must have been foremost in the minds of the legislators in the First Congress indicated the popular demand for an end to preferential treatment to religions."[47]

He also correctly insisted that the establishment clause should not be separated from its historical context.[48] He meant that one should also look at the state constitutions for what insights they might yield, at public opinion surrounding ratification of the Bill of Rights, and at the government practices of the time that supported religion. "It is revealing," he wrote, "to note that in every state constitution in force between 1776 and 1789 where 'establishment' was mentioned, it was equated or used in conjunction with 'preference.' "[49] He meant, of course, that nonpreferential support was not considered an establishment; but the Massachusetts experience destroys that point.

Indeed the basic law of New Hampshire, Vermont, Maryland, Georgia, South Carolina, and even Connecticut, all of which lawfully permitted multiple establishments, as did Massachusetts, mentioned no favored church. In the classic sense of an establishment of religion, one denomination received preference, not Christianity or Protestantism. There is no doubt whatever that establishments of religion existed in the four New England states, actually as well as theoretically. They disprove the nonpreferentialist interpretation that the absence of preference in government aid to religion denotes the absence of an establishment.

Interestingly, when Antieau named the six states that mentioned "establishment" in connection with the idea of preference, the five besides Massachusetts were Pennsylvania, New Jersey, North Carolina, Delaware, and New York. That they were the five is interesting because none of them maintained an establishment after 1776; yet all five, including the three that never had an establishment at any time in their histories, placed the support of religion on a purely private, voluntary basis. In other words, they believed that a constitutional provision ensuring no subordination of one sect to another or providing no preference of one over another signified a constitutional ban on government aid to religion. Thomas J. Curry made that point. He observed too that Rhode Island, where voluntarism in the support of religion had been entrenched the longest, thought it was endorsing that principle when recommending belatedly that the Constitution be amended to include a provision against government preference of one sect over another.[50]

Indeed, the facts show that the treasured principle of no preference, which nonpreferentialists converted wrongly into an allowance of government aid on an impartial basis, was, in effect, irrelevant, because states with no history of establishments (Rhode Island, Pennsylvania, Delaware, and New Jersey) endorsed the no-preference principle yet kept religion privately supported, while Massachusetts, New Hampshire, and Vermont endorsed the same principle yet maintained tax-supported compulsory public worship. Consider Rhode Island and Connecticut, the two states that had no written constitutions. Although the laws of neither provided preference, one always had an establishment and one never did.

Two hundred years ago, when America was substantially a nation of Protestants and the links between government and religion were close in many ways, people did not quibble as we do about whether the integrity of the principle of separation depended on the use of the definite or the indefinite article or whether the law provided for absolutist language or language that by logical deduction allowed for important exceptions. The significant case of Isaac Backus, the great Baptist leader of Massachusetts, illustrates. Of him it has been said that "no individual in America since Roger Williams stands out so preeminently as the champion of religious liberty."[51]

Backus, a veteran of the struggle against the establishment provision of the Massachusetts constitution of 1780, was a member of the Massachusetts ratifying convention in 1788 and supported ratification secure in the knowledge that the United States had no power to legislate on the subject of religion. In his *History of New England, with Particular Reference to the Denomination of Christians Called Baptists* (3 vols., 1777–1796) and in the later one-volume abridgment (1804), he misquoted the First Amendment entirely by stating that it said: "Congress shall make no law, establishing articles of faith, or a mode of worship, or prohibiting the free exercise of religion."[52] The point is that he regarded such language, which the Senate had adopted at one point, as sufficient to condemn the establishments of religion in Massachusetts and Connecticut.[53]

Nonpreferentialists would construe that language as the narrowest proposed during the entire legislative history of the First Amendment, logically allowing impartial government aid to religion of the sort that Backus thought such language prohibited. Backus was misinformed but not naive; he was a veteran of the separationists' campaign to make the support of religion purely voluntary. As Thomas J. Curry noted, the Senate debate in its historical context "represented no sharply divided opinions about the nature of the amendment on religion. Senators who believed that religion should be supported voluntarily could subscribe to the formula banning an establishment of 'One Religious Sect or Society in preference to others' as readily as their colleagues, especially from New England, who believed that the states should make provisions for the support of religion." Senators from states whose constitutions had separated government and religion and left the support of religion to private conscience, Curry concluded, may well have preferred to use the no-preference language of those constitutions, just as New Englanders may have wanted the terminology most familiar to them, proscribing articles of faith or modes of worship.[54]

Curry observed that legislators in several states that opposed a preference for one religion did not propose an assistance to all, and their constitutions "clearly banned any state support for religion whatsoever. On the other hand, proponents of a general assessment

never viewed a ban on preferential establishments as enabling legislation for their cause." In no instance, he added, did such people claim
that no preference could justify the establishment of several or all
religions rather than one. "Opponents of tax support for religion,"
Curry showed, "never saw in the 'no subordination of any one sect'
clause a threat to their own stance." Staunch separationists on matters
of government-aided religion "not only avoided criticizing the provision, but clearly approved of it."[55] Massachusetts towns opposing the
establishment article of the proposed state constitution of 1780 favorably quoted the no-subordination principle.[56] Accordingly, Curry
concluded, although that principle denying preference

> appears when lifted out of its historical context to favor or
> permit a broad involvement of government with religion, [it]
> meant quite the opposite in its time. Those most against any
> state support for religion used language prohibiting prefer-
> ential establishment to express a negation of all state favors
> or financial assistance to churches.[57]

The First Amendment as a Limitation on Power

Congress considered and rejected the phraseology that nonpreferentialists emphasize as indicative of a narrow interpretation. The House
rejected the Senate's version, showing that the House under no circumstances can be understood as having framed an amendment that
merely banned preference. The Senate, having accepted a phrasing
that lends itself to the narrow interpretation (when abstracted from its
historical context), abandoned it in the face of uncompromising opposition from the House. When the amendment emerged from the
joint conference committee and received approbation from both
chambers, it meant something broader than no preference. And,
however it was phrased, it made an exception to a power that did not
exist. Construing the establishment clause as the nonpreferentialists
do in effect amends it by adding the word "exclusive," which is not
there, so that it reads: Congress shall make no law respecting an
exclusive establishment of religion. Awed stupefaction is an appropriate response to the nonpreferentialists' achievement in meta-
morphosizing the clause into a source of positive power.

Black magic—not historical evidence, grammatical analysis, or
logical deductions—black magic and only that can turn the First
Amendment into a repository of government power. Plainly it is a
limitation on power. The fact that outstanding constitutional scholars
like Antieau and Berns could even think that it authorized government aids to religion shows how desperately unable they were to

control their policy preferences, which they read back into the past and into the words of the amendment. Antieau sought to avoid dogmatism when he declared that any historical interpretation of the establishment clause was reasonable and that all interpretations are conjectural. Some, however, are more reasonable than others and less conjectural.

It is a fact, not an interpretation, that the unamended Constitution vests no power over religion and that the First Amendment vests no power whatever. It is a fact that the framers of the Constitution insisted that no limitations on the government's power over religion were necessary, because the government possessed only delegated authority, plus the authority necessary to execute the delegated powers; under no circumstances, argued the framers, could the government legislate on the subject of religion. They believed that nonexistent powers could not be exercised or abused, making all provisions against such a possibility superfluous. They believed that no need existed to declare that things shall not be done that there is no power to do.[58] They believed that the government was entirely without authority over religion. It was powerless, therefore, *even in the absence of the First Amendment*, to enact laws benefiting religion, with or without preference.

James Wilson of Pennsylvania responded to an allegation that the Constitution if ratified without amendment would not secure the rights of conscience by saying, "I ask the honorable gentleman, what part of this system puts it in the power of Congress to attack those rights?"[59] Edmund Randolph of Virginia asserted that "no power is given expressly to Congress over religion" and that only powers given could be exercised.[60] Madison said, "There is not a shadow of right in the general government to intermeddle with religion."[61] Richard Dobbs Spaight of North Carolina, who had also signed the Constitution, said of religion, "No power is given the general government to interfere with it at all. Any act of Congress on this subject would be a usurpation."[62]

When introducing the amendments that became the Bill of Rights, Madison explicitly said that the "great object" was to "limit and qualify the powers of Government" to ensure that powers granted could not be exercised in forbidden fields such as religion.[63] He told Jefferson that a bill of rights should be "so framed as not to imply powers not meant to be included in the enumeration."[64] To argue as the nonpreferentialists do that the establishment clause should be construed to permit nondiscriminatory aid to religion leads to the impossible conclusion that the First Amendment *added* to the powers of Congress even though it was framed to restrict Congress. It is not only an impossible conclusion; it is ridiculous. Not one state would have ratified such an enhancement of national authority, especially if it increased the tax power. The nonpreferentialists' feat of transforming the words "Congress shall make no law" into an augmentation of power vindicates the prophecy of Federalist leaders that, in Madison's words, "if an enumeration be made of our rights, will it not be implied, that everything omitted, is given to the general government?"[65]

Citing Justice Joseph Story's *Commentaries on the Constitution* is fashionable among the nonpreferentialists who think his authority is on their side.[66] Cord invokes Story as part of his evidence that the First Amendment was not meant "to preclude Federal governmental aid to religion when it was provided on a nondiscriminatory basis."[67] Story did state that "Christianity ought to receive encouragement from the [national] State," but he did not mention which provision of the Constitution authorized that encouragement. In fact, Cord also quoted him as saying that "it was deemed advisable to exclude from the national government all power to act upon the subject. . . . Thus the whole power over the subject of religion is left exclusively to the State governments."[68]

Cord also quoted Madison as saying that the national government had not the shadow of a power to meddle with religion, and Cord himself declared "that the First Amendment originally left the entire issue of governmental involvement with religion to the States."[69] What then is the source of the government's authority to provide nonpreferential aid to religion? The nonpreferentialists, who tend to be conservatives, surely do not believe that the government can do whatever is not expressly prohibited to it; on the contrary, it should do only what is enumerated or necessary to carry out delegated powers.

The Incorporation Doctrine

If the United States has no constitutional power to benefit religion and if under the incorporation doctrine the Fourteenth Amendment imposes on the states the same limitations as the First Amendment places on the United States, where do the states derive a constitutional power to aid religion? Because the states have none, nonpreferentialists break a lance against the incorporation of the First Amendment's establishment clause into the Fourteenth as a limitation on the states. Without the incorporation the states would be free from the restraints of the United States Constitution and would be able to enact any measure concerning religion, subject only to such limitations as might exist in the individual state constitutions.

To expect the Supreme Court to turn back the clock by scrapping the entire incorporation doctrine is so unrealistic as not to warrant consideration. James McClellan and other reactionaries indulge their emotions when denouncing the Court for its "revolutionary course" in making the First Amendment applicable to the states in the cases beginning with *Gitlow* v. *New York*[70] and in "arbitrarily" assuming religious liberty and freedom from establishments of religion to be within the liberty of the Fourteenth Amendment's due process clause.[71] But such extravagance of language persuades no one who remembers that the revolutionists were led not by Earl Warren but by Edward T. Sanford, joined by James C. McReynolds, George Sutherland, Pierce Butler, Joseph McKenna, Willis Vandevanter, and William Howard Taft, among others; and the *Gitlow* Court was unanimous as to the incorporation doctrine. The *Cantwell* Court, which incorporated the free exercise clause and, by dictum, the establishment clause, spoke unanimously through Owen Roberts.[72] The *Everson* Court too was unanimous on the incorporation issue.[73]

McClellan, Cord, and others complained that incorporation began belatedly in 1925 with *Gitlow*.[74] In fact it began in the late nineteenth century to protect property rights; in 1894 the Court read the equal protection clause of the Fourteenth Amendment to include the takings clause of the Fifth Amendment, to strike down rate regulation,[75] and then the Court crammed the takings clause into the Fourteenth's due process clause to achieve the same end.[76] The incorporation doctrine has a history so aged and fixed that overthrowing it is as likely as bagging snarks on the roof of the Court's building. Of all the amendments constituting the Bill of Rights, the First Amendment is the least likely to be thrown out of its nesting place within the word "liberty" of the Fourteenth. The Hughes Court unanimously awarded the First Amendment the laurels of uttermost fundamentality: no freedoms are more precious or more basic than those in the First.[77]

Even so, Edward S. Corwin, Robert G. McCloskey, and McClellan, among others, have suggested that a principled distinction can be made between the establishment clause and the other clauses of the First Amendment, allowing the disincorporation of the establishment clause. Their point is that the clause does not protect an individual freedom; it does not provide a right to do something. Government may violate one's personal right to speak freely or worship as he pleases if he pleases, but government cannot violate one's right not to be subject to an establishment of religion. But why not? Advocates of this view state it as if it were self-evidently true. As McCloskey said, "It requires a semantic leap to translate 'liberty' into 'disestablishment' when by definition the forbidden establishment need involve no restriction of the liberty of any individual."[78] By what definition? The semantic leap covers about a millimeter of space: freedom from an establishment, even a nonpreferential one, is an indispensable attribute of liberty.

That was the principal theme of Madison's Remonstrance and a theme of the Virginia Statute for Religious Freedom. An establishment, Madison argued, "violated the free exercise of religion" and would "subvert public liberty."[79] That view of the matter was not just the product of rationalists who cared little about revealed religion. From Roger Williams and John Clarke to Isaac Backus and John Leland (the only man to have fought for separation of church and state in Virginia, Connecticut, and Massachusetts), some evangelicals who profoundly cared about the purity of religious faith had warned against the corrupting embrace of government and, to defend religion, had advocated separation. To them the integrity of religion and of religious liberty depended on the promptings of private conscience untarnished by the assistance of government. Christ's kingdom, argued devout evangelicals, is not of this world, and government should have no jurisdiction over it. Madison's Remonstrance bore the influence of his Orange County neighbor John Leland, as well as that of the deistic Jefferson, who cared more about the purity of public liberty.

The aggressive personal liberties of the First Amendment, we are also told, must be exercised to be enjoyed, and therefore they seem to be distinguishable from establishment as a form of liberty. Freedom *of* religion, from this viewpoint, is unlike freedom *from* establishment. But that is only a partial truth, because freedom of religion and the freedoms of speech, press, and assembly are also freedoms from government ("Congress shall make no law . . .")—from government impositions and measures that create a suffocating civic environment within which the possibility of exercising and enjoying personal freedoms has been diminished. Freedom from seditious libel laws, from taxes on knowledge, from prosecutions for blasphemy, from censorship, and from disabilities arising because of one's associations or religion are similar in nature to freedom from establishments in the sense that the First Amendment creates immunities that form a wall within which freedom can flourish. What Zechariah Chafee called "the most important human right in the Constitution" is a "freedom from" or an immunity: the right to the writ of habeas corpus or freedom from arbitrary arrest.[80]

Numerous rights deemed fundamental by the Supreme Court are immunities that cannot be exercised by individuals. No one can affirmatively exercise a negative right, such as the right to be free from compulsory self-incrimination or from cruel and unusual punishments. These are, nevertheless, personal rights, in the sense that specific individuals are the butt of a denial of freedom from compulsory self-incrimination or from cruel and unusual punishment.

All rights, however personal, have another and equally important dimension. They have a social or civic nature. By imposing restraints upon government, they enhance the right of the body politic to be free for private and voluntary judgments by all members. Public as well as private liberty is the beneficiary. Taxes spent for religion violate the right to support religion voluntarily and privately. Religious exercises in the public schools are intimidating to those who must voluntarily decline to participate. Such aids to religion therefore damage public liberty. As Madison said, an establishment "violates equality by subjecting some to peculiar burdens." The fruits of an establishment, he argued, include "bigotry and persecution" and "will destroy that moderation and harmony which the forbearance of our laws to intermeddle with Religion has produced among its several sects."[81] Public liberty and personal civil liberty require an exemption from government-sponsored programs that spur bigotry.

Those who expect a conservative Supreme Court, likely to become more conservative in its personnel, to overrule the incorporation doctrine with respect to the establishment clause underestimate the political shrewdness of the Court, whether liberal or conservative activists dominate it. The precipitate repudiations of entrenched doctrines would appear too obviously the result of subjective choices. Wherever possible the court will avoid a dramatic overruling of its precedents. In the art of judging, a proper regard for appearances counts. The Court must seem to appreciate the values of coherence, stability, and continuity with the past. Judges, especially conservative ones, prefer to avoid sudden shifts in constitutional law. Any person who reaches the highest court is sophisticated enough to appreciate the strategic and political values of achieving desired results by indirection. Overruling is a device of last resort, employed only when other alternatives are unavailable or unavailing. The Court will not overrule the incorporation doctrine; it will not turn back the clock. But it is quite likely to reinterpret precedents, distinguishing away some, blunting others, and making new law without the appearance of overruling or disrespecting the past. The Court will nourish the impression that it is for standing pat. It merely refuses to endorse further expansion of rights but faithfully hews to fundamental doctrines.

Perhaps the chief reason that the incorporation doctrine will continue undiminished in vitality is that no need exists to overthrow it to achieve the results that promote religious interests. Malbin misleadingly declared that the framers of the First Amendment did not mean to prevent the United States from giving nonpreferential aid to religion if the aid is incidental to the performance of a delegated power, but he stumbled on a truth about the politics of constitutional law.[82] Power that is illegitimately exercised under one constitutional rubric may be valid under another. Although Congress has no constitutional authority to legislate on religion as such or make it the beneficiary of legislation, the blunt fact is that regardless of what the framers intended and regardless of the absence of a power to legislate on religion, the United States does possess constitutional powers to benefit or burden religion as an indirect or incidental result of the exercise of delegated powers.

The First Congress, for example, in the course of debating the amendments that became the Bill of Rights, reenacted the Northwest Ordinance, passed in 1787 by the Congress of the Confederation; that statute included a clause providing that schools and the means of education should be encouraged because religion, like morality and knowledge, is "necessary to good government and the happiness of mankind." And without doubt religion (Protestantism) constituted an important part of the curriculum at that time. Significantly, however, Congress in 1789 did not reenact the provision of 1787 by which one lot in each township was to be set aside "perpetually for the purposes of religion."[83] Congress could constitutionally benefit religion indirectly in the reenactment of the Northwest Ordinance by virtue of an express power to make "needful rules" for the governance of the territories.

Similarly, under the power to "make rules for the government and regulation" of the armed forces, Congress provided for military and naval chaplains and paid them from public taxes. Under the power to govern its own proceedings, both chambers of Congress provided for legislative chaplains. So too the necessity to punish violators of federal laws by imprisonment enabled Congress to build prisons and provide chaplains for their inmates. Congress may close government buildings on the Sabbath and on religious holidays, because it controls federal property. Under the power to coin money, Congress placed a theistic motto on U.S. coins and currency. Under the power to levy taxes, Congress can make exemptions for churches and clergymen. It has the power to raise armies and therefore the power to lay down the terms for conscription, including exemptions for conscientious objectors and clergymen. By the exercise of the treaty power the government can make treaties with the Indians and implement those treaties by appropriations for religion, ostensibly for the purpose of civilizing, Christianizing, and pacifying the Indians.[84] The examples can be extended almost indefinitely.

The same authority that can incidentally benefit religion by the exercise of legitimate powers may also burden religion. A power to help is a power to hinder. Congress could draft conscientious objectors or tax church property, for example. That it does not do so is a matter of politics, not a result of a lack of constitutional power. Those who clamor for additional government support of religion should beware of the risks to religion from government entanglements.

Conclusion

The limits on the employment of authorized powers include the proscription against establishments of religion. At the time the First Amendment was framed government and religion were much closer than they are today, but nothing was clearer than that financial aid to religion constituted an establishment of religion. The establishment clause should be far broader in meaning now than it was when adopted, because the nation is far more religiously pluralistic and is growing ever more so. Then for all practical purposes religion meant Christianity, and Christianity meant Protestantism. But Roman Catholics are now the largest single denomination in the nation, and about 6 million American citizens are Jews; and there are several scores of sects and substantial numbers of adherents of religions that were unknown in 1789, from Mormons and Christian Scientists to Pentecostalists, Jehovah's Witnesses, and members of the Unification Church; the number of Muslims, as well as Buddhists, Confucianists, Hindus, Sikhs, and Shintoists, is increasing.

We should not want the ban on establishments to mean only what it meant in 1789 or only what its framers intended. As Holmes said, "historical continuity with the past is not a duty, it is only a necessity."[85] That Delphic statement can be construed to mean that we cannot escape history because it has shaped us and guides our policies, but we are not obliged to remain static. Two hundred years of expanding the meaning of democracy should have some constitutional effect. We are not bound by the wisdom of the framers; we are bound only to consider whether the purposes they had in mind still merit political respect and constitutional obedience.

Justice Byron White said that judges "have carved out what they deemed to be the most desirable national policy governing various aspects of church-state relationships."[86] The judges of the Supreme Court are supposed to enforce constitutional limitations, not make national policy or determine what policy is desirable for the nation. The establishment clause may not be self-defining, but it embodies a policy that time has proved to be best. Despite continuing complaints about the wall of separation between government and religion, that is the policy embodied by the establishment clause. The Constitution erected that wall.

If the fact that it is the policy of the Constitution does not satisfy, history helps validate it. A page of history is supposed to be worth a volume of logic. The page is from Tocqueville. Not much more than half a century after independence he wrote that "the religious atmosphere of the country was the first thing that struck me on my arrival in the United States." He expressed "astonishment" because in Europe religion and freedom marched in "opposite directions." Questioning the "faithful of all communions," including clergymen, especially Roman Catholic priests, he found that

> they all agreed with each other except about details; all thought that the main reason for the quiet sway of religion over their country was the *complete separation of church and state*. I have no hesitation in stating that throughout my stay in America I met nobody, lay or cleric, who did not agree about that.[87]

Religion in the United States, like religious liberty, thrives mightily, far more than 200 years ago, when the vast majority of Americans were religiously unaffiliated. In a famous letter to the Baptists of Danbury, Connecticut, Jefferson spoke of the "wall of separation" between church and state. He cared for the rights of conscience but also for the government's freedom from religion.[88] Roger Williams, however, who cared even more deeply about religion, had spoken of the "wall of separation" more than a century and a half before Jefferson. In 1644 Williams wrote that the wall existed to preserve the integrity of religion by walling out corrupting influences:

> First, the faithful labors of many witnesses of Jesus Christ, extant to the world, abundantly proving that the church of the Jews under the Old Testament in the type and the church of the Christians under the New Testament in the antitype

were both separate from the world; and that when they have opened a gap in the hedge or *wall of separation* between the garden of the church and the wilderness of the world, God hath ever broke down the wall itself, removed the candlestick, and made His garden a wilderness, as at this day. And that therefore if He will ever please to restore His garden and paradise again, it must of necessity be walled in peculiarly unto Himself from the world; and that all that shall be saved out of the world are to be transplanted out of the wilderness of the world, and added unto His church or garden.[89]

Thus the wall of separation had the allegiance of a most profound sectarian impulse as well as a secular one. It ensures the government's freedom from religion and the individual's freedom of religion. The second probably cannot flourish without the first.

Separation has other bountiful results. Government and religion in America are mutually independent, much as Jefferson and Madison hoped they would be. Government maintains a benign neutrality toward religion without promoting or serving religion's interests in any significant way except, perhaps, for the policy of tax exemption. To be sure, government's involvement with religion takes many forms. The Joint Chiefs of Staff supposedly begin their meetings with prayer, as do our legislatures, and the Supreme Court opens its session with the incantation "God save the United States and this honorable Court." But "In God We Trust" and its relatives are of trifling significance in the sense that they have little genuine religious content. Caesar exploits, secularizes, and trivializes but leaves organized religion alone. Free of government influence, organized religion in turn does not use government for religious ends or advance the ends of government. Thus history has made the wall of separation real. It is not just a metaphor. It has constitutional existence. Despite its detractors and its archways, the wall ranks as one of the mightiest monuments of constitutional government in this nation. Robert Frost notwithstanding, something there is that loves a wall.

Notes

1. James O'Neill, *Religion and Education under the Constitution* (New York: Harper and Brothers, 1949). Da Capo Press of New York reprinted O'Neill's book in 1972 in a series, Civil Liberties in America, under my editorship.

2. Chester J. Antieau, Arthur T. Downey, and Edward C. Roberts, *Freedom from Federal Establishment: Formation and Early History of the First Amendment Religious Clauses* (Milwaukee: Bruce Publishing Co., 1964); Michael J. Malbin, *Religion and Politics: The Intention of the Authors of the First Amendment* (Washington, D.C.: American Enterprise Institute, 1978); Walter Berns, *The First*

Amendment and the Future of American Democracy (New York: Basic Books, 1976); James McClellan, "The Making and the Unmaking of the Establishment Clause," in Patrick B. McGuigan, and R. R. Rader, eds., *A Blueprint for Judicial Reform* (Washington, D.C.: Free Congress Education and Research Foundation, 1981); and Robert L. Cord, *Separation of Church and State: Historical Fact and Current Fiction* (New York: Lambeth Press, 1982).

3. Edward S. Corwin, "The Supreme Court as National School Board," *Law and Contemporary Problems*, vol. 14 (1949), pp. 10, 20. Everson v. Board of Education, 330 U.S. 1, 15 (1947).

4. I published an essay, "No Establishment of Religion: The Original Understanding," in an anthology of my writings, *Judgments: Essays on Constitutional History* (Chicago: Quadrangle Press, 1972), pp. 169–224. Berns, *The First Amendment*, dealt with my work on freedom of the press but ignored my essay on the establishment clause. Malbin, *Religion and Politics*, cited the essay once, p. 3, n. 7, in a short list of works supporting *Everson's* reading of history but wholly ignored my argument. McClellan, "The Making and the Unmaking," cited my essay once, oddly, to support a quotation from the Virginia Statute for Religious Freedom but otherwise ignored the essay. Cord, *Separation*, did not mention my essay at all, although at p. 11, n. 34, he quoted C. Herman Pritchett, *The American Constitution*, 3d ed. (New York: McGraw-Hill, 1977), which stated my multiple-establishment interpretation. Cord, to his credit, confronted Leo Pfeffer, *Church, State, Freedom*, rev. ed. (Boston: Beacon Press, 1967), but Pfeffer did not present the multiple-establishment interpretation, summarized here. Cord dismissed the point by Pritchett in a footnote: "This plural interpretation of American 'established' churches appears to be at odds with [Richard B.] Morris, *The Encyclopedia of American History* and [Samuel E.] Morison, *The Oxford History of the American People*, both of which indicated, that for the most part single 'establishments' existed in States which had established churches." Scholars should work from primary sources and specialized monographs, not textbooks and surveys. When they ignore the work of other scholars who present views supported by evidence, they forfeit readers' confidence. Although I wrote the essay mentioned in this note in 1958, I did not publish it until 1972. Therefore Antieau had no need to confront my work, and this is my first response to his.

5. Berns, McClellan, and Cord ignored Antieau's book; Malbin mentioned Antieau in notes, in passing, but did not acknowledge a debt to him. Those who borrowed so heavily from his book should have acknowledged it.

6. They also opposed the wall of separation between government and religion, and although they found triumphal archways through it, they wanted it down enough to allow a variety of nonpreferential aids to religion; finally, they lambasted the incorporation doctrine of *Everson*, which applies to the states the First Amendment's ban on an establishment of religion.

7. Antieau et al., *Freedom from Establishment*, p. 49.

8. Ibid., p. 52. The tiny group of Jews in Richmond probably had no idea that Virginia was so heavily populated with solicitous Christian friends. Under the proposed general assessment bill of 1784, which embodied the idea of a multiple establishment, every person was taxed for the church of his

choice. The bill declared the "liberal principle" that all Christian sects and denominations were equal before the law and none preferred over others, did not speak of the "established religion" of the state, and did not prescribe articles of faith, as did a general assessment bill of 1779. Malbin, *Religion and Politics*, p. 23, confused the 1784 bill with the 1779 one. Both bills are reprinted in Thomas Buckley, *Church and State in Revolutionary Virginia, 1776–1787* (Charlottesville: University Press of Virginia, 1977), pp. 185–89.

9. Cord, *Separation*, pp. 5, 6, 10.

10. Ibid., p. 5.

11. Antieau et al., *Freedom from Establishment*, p. 136.

12. Malbin, *Religion and Politics*, pp. 1, 3.

13. Ibid., p. 14.

14. Jefferson to Samuel Miller, Jan. 23, 1808, *The Writings of Thomas Jefferson*, ed. Albert E. Burgh (Washington, D.C.: Thomas Jefferson Memorial Association, 1907), vol. 11, p. 428. My emphasis. See Marion Tinling, "Thomas Lloyd's Report of the First Federal Congress," *William and Mary Quarterly*, 3d ser., vol. 18 (October 1961), p. 530, on the omission of articles, and pp. 530–38 for contemporary criticism of Lloyd's reporting, including Madison's remarks about "mutilation and perversion."

15. James Madison, Message of February 28, 1811, in James D. Richardson, ed., *A Compilation of the Messages and Papers of the Presidents* (Washington, D.C.: Bureau of National Literature, 1896), vol. 1, p. 490.

16. Ibid., Message of February 21, 1811, p. 489.

17. Reprinted in "Madison's 'Detached Memoranda,' " ed. Elizabeth Fleet, *William and Mary Quarterly*, 3d ser., vol. 3 (1946), p. 558.

18. Ibid.

19. Ibid., pp. 558–60.

20. Cord, *Separation*, p. 10.

21. Jonathan Elliot, ed., *The Debates in the Several State Conventions* (Philadelphia, 1836), vol. 3, p. 330.

22. Cord, *Separation*, p. 8.

23. Ibid., p. 20.

24. Berns, *The First Amendment*, p. 9.

25. Cord, *Separation*, p. 23. For the Memorial and Remonstrance, *Papers of James Madison*, ed. Robert Rutland (Chicago: University of Chicago Press, 1973), vol. 8, pp. 298–314, or see appendix to this volume.

26. John Courtney Murray, "Law or Prepossessions," *Law and Contemporary Problems*, vol. 14 (1949), p. 29.

27. Madison to James Monroe, May 29, 1785, in *Papers of Madison*, vol. 8, p. 286.

28. Madison to Jefferson, February 14, 1790, quoted in Irving Brant, *James Madison: Father of the Constitution* (Indianapolis: Bobbs-Merrill, 1950), p. 272.

29. Madison to Edward Livingston, July 10, 1822, in *The Writings of James Madison*, ed. Gaillard Hunt (New York: G. P. Putnam, 1919), vol. 9, p. 100.

30. Cord, *Separation*, p. 23; and Antieau et al., *Freedom from Establishment*, pp. 180–81. In Marsh v. Chambers, 463 U.S. 783, 788 n. 8 (1983), Chief Justice Burger for the Court, citing "1 Annals of Cong. 891 (1789)," declared that

Madison voted for the statute authorizing chaplains. In fact the Annals of Congress does not record the vote or say how any member voted, and the citation should be to p. 1077 for January 7, 1790.

31. Cord, *Separation*, p. 11 (his emphasis).

32. Berns, *The First Amendment*, p. 7.

33. Ibid., p. 9. Chief Justice William H. Rehnquist, the judicial leader of the nonpreferentialists, presented their view in a dissenting opinion of 1985 (reproduced in chap. 5 of this volume) when he declared, wrongly, that the "well accepted meaning" of the establishment clause is that it prohibited the establishment of a "national religion," which he defined as the official "designation of any church as a national one." The clause also "forbade preference among religious sects or denominations." But it created no wall of separation between government and religion, not even between church and state. "The Establishment Clause," Rehnquist wrote, "did not require government neutrality between religion and irreligion nor did it prohibit the federal government from providing non-discriminatory aid to religion." Wallace v. Jaffree, 105 S. Ct. 2479, 2516, 2520 (1985). Edwin Meese III, the attorney general of the United States and a preeminent political leader of the nonpreferentialists, claims that "the First Amendment forbade the establishment of a particular religion or a particular church. It also precluded the federal government from favoring one church, or one church group over another. That's what the First Amendment did, but it did not go further. It did not, for example, preclude federal aid to religious groups so long as that assistance furthered a public purpose and so long as it did not discriminate in favor of one religious group against another." Meese, "Address before the Christian Legal Society," San Diego, September 29, 1985, pp. 8–9. Department of Justice transcript. Nonpreferentialists do not trifle to state what part of the Constitution empowers the government to aid religion nonpreferentially.

34. Bernard Schwartz, ed., *The Bill of Rights: A Documentary History* (New York: Chelsea House, 1971), p. 1024. The speech is at pp. 1023–34.

35. Ibid., p. 1089.

36. Elliot, *Debates*, vol. 4, p. 192.

37. Ibid., vol. 2, p. 148.

38. Ibid., vol. 3, pp. 436, 448–49.

39. Ibid., pp. 593, 659.

40. Leonard W. Levy, "Bill of Rights," in *Encyclopedia of American Political History*, ed. Jack Greene (New York: Charles Scribner's Sons, 1984), vol. 1, pp. 104–25, is my full statement on the subject.

41. Madison to Richard Peters, August 19, 1789, *Papers of Madison*, vol. 12, pp. 346–47.

42. Max Farrand, ed., *Records of the Federal Convention* (New Haven, Conn.: Yale University Press, 1911), vol. 2, p. 479, for the statement of August 31, 1787, about his right hand, and p. 640 for the statement of September 12 that congressional control over commerce by majority vote constituted "an insuperable objection."

43. Cord, *Separation*, p. 6.

44. Charles C. Tansill, ed., *Documents Illustrative of the Formation of the Union*

of the American States (Washington, D.C., 1927), pp. 1009–59, reprints all state ratification documents.

45. Antieau et al., *Freedom from Establishment*, p. 142.

46. Ibid., p. 132.

47. Ibid.

48. Ibid., p. 143.

49. Ibid., p. 132.

50. Thomas J. Curry, "The First Freedoms" (Ph.D. dissertation, Claremont Graduate School, 1983), pp. 645–51. The best book on the subject is Curry's *First Freedoms: Church and State in America to the Passage of the First Amendment* (New York: Oxford University Press, 1986). Monsignor Curry and I agree on major First Amendment issues, especially on the point that nonpreferential government aid to religion violates the amendment, but we disagree about multiple establishments. He believes that the concept of a preferential establishment still dominated American thinking at the time of the framing of the First Amendment and even later. Nevertheless, he concludes his book by saying that "the people of almost every state that ratified the First Amendment believed that religion should be maintained and supported voluntarily. They saw government attempts to organize and regulate such support as a usurpation of power, as a violation of liberty of conscience and free exercise of religion, and as falling within the scope of what they termed an establishment of religion." Ibid., p. 222.

51. *Dictionary of American Biography*, vol. 1, p. 470. The best works on Backus are William G. McLoughlin, *Isaac Backus and the American Pietistic Tradition* (Boston: Little, Brown, and Co., 1967); and McLoughlin, *New England Dissent, 1630–1833* (Cambridge, Mass.: Harvard University Press, 1971).

52. Quoted in McLoughlin, *New England Dissent*, vol. 2, p. 783.

53. Ibid., pp. 783–84.

54. Curry, "First Freedoms," p. 829; see his book of the same title, p. 214.

55. Curry, "First Freedoms," pp. 649–50; see book of the same title, p. 212.

56. Oscar and Mary Handlin, eds., *The Popular Source of Political Authority* (Cambridge, Mass.: Harvard University Press, 1966), p. 819, for the town of Charlton. See also ibid., pp. 618–19 (West Springfield), p. 674 (Sherborn), pp. 727–28 (Berwick), p. 785 (Medway), and p. 855 (Petersham). Art. III is in ibid., pp. 442–43.

57. Curry, "First Freedoms," p. 651; see also pp. 783–84; and see his book, pp. 211–12.

58. *Federalist* No. 84.

59. Elliot, *Debates*, vol. 2, p. 455.

60. Ibid., vol. 3, p. 204; see also p. 469.

61. Ibid., p. 330.

62. Ibid., vol. 4, p. 208; and see James Iredell, ibid., p. 94.

63. Schwartz, *Bill of Rights*, vol. 2, p. 1029.

64. Madison to Jefferson, October 17, 1788, in *Papers of Madison*, vol. 11, p. 297.

65. Elliot, *Debates*, vol. 3, p. 620.

66. Cord, *Separation*, pp. 12–15; McClellan, "The Making and the Unmaking," p. 295; Berns, *The First Amendment*, pp. 59–60, 71; and Antieau et al., *Freedom from Establishment*, p. 160.

67. Cord, *Separation*, p. 15.

68. Ibid., quoting *Commentaries on the Constitution*, secs. 1874, 1879.

69. Ibid., p. 14.

70. 268 U.S. 652 (1925).

71. McClellan, "The Making and the Unmaking," p. 316, and in his essay in this volume. The earlier essay is littered with errors, great and small, some of them howlers. McClellan grossly distorts history, gets nuances wrong, and says silly things. He scarcely understands what an establishment of religion is. He thinks Protestants had a preferred status over Dissenters, not knowing that the Dissenters were Protestants, and he thinks that every state but Rhode Island rejected "the Jeffersonian system of church-state relations." McClellan's essay in this volume briefly summarizes the mistaken history of the earlier essay.

72. Cantwell v. Connecticut, 310 U.S. 296 (1940).

73. 330 U.S. 1 (1947).

74. Cord, *Separation*, p. 99.

75. Reagan v. Farmer's Loan & Trust Co., 154 U.S. 362, 399 (1894).

76. In Chicago, Burlington & Quincy R.R. v. Chicago, 166 U.S. 226 (1897), the Court read the eminent domain clause of the Fifth Amendment into the due process clause of the Fourteenth Amendment. See also Smyth v. Ames, 169 U.S. 466 (1898). In United Rys v. West, 280 U.S. 234 (1930), the Court struck down as confiscatory a government fixed-rate schedule that allowed a profit of 6.26 percent. Protecting First Amendment freedoms from state abridgment seems no more revolutionary or arbitrary than protecting property rights.

77. Palko v. Conn., 302 U.S. 319 (1937). In Wallace v. Jaffree, 105 S. Ct. 2479, 2484–86 (1985), the Court, without dissent on the point, explicitly reaffirmed the incorporation doctrine and repudiated a disincorporation doctrine.

78. Robert G. McCloskey, "Principles, Powers, and Values: the Establishment Clause and the Supreme Court," in Donald A. Giannella, ed., *1964 Religion and the Public Order* (Chicago: University of Chicago Press, 1965), p. 11. See also Edward S. Corwin, *A Constitution of Powers in a Secular State* (Charlottesville, Va.: Michie Co., 1951), pp. 113–16.

79. Madison, *Papers of Madison*, vol. 8, pp. 300, 304.

80. Zechariah Chafee, *How Human Rights Got into the Constitution* (Boston: Boston University Press, 1952), p. 51. Article I, section 9, protects the "Privilege of the Writ" from being suspended except when the public safety requires suspension. Parsing the provision the way nonpreferentialists analyze the establishment clause would reduce the "privilege" to a nullity.

81. Madison, *Papers of Madison*, vol. 8, pp. 300, 301, 302.

82. Malbin (*Religion and Politics*, p. 17) wrote that all the framers of the First Amendment agreed that it gave "no direct power" to deal with the subject of religion, implying that it gave an indirect power. He added that they dis-

agreed over what Congress should be allowed to do in accordance with some delegated power; but they did not discuss the subject of aiding religion indirectly by exercising any delegated power.

83. *Journals of the Continental Congress,* ed. Worthington C. Ford et al. (Washington, D.C., 1904–1937), vol. 33, pp. 399–400.

84. Cord, *Separation of Church and State,* pp. 57–80, grossly exaggerates the significance of federal aid to religion among Indians as if it somehow justified aid to religion among citizens. Aid to Indians, under either the treaty power or the power to regulate Indian affairs, is not worth two cents as a precedent for anything else.

85. "Learning and Science" (1895) in Oliver Wendell Holmes, *Collected Legal Papers* (New York: Harcourt, Brace, and Co., 1920), p. 139.

86. Comm. for Pub. Ed. v. Nyquist, 413 U.S. 756, 820 (1973).

87. Alexis de Tocqueville, *Democracy in America,* ed. J. P. Mayers and Max Lerner, trans. George Lawrence (New York: Harper & Row, 1969), pp. 271–72. Emphasis added.

88. Jefferson to Nehemiah Dodge et al., January 1, 1802, in *Writings of Jefferson,* vol. 16, pp. 281–82.

89. Roger Williams, "A Letter of Mr. John Cottons" (1643), in *The Complete Writings of Roger Williams* (New York: Russell and Russell, 1963), vol. 1, p. 392. I have followed the modernized version of Perry Miller, *Roger Williams: His Contribution to the American Tradition* (New York: Bobbs-Merrill, 1962), p. 98. Emphasis added.

5

The True Meaning of the Establishment Clause: A Dissent

William H. Rehnquist

Thirty-eight years ago this Court, in *Everson* v. *Board of Education*, 330 U.S. 1, 16 (1947) summarized its exegesis of Establishment Clause doctrine thus:

> "In the words of Jefferson, the clause against establishment of religion by law was intended to erect 'a wall of separation between church and State.' *Reynolds* v. *United States*, [98 U.S. 145, 164, (1879)]."

This language from *Reynolds*, a case involving the Free Exercise Clause of the First Amendment rather than the Establishment Clause, quoted from Thomas Jefferson's letter to the Danbury Baptist Association the phrase "I contemplate with sovereign reverence that act of the whole American people which declared that their legislature should 'make no law respecting an establishment of religion, or prohibiting the free exercise thereof,' thus building a wall of separation between church and State." 8 Writings of Thomas Jefferson 113 (H. Washington ed. 1861).[1]

It is impossible to build sound constitutional doctrine upon a mistaken understanding of constitutional history, but unfortunately the Establishment Clause has been expressly freighted with Jefferson's misleading metaphor for nearly forty years. Thomas Jefferson was of course in France at the time the constitutional amendments known as the Bill of Rights were passed by Congress and ratified by

---

On June 4, 1985, the Supreme Court of the United States ruled, 6–3, that an Alabama statute authorizing a one-minute period of silence in all public schools "for meditation or voluntary prayer" was unconstitutional. The Court held that the statute was a law respecting an establishment of religion and thus violated the First Amendment. *Wallace v. Jaffree*, 472 U.S. 38 (1985). This chapter is taken from the dissenting opinion in the case by William H. Rehnquist, then associate justice and now chief justice——*Eds.*

the states. His letter to the Danbury Baptist Association was a short note of courtesy, written fourteen years after the amendments were passed by Congress. He would seem to any detached observer as a less than ideal source of contemporary history as to the meaning of the Religion Clauses of the First Amendment.

Jefferson's fellow Virginian James Madison, with whom he was joined in the battle for the enactment of the Virginia Statute of Religious Liberty of 1786, did play as large a part as anyone in the drafting of the Bill of Rights. He had two advantages over Jefferson in this regard: he was present in the United States, and he was a leading member of the First Congress. But when we turn to the record of the proceedings in the First Congress leading up to the adoption of the Establishment Clause of the Constitution, including Madison's significant contributions thereto, we see a far different picture of its purpose than the highly simplified "wall of separation between church and State."

During the debates in the thirteen colonies over ratification of the Constitution, one of the arguments frequently used by opponents of ratification was that without a Bill of Rights guaranteeing individual liberty the new general government carried with it a potential for tyranny. The typical response to this argument on the part of those who favored ratification was that the general government established by the Constitution had only delegated powers, and that these delegated powers were so limited that the government would have no occasion to violate individual liberties. This response satisfied some, but not others, and of the eleven colonies which ratified the Constitution by early 1789, five proposed one or another amendments guaranteeing individual liberty. Three—New Hampshire, New York, and Virginia—included in one form or another a declaration of religious freedom. See 3 J. Elliot, Debates on the Federal Constitution 659 (1891); 1 *id.*, at 328. Rhode Island and North Carolina flatly refused to ratify the Constitution in the absence of amendments in the nature of a Bill of Rights. 1 *id.*, at 334; 4 at 244. Virginia and North Carolina proposed identical guarantees of religious freedom:

> "[A]ll men have an equal, natural and unalienable right to the free exercise of religion, according to the dictates of conscience, and that no particular religious sect or society ought to be favored or established, by law, in preference to others." 3 *id.*, at 659; 4 *id.*, at 244.[2]

On June 8, 1789, James Madison rose in the House of Representatives and "reminded the House that this was the day that he had heretofore named for bringing forward amendments to the Constitution." 1 Annals of Cong. 424. Madison's subsequent remarks in urging the House to adopt his drafts of the proposed amendments were less those of a dedicated advocate of the wisdom of such measures than those of a prudent statesman seeking the enactment of measures sought by a number of his fellow citizens which could surely do no harm and might do a great deal of good. He said, *inter alia:*

> "It appears to me that this House is bound by every motive of prudence, not to let the first session pass over without proposing to the State Legislatures, some things to be incorporated into the Constitution, that will render it as acceptable to the whole people of the United States, as it has been found acceptable to a majority of them. I wish, among other reasons why something should be done, that those who had been friendly to the adoption of this Constitution may have the opportunity of proving to those who were opposed to it that they were as sincerely devoted to liberty and a Republican Government, as those who charged them with wishing the adoption of this Constitution in order to lay the foundation of an aristocracy or despotism. It will be a desirable thing to extinguish from the bosom of every member of the community, any apprehensions that there are those among his countrymen who wish to deprive them of the liberty for which they valiantly fought and honorably bled. And if there are amendments desired of such a nature as will not injure the Constitution, and they can be ingrafted so as to give satisfaction to the doubting part of our fellow-citizens, the friends of the Federal Government will evince that spirit of deference and concession for which they have hitherto been distinguished." *Id.*, at 431–432.

The language Madison proposed for what ultimately became the Religion Clauses of the First Amendment was this:

> "The civil rights of none shall be abridged on account of religious belief or worship, nor shall any national religion be established, nor shall the full and equal rights of conscience be in any manner, or on any pretext, infringed." *Id.*, at 434.

On the same day that Madison proposed them, the amendments which formed the basis for the Bill of Rights were referred by the House to a committee of the whole, and after several weeks' delay were then referred to a Select Committee consisting of Madison and ten others. The Committee revised Madison's proposal regarding the establishment of religion to read:

> "[N]o religion shall be established by law, nor shall the equal rights of conscience be infringed." *Id.*, at 729.

The Committee's proposed revisions were debated in the House on August 15, 1789. The entire debate on the Religion Clauses is contained in two full columns of the "Annals," and does not seem particularly illuminating. See *id.*, at 729–731. Representative Peter Sylvester of New York expressed his dislike for the revised version, because it might have a tendency "to abolish religion altogether." Representative John Vining suggested that the two parts of the sentence be transposed; Representative Elbridge Gerry thought the language should be changed to read "that no religious doctrine shall be established by law." *Id.*, at 729. Roger Sherman of Connecticut had the traditional reason for opposing provisions of a Bill of Rights—that Congress had no delegated authority to "make religious establishments"—and therefore he opposed the adoption of the amendment. Representative Daniel Carroll of Maryland thought it desirable to adopt the words proposed, saying "[h]e would not contend with gentlemen about the phraseology, his object was to secure the substance in such a manner as to satisfy the wishes of the honest part of the community."

Madison then spoke, and said that "he apprehended the meaning of the words to be, that Congress should not establish a religion, and enforce the legal observation of it by law, nor compel men to worship God in any manner contrary to their conscience." *Id.*, at 730. He said that some of the state conventions had thought that Congress might rely on the "necessary and proper" clause to infringe the rights of conscience or to establish a national religion, and "to prevent these effects he presumed the amendment was intended, and he thought it as well expressed as the nature of the language would admit." *Ibid.*

Representative Benjamin Huntington then expressed the view that the Committee's language might "be taken in such latitude as to be extremely hurtful to the cause of religion. He understood the amendment to mean what had been expressed by the gentleman from Virginia; but others might find it convenient to put another construction upon it." Huntington, from Connecticut, was concerned that in the New England states, where state established religions were the rule rather than the exception, the federal courts might not be able to entertain claims based upon an obligation under the bylaws of a religious organization to contribute to the support of a minister or the building of a place of worship. He hoped that "the amendment would be made in such a way as to secure the rights of conscience, and a free exercise of the rights of religion, but not to patronise those who professed no religion at all." *Id.*, at 730–731.

Madison responded that the insertion of the word "national" before the word "religion" in the Committee version should satisfy the minds of those who had criticized the language. "He believed that the people feared one sect might obtain a pre-eminence, or two combine together, and establish a religion to which they would compel others to conform. He thought that if the word 'national' was introduced, it would point the amendment directly to the object it was intended to prevent." *Id.,* at 731. Representative Samuel Livermore expressed himself as dissatisfied with Madison's proposed amendment, and thought it would be better if the Committee language were altered to read that "Congress shall make no laws touching religion, or infringing the rights of conscience." *Ibid.*

Representative Gerry spoke in opposition to the use of the word "national" because of strong feelings expressed during the ratification debates that a federal government, not a national government, was created by the Constitution. Madison thereby withdrew his proposal but insisted that his reference to a "national religion" only referred to a national establishment and did not mean that the government was a national one. The question was taken on Representative Livermore's motion, which passed by a vote of 31 for and 20 against. *Ibid.*

The following week, without any apparent debate, the House voted to alter the language of the Religion Clause to read "Congress shall make no law establishing religion, or to prevent the free exercise thereof, or to infringe the rights of conscience." *Id.,* at 766. The floor debates in the Senate were secret, and therefore not reported in the Annals. The Senate on September 3, 1789 considered several different forms of the Religion Amendment, and reported this language back to the House.

> "Congress shall make no law establishing articles of faith or a mode of worship, or prohibiting the free exercise of religion."

C. Antieau, A. Downey, & E. Roberts, Freedom From Federal Establishment 130 (1964).

⌐ The House refused to accept the Senate's changes in the Bill of Rights and asked for a conference; the version which emerged from the conference was that which ultimately found its way into the Constitution as a part of the First Amendment.

> "Congress shall make no law respecting an establishment of religion, or prohibiting the free exercise thereof."

The House and the Senate both accepted this language on successive days, and the amendment was proposed in this form.

On the basis of the record of these proceedings in the House of Representatives, James Madison was undoubtedly the most important architect among the members of the House of the amendments which became the Bill of Rights, but it was James Madison speaking as an advocate of sensible legislative compromise, not as an advocate of incorporating the Virginia Statute of Religious Liberty into the United States Constitution. During the ratification debate in the Virginia Convention, Madison had actually opposed the idea of any Bill of Rights. His sponsorship of the amendments in the House was obviously not that of a zealous believer in the necessity of the Religion Clauses, but of one who felt it might do some good, could do no harm, and would satisfy those who had ratified the Constitution on the condition that Congress propose a Bill of Rights.[3] His original language "nor shall any national religion be established" obviously does not conform to the "wall of separation" between church and State idea which latter day commentators have ascribed to him. His explanation on the floor of the meaning of his language—"that Congress should not establish a religion, and enforce the legal observation of it by law" is of the same ilk. When he replied to Huntington in the debate over the proposal which came from the Select Committee of the House, he urged that the language "no religion shall be established by law" should be amended by inserting the word "national" in front of the word "religion."

It seems indisputable from these glimpses of Madison's thinking, as reflected by actions on the floor of the House in 1789, that he saw the amendment as designed to prohibit the establishment of a national religion, and perhaps to prevent discrimination among sects. He did not see it as requiring neutrality on the part of government between religion and irreligion. Thus the Court's opinion in *Everson*— while correct in bracketing Madison and Jefferson together in their exertions in their home state leading to the enactment of the Virginia Statute of Religious Liberty—is totally incorrect in suggesting that Madison carried these views onto the floor of the United States House of Representatives when he proposed the language which would ultimately become the Bill of Rights.

The repetition of this error in the Court's opinion in *Illinois ex rel. McCollum* v. *Board of Education*, 333 U.S. 203 (1948), and, *inter alia, Engel* v. *Vitale*, 370 U.S. 421 (1962), does not make it any sounder historically. Finally, in *Abington School District* v. *Schempp*, 374 U.S. 203, 214 (1963) the Court made the truly remarkable statement that "the views of Madison and Jefferson, preceded by Roger Williams came to be incorporated not only in the Federal Constitution but likewise in those of most of our States" (footnote omitted). On the basis of what evidence we have, this statement is demonstrably incorrect as a matter of history.[4] And its repetition in varying forms in succeeding opinions of the Court can give it no more authority than it possesses as a matter of fact; *stare decisis* may bind courts as to matters of law, but it cannot bind them as to matters of history.

None of the other Members of Congress who spoke during the August 15th debate expressed the slightest indication that they thought the language before them from the Select Committee, or the evil to be aimed at, would require that the Government be absolutely neutral as between religion and irreligion. The evil to be aimed at, so far as those who spoke were concerned, appears to have been the establishment of a national church, and perhaps the preference of one religious sect over another; but it was definitely not concern about whether the Government might aid all religions evenhandedly. If one were to follow the advice of JUSTICE BRENNAN, concurring in *Abington School District* v. *Schempp, supra* at 236, and construe the Amendment in the light of what particular "practices . . . challenged threaten those consequences which the Framers deeply feared; whether, in short, they tend to promote that type of interdependence between religion and state which the First Amendment was designed to prevent," one would have to say that the First Amendment Establishment Clause should be read no more broadly than to prevent the establishment of a national religion or the governmental preference of one religious sect over another.

The actions of the First Congress, which re-enacted the North-west Ordinance for the governance of the Northwest Territory in 1789, confirm the view that Congress did not mean that the Government should be neutral between religion and irreligion. The House of Representatives took up the Northwest Ordinance on the same day as Madison introduced his proposed amendments which became the Bill of Rights; while at that time the Federal Government was of course not bound by draft amendments to the Constitution which had not yet been proposed by Congress, say nothing of ratified by the States, it seems highly unlikely that the House of Representatives would simultaneously consider proposed amendments to the Constitution and enact an important piece of territorial legislation which conflicted with the intent of those proposals. The Northwest Ordinance, 1 Stat. 50, reenacted the Northwest Ordinance of 1787 and provided that "[r]eligion, morality, and knowledge, being necessary to good government and the happiness of mankind, schools and the means of education shall forever be encouraged." *Id.*, at 52, n.(a). Land grants for schools in the Northwest Territory were not limited to public schools. It was not until 1845 that Congress limited land grants in the new States and Territories to nonsectarian schools. 5 Stat. 788; Antieau, Downey, & Roberts, Freedom From Federal Establishment, at 163.

On the day after the House of Representatives voted to adopt the form of the First Amendment Religion Clause which was ultimately proposed and ratified, Representative Elias Boudinot proposed a resolution asking President George Washington to issue a Thanksgiving Day proclamation. Boudinot said he "could not think of letting the session pass over without offering an opportunity to all the citizens of the United States of joining with one voice, in returning to Almighty God their sincere thanks for the many blessings he had poured down upon them." 1 Annals of Cong. 914 (1789). Representative Aedanas Burke objected to the resolution because he did not like "this mimicking of European customs"; Representative Thomas Tucker objected that whether or not the people had reason to be satisfied with the Constitution was something that the states knew better than the Congress, and in any event "it is a religious matter, and, as such, is proscribed to us." *Id.*, at 915. Representative Sherman supported the resolution "not only as a laudable one in itself, but as warranted by a number of precedents in Holy Writ: for instance, the solemn thanksgivings and rejoicings which took place in the time of Solomon, after the building of the temple, was a case in point. This example, he thought, worthy of Christian imitation on the present occasion. . . ." *Ibid.*

Boudinot's resolution was carried in the affirmative on September 25, 1789. Boudinot and Sherman, who favored the Thanksgiving proclamation, voted in favor of the adoption of the proposed amendments to the Constitution, including the Religion Clause; Tucker, who opposed the Thanksgiving proclamation, voted against the adoption of the amendments which became the Bill of Rights.

Within two weeks of this action by the House, George Washington responded to the Joint Resolution which by now had been changed to include the language that the President "recommend to the people of the United States a day of public thanksgiving and prayer, to be observed by acknowledging with grateful hearts the many and signal favors of Almighty God, especially by affording them an opportunity peaceably to establish a form of government for their safety and happiness." 1 J. Richardson, Messages and Papers of the Presidents, 1789–1897, p. 64 (1897). The Presidential proclamation was couched in these words:

> "Now, therefore, I do recommend and assign Thursday, the 26th day of November next, to be devoted by the people of these States to the service of that great and glorious Being who is the beneficent author of all the good that was, that is, or that will be; that we may then all unite in rendering unto Him our sincere and humble thanks for His kind care and

protection of the people of this country previous to their becoming a nation; for the signal and manifold mercies and the favorable interpositions of His providence in the course and conclusion of the late war; for the great degree of tranquility, union, and plenty which we have since enjoyed; for the peaceable and rational manner in which we have been enabled to establish constitutions of government for our safety and happiness, and particularly the national one now lately instituted; for the civil and religious liberty with which we are blessed, and the means we have of acquiring and diffusing useful knowledge; and, in general, for all the great and various favors which He has been pleased to confer upon us.

"And also that we may then unite in most humbly offering our prayers and supplications to the great Lord and Ruler of Nations, and beseech Him to pardon our national and other transgressions; to enable us all, whether in public or private stations, to perform our several and relative duties properly and punctually; to render our National Government a blessing to all the people by constantly being a Government of wise, just, and constitutional laws, discreetly and faithfully executed and obeyed; to protect and guide all sovereigns and nations (especially such as have shown kindness to us), and to bless them with good governments, peace, and concord; to promote the knowledge and practice of true religion and virtue, and the increase of science among them and us; and, generally, to grant unto all mankind such a degree of temporal prosperity as He alone knows to be best." *Ibid.*

George Washington, John Adams, and James Madison all issued Thanksgiving proclamations; Thomas Jefferson did not, saying:

"Fasting and prayer are religious exercises; the enjoining them an act of discipline. Every religious society has a right to determine for itself the times for these exercises, and the objects proper for them, according to their own particular tenets; and this right can never be safer than in their own hands, where the Constitution has deposited it." 11 Writings of Thomas Jefferson 429 (A. Lipscomb ed. 1904).

As the United States moved from the 18th into the 19th century, Congress appropriated time and again public moneys in support of sectarian Indian education carried on by religious organizations. Typical of these was Jefferson's treaty with the Kaskaskia Indians, which provided annual cash support for the Tribe's Roman Catholic priest and church.[5] It was not until 1897, when aid to sectarian education for Indians had reached $500,000 annually, that Congress decided thereafter to cease appropriating money for education in sectarian schools. See Act of June 7, 1897, 30 Stat. 62, 79.; cf. *Quick Bear* v. *Leupp,* 210 U.S. 50, 77–79 (1908); J. O'Neill, Religion and Education Under the Constitution 118–119 (1949). See generally R. Cord, Separation of Church and State 61–82 (1982). This history shows the fallacy of the notion found in *Everson* that "no tax in any amount" may be levied for religious activities in any form. 330 U.S. at 15–16.

Joseph Story, a member of this Court from 1811 to 1845, and during much of that time a professor at the Harvard Law School, published by far the most comprehensive treatise on the United States Constitution that had then appeared. Volume 2 of Story's Commentaries on the Constitution of the United States 630–632 (5th ed. 1891) discussed the meaning of the Establishment Clause of the First Amendment this way:

> "Probably at the time of the adoption of the Constitution, and of the amendment to it now under consideration [First Amendment], the general if not the universal sentiment in America was, that Christianity ought to receive encouragement from the State so far as was not incompatible with the private rights of conscience and the freedom of religious worship. An attempt to level all religions, and to make it a matter of state policy to hold all in utter indifference, would have created universal disapprobation, if not universal indignation.
>
> "The real object of the [First] [A]mendment was not to countenance, much less to advance, Mahometanism, or Judaism, or infidelity, by prostrating Christianity; but to exclude all rivalry among Christian sects, and to prevent any national ecclesiastical establishment which should give to a hierarchy the exclusive patronage of the national government. It thus cut off the means of religious persecution (the vice and pest of former ages), and of the subversion of the rights of conscience in matters of religion, which had been trampled upon almost from the days of the Apostles to the present age. . . ." (Footnotes omitted.)

Thomas Cooley's eminence as a legal authority rivaled that of Story. Cooley stated in his treatise entitled Constitutional Limitations that aid to a particular religious sect was prohibited by the United States Constitution, but he went on to say:

> "But while thus careful to establish, protect, and defend religious freedom and equality, the American constitutions contain no provisions which prohibit the authorities from such solemn recognition of a superintending Providence in public transactions and exercises as the general religious

sentiment of mankind inspires, and as seems meet and proper in finite and dependent beings. Whatever may be the shades of religious belief, all must acknowledge the fitness of recognizing in important human affairs the superintending care and control of the Great Governor of the Universe, and of acknowledging with thanksgiving his boundless favors, or bowing in contrition when visited with the penalties of his broken laws. No principle of constitutional law is violated when thanksgiving or fast days are appointed; when chaplains are designated for the army and navy; when legislative sessions are opened with prayer or the reading of the Scriptures, or when religious teaching is encouraged by a general exemption of the houses of religious worship from taxation for the support of State government. Undoubtedly the spirit of the Constitution will require, in all these cases, that care be taken to avoid discrimination in favor of or against any one religious denomination or sect; but the power to do any of these things does not become unconstitutional simply because of its susceptibility to abuse. . . ." *Id.*, at 470–471.

Cooley added that,

"[t]his public recognition of religious worship, however, is not based entirely, perhaps not even mainly, upon a sense of what is due to the Supreme Being himself as the author of all good and of all law; but the same reasons of state policy which induce the government to aid institutions of charity and seminaries of instruction will incline it also to foster religious worship and religious institutions, as conservators of the public morals and valuable, if not indispensable, assistants to the preservation of the public order." *Id.*, at 470.

It would seem from this evidence that the Establishment Clause of the First Amendment had acquired a well-accepted meaning: it forbade establishment of a national religion, and forbade preference among religious sects or denominations. Indeed, the first American dictionary defined the word "establishment" as "the act of establishing, founding, ratifying or ordainin(g,") such as in "[t]he episcopal form of religion, so called, in England." 1 N. Webster, American Dictionary of the English Language (1st ed. 1828). The Establishment Clause did not require government neutrality between religion and irreligion nor did it prohibit the federal government from providing non-discriminatory aid to religion. There is simply no historical foundation for the proposition that the Framers intended to build the "wall of separation" that was constitutionalized in *Everson*.

Notwithstanding the absence of an historical basis for this theory of rigid separation, the wall idea might well have served as a useful albeit misguided analytical concept, had it led this Court to unified and principled results in Establishment Clause cases. The opposite, unfortunately, has been true; in the 38 years since *Everson* our Establishment Clause cases have been neither principled nor unified. Our recent opinions, many of them hopelessly divided pluralities,[6] have with embarrassing candor conceded that the "wall of separation" is merely a "blurred, indistinct, and variable barrier," which "is not wholly accurate" and can only be "dimly perceived." *Lemon* v. *Kurtzman*, 403 U.S. 602, 614 (1971); *Tilton* v. *Richardson*, 403 U.S. 672, 677–678 (1971); *Wolman* v. *Walter*, 433 U.S. 229, 236 (1977); *Lynch* v. *Donnelly*, 465 U.S. ——, (1984).

Whether due to its lack of historical support or its practical unworkability, the *Everson* "wall" has proven all but useless as a guide to sound constitutional adjudication. It illustrates only too well the wisdom of Benjamin Cardozo's observation that "[m]etaphors in law are to be narrowly watched, for starting as devices to liberate thought, they end often by enslaving it." *Berkey* v. *Third Avenue R. Co.*, 244 N.Y. 84, 94, 155 N.E. 58, 61 (1926).

But the greatest injury of the "wall" notion is its mischievous diversion of judges from the actual intentions of the drafters of the Bill of Rights. The "crucible of litigation," ante at 14, is well adapted to adjudicating factual disputes on the basis of testimony presented in court, but no amount of repetition of historical errors in judicial opinions can make the errors true. The "wall of separation between church and State" is a metaphor based on bad history, a metaphor which has proved useless as a guide to judging. It should be frankly and explicitly abandoned.

The Court has more recently attempted to add some mortar to *Everson*'s wall through the three-part test of *Lemon* v. *Kurtzman, supra,* at 614–615, which served at first to offer a more useful test for purposes of the Establishment Clause than did the "wall" metaphor. Generally stated, the *Lemon* test proscribes state action that has a sectarian purpose or effect, or causes an impermissible governmental entanglement with religion. . . .

. . . The *Lemon* test has no more grounding in the history of the First Amendment than does the wall theory upon which it rests. The three-part test represents a determined effort to craft a workable rule from an historically faulty doctrine; but the rule can only be as sound as the doctrine it attempts to service. The three-part test has simply not provided adequate standards for deciding Establishment Clause cases, as this Court has slowly come to realize. Even worse, the *Lemon* test has caused this Court to fracture into unworkable plurality opinions, see *supra*, n. 6, depending upon how each of the three factors applies to a certain state action. The results from our school services cases show the difficulty we have encountered in making the *Lemon* test yield principled results.

For example, a State may lend to parochial school children geography textbooks[7] that contain maps of the United States, but the State may not lend maps of the United States for use in geography class.[8] A State may lend textbooks on American colonial history, but it may not lend a film on George Washington, or a film projector to show it in history class. A State may lend classroom workbooks, but may not lend workbooks in which the parochial school children write, thus rendering them nonreusable.[9] A State may pay for bus transportation to religious schools[10] but may not pay for bus transportation from the parochial school to the public zoo or natural history museum for a field trip.[11] A State may pay for diagnostic services conducted in the parochial school but therapeutic services must be given in a different building; speech and hearing "services" conducted by the State inside the sectarian school are forbidden, *Meek* v. *Pittenger*, 421 U.S. 349, 367, 371 (1975), but the State may conduct speech and hearing diagnostic testing inside the sectarian school. *Wolman*, 433 U.S., at 241. Exceptional parochial school students may receive counseling, but it must take place outside of the parochial school,[12] such as in a trailer parked down the street. *Id.*, at 245. A State may give cash to a parochial school to pay for the administration of State-written tests and state-ordered reporting services,[13] but it may not provide funds for teacher-prepared tests on secular subjects.[14] Religious instruction may not be given in public school,[15] but the public school may release students during the day for religion classes elsewhere, and may enforce attendance at those classes with its truancy laws.[16]

These results violate the historically sound principle "that the Establishment Clause does not forbid governments . . . to [provide] general welfare under which benefits are distributed to private individuals, even though many of those individuals may elect to use those benefits in ways that 'aid' religious instruction or worship." *Committee for Public Education* v. *Nyquist*, 413 U.S. 756, 799 (1973) (BURGER, C. J., concurring in part and dissenting in part). It is not surprising in the light of this record that our most recent opinions have expressed doubt on the usefulness of the *Lemon* test. . . .

The true meaning of the Establishment Clause can only be seen in its history. See *Walz*, 397 U.S., at 671–673; see also *Lynch*, *supra*, at —— ——. As drafters of our Bill of Rights, the Framers inscribed the principles that control today. Any deviation from their intentions frustrates the permanence of that Charter and will only lead to the type of unprincipled decisionmaking that has plagued our Establishment Clause cases since *Everson*.

The Framers intended the Establishment Clause to prohibit the designation of any church as a "national" one. The Clause was also designed to stop the Federal Government from asserting a preference for one religious denomination or sect over others. Given the "incorporation" of the Establishment Clause as against the States via the Fourteenth Amendment in *Everson*, States are prohibited as well from establishing a religion or discriminating between sects. As its history abundantly shows, however, nothing in the Establishment Clause requires government to be strictly neutral between religion and irreligion, nor does that Clause prohibit Congress or the States from pursuing legitimate secular ends through nondiscriminatory sectarian means.

The Court strikes down the Alabama statute in No. 83-812, *Wallace* v. *Jaffree*, because the State wished to "endorse prayer as a favored practice." *Ante*, at 21. It would come as much of a shock to those who drafted the Bill of Rights as it will to a large number of thoughtful Americans today to learn that the Constitution, as construed by the majority, prohibits the Alabama Legislature from "endorsing" prayer. George Washington himself, at the request of the very Congress which passed the Bill of Rights, proclaimed a day of "public thanksgiving and prayer, to be observed by acknowledging with grateful hearts the many and signal favors of Almighty God." History must judge whether it was the father of his country in 1789, or a majority of the Court today, which has strayed from the meaning of the Establishment Clause.

The State surely has a secular interest in regulating the manner in which public schools are conducted. Nothing in the Establishment Clause of the First Amendment, properly understood, prohibits any such generalized "endorsement" of prayer. I would therefore reverse the judgment of the Court of Appeals in *Wallace* v. *Jaffree*.

Notes

1. *Reynolds* is the only authority cited as direct precedent for the "wall of separation theory." 330 U.S., at 16. *Reynolds* is truly inapt; it dealt with a Mormon's Free Exercise Clause challenge to a federal polygamy law.

2. The New York and Rhode Island proposals were quite similar. They stated that no particular "religious sect or society ought to be favored or established by law in preference to others." 1 Elliot's Debates, at 328; *id.*, at 334.

3. In a letter he sent to Jefferson in France, Madison stated that he did not see much importance in a Bill of Rights but he planned to support it because it

was "anxiously desired by others . . . [and] it might be of use, and if properly executed could not be of disservice." 5 Writings of James Madison 271 (G. Hunt ed. 1904).

4. State establishments were prevalent throughout the late Eighteenth and early Nineteenth Centuries. See Massachusetts Constitution of 1780, Part 1, Art. III; New Hampshire Constitution of 1784, Art. VI; Maryland Declaration of Rights of 1776, Art. XXXIII; Rhode Island Charter of 1633 (superseded 1842).

5. The Treaty stated in part:
"*And whereas*, the greater part of said Tribe have been baptized and received into the Catholic church, to which they are much attached, the United States will give annually for seven years one hundred dollars towards the support of a priest of that religion . . . [a]nd . . . three hundred dollars, to assist the said Tribe in the erection of a church." 7 Stat. 79.

From 1789 to 1823 the U.S. Congress had provided a trust endowment of up to 12,000 acres of land "for the Society of the United Bretheren for propagating the Gospel among the Heathen." See, *e.g.*, ch. 46, 1 Stat. 490. The Act creating this endowment was renewed periodically and the renewals were signed into law by Washington, Adams, and Jefferson.

Congressional grants for the aid of religion were not limited to Indians. In 1787 Congress provided land to the Ohio Company, including acreage for the support of religion. This grant was reauthorized in 1792. See 1 Stat. 257. In 1833 Congress authorized the State of Ohio to sell the land set aside for religion and use the proceeds "for the support of religion . . . and for no other use or purpose whatsoever. . . ." 4 Stat. 618–619.

6. *Tilton* v. *Richardson* 403 U.S. 672, 677 (1971); *Meek* v. *Pittenger*, 421 U.S. 349 (1975) (partial); *Roemer* v. *Board of Public Works of Maryland*, 426 U.S. 736 (1976); *Wolman* v. *Walter*, 433 U.S. 229 (1977).

Many of our other Establishment Clause cases have been decided by bare 5–4 majorities. *Committee for Public Education* v. *Regan*, 444 U.S. 646 (1980); *Larson* v. *Valente*, 456 U.S. 228 (1982); *Mueller* v. *Allen*, 463 U.S. 388 (1983); *Lynch* v. *Donnelly*, 465 U.S. ——— (1984); *cf. Levitt* v. *Committee for Public Education*, 413 U.S. 472 (1973).

7. *Board of Education* v. *Allen*, 392 U.S. 236 (1968).

8. *Meek*, 421 U.S., at 362–366. A science book is permissible, a science kit is not. See *Wolman*, 433 U.S., at 249.

9. See *Meek*, *supra*, at 354–355, nn. 3, 4, 362–366.

10. *Everson* v. *Board of Education*, 330 U.S. 1 (1947).

11. *Wolman*, *supra*, at 252–255.

12. *Wolman*, *supra*, at 241–248; *Meek*, *supra*, at 352, n. 2, 367–373.

13. *Regan*, 444 U.S., at 648, 657–659.

14. *Levitt*, 413 U.S., at 479–482.

15. *Illinois ex rel. McCollum* v. *Board of Education*, 333 U.S. 203 (1948).

16. *Zorach* v. *Clauson*, 343 U.S. 306 (1952).

6

Free Enterprise in Religion, or How the Constitution Protects Religion and Religious Freedom

Dean M. Kelley

Some (Recent) "Restorationists" of the Religion Clauses

In every generation there are those who cavil at some current course of constitutional interpretation by the Supreme Court and contend that it has departed from the compact entered into by the founders, leading the nation down some vagrant trail of its own imagining—legislating rather than adjudicating. They wish to restore the pristine, primordial purity of the founders' intent by an appeal to history. (The only trouble is that these various would-be restorationists do not always agree among themselves about where the Court went wrong or what the history appealed to is supposed to prove.)

Two restorationist themes have recently (re)appeared with respect to the religion clauses of the First Amendment. A brief critique of them may help to lead us into a consideration of the main burden of this essay.

"The Founders Intended Only to Prevent the Establishment of a National Church." Several recent writers have reviewed the history of the First Amendment (and of contemporaneous events, state enactments, and the like) and have claimed to discover evidence that persuades them that the founders intended only to prohibit the establishment of a single sect or denomination as the national religion of the United States but did not intend to preclude the government's encouragement of the people's religious proclivities or nonpreferential assistance to all religions.[1] In advancing this view, they are following a series of restorationist writers going back to Edward S. Corwin and Erwin N. Griswold, if not even further back to T. M. Cooley and Joseph Story.[2] They have added an important insight by showing that

114

the founders used the word "respecting" ("Congress shall make no law *respecting* an establishment of religion") to prevent the new federal government from interfering with the existing establishments of religion in those states, such as Connecticut and Massachusetts, that still had them.[3] But two facts militate against the acceptance of this restorationist theme.

First, the First Congress was not without opportunities to enact the limited kind of no-establishment clause that the restorationists say was intended. The first House of Representatives had before it several wordings of that sort, and so did the first Senate.

• Madison's proposal (House of Representatives), June 7, 1789: "nor shall any national religion be established."

• Substitute amendment (Senate), September 3, 1789: "Congress shall make no law establishing one religious sect or society in preference to others." (This version was defeated, then adopted, later lost again.)

• Second amendment (Senate), September 3, 1789: "Congress shall not make any law . . . establishing any religious sect or society."

• Third amendment (Senate), September 3, 1789: "Congress shall make no law establishing any particular denomination of religion in preference to another."

• Fourth version (Senate), September 9, 1789: "Congress shall make no law establishing articles of faith or a mode of worship."[4]

The point is that none of these was enacted. The First Congress wanted to prevent *more* than the establishment of a national religion, a single sect in preference to others, or an official creed or mode of worship. It wanted to keep the national government away from the religious business altogether. So it finally settled on "Congress shall make no law [even] *respecting* an establishment of religion."

Second, presumably the kind of national "establishment of religion" the First Congress wished to ban was the kind with which they were then familiar in the states, and that kind was not a preferential establishment of one sect or faith. As Leonard W. Levy points out:

> Four states had never experienced establishments of religion. Of the remaining states, three completely abolished their establishments during the Revolution, and the other six— Massachusetts, New Hampshire, Connecticut, Maryland, South Carolina and Georgia—converted to comprehensive or multiple establishments. Significantly, *every one of the six states explicitly provided that no sect or denomination should be subordinated to any other;* all denominations enjoyed equal status before the law on a wholly nonpreferential basis.[5]

115

They apparently did not want for the nation even the kind of non-preferential plural establishments they then saw in effect in the six states that had establishments of religion. And in those six states even that plural establishment of religion was eventually eliminated by action of the state legislatures, the last being Massachusetts in 1833. Are the restorationists now trying to restore what the several states on their own motion got rid of over a century and a half ago?

"The Prohibition against Establishment of Religion Was Intended to Apply Only to Congress, Not to the States." One could hardly dispute that the First Amendment as written is a restriction solely on the powers of the federal government, not of the states. What is at issue is the incorporation of the religion clauses—particularly the no-establishment clause—into the Fourteenth Amendment, making them applicable to the states as well. It is not necessary to rehearse here the long and acrimonious arguments over the incorporation of the various clauses of the Bill of Rights into the Fourteenth Amendment to respond to the contention that the states should be left free of federal judicial interference to arrange whatever accommodations to the religious needs of their citizens they deem appropriate within their borders.

That may once have been an acceptable view of the federal-state relationship, but two centuries of experience have suggested otherwise. The American people have learned by bitter experience—including a bloody Civil War and subsequent violent civil rights struggles—that the several states cannot always be relied on to protect all the rights of all their citizens. Those citizens who are disadvantaged by the unwillingness of the states where they live to grant them the basic rights enjoyed by others may appeal to the federal Constitution to protect the rights they enjoy by virtue of their federal citizenship.

Learned legal debate will doubtless continue over the circumstances and grounds on which such appeals can be effective and on the reach and force of the due process clause of the Fourteenth Amendment. (To the lay mind the privileges and immunities clause seems a likelier vehicle—but the Supreme Court has eschewed that route.) But the bottom line is clear even to the man and woman in the street: they do not want their own basic rights and liberties to be subject to "local option." They all want to be fully free and equal American citizens regardless of where in the United States they may happen to reside, and that includes the right not to be subjected to an establishment of religion and the right to "the free exercise thereof."

The Supreme Court Has Long Since Moved beyond These Restorationist Contentions. Although the Supreme Court has had the benefit of the advice of so many learned restorationists over the years, it has not acceded to their urgings. In fact, in 1963 the Court explicitly rejected both these contentions about the religion clauses. Justice Tom Clark, writing for the Court, explained:

> First, this Court has decisively settled that the First Amendment's mandate that "Congress shall make no law respecting an establishment of religion, or prohibiting the free exercise thereof" has been made wholly applicable to the states by the Fourteenth Amendment. . . . In a series of cases since *Cantwell* [v. *Connecticut*, 1940] the Court has repeatedly reaffirmed that doctrine, and we do so now. . . .
>
> Second, this Court has rejected unequivocally the contention that the establishment clause forbids only governmental preference of one religion over another. Almost 20 years ago in *Everson* . . . the Court said that "[n]either a state nor the Federal government can set up a church. Neither can pass laws which aid one religion, aid all religions, or prefer one religion over another." . . . The same conclusion has been firmly maintained ever since that time, . . . and we reaffirm it now.
>
> While none of the parties to either of these cases has questioned these basic conclusions of the Court, both of which have been long established, others continue to question their history, logic and efficacy. Such contentions, in the light of the consistent interpretation in cases of this Court, seem entirely untenable and of value only as academic exercises.[6]

The restorationist appeal to history is engaging—in an academic way—but not persuasive. Even if the restorationists' contentions about the founders' intent were based on evidence that was unambiguous, which it is not, it would not necessarily follow that that intent is fully and obviously applicable in only one undebatable way today. The words of the Constitution are clear and unchanging (except by the arduous course of amendment); their meaning and their application to new circumstances unknown to the founders (such as radio, television, space travel—and public schools) are not. We are fortunate to have an agency of government—the Supreme Court—to adjudicate disputes over the application of these basic ground rules of our society to changing circumstances.

No one will agree with all their conclusions. Even when we disagree, however, we should be thankful that we have a body of nine conscientious, capable, and articulate men and women—who do not have to stand for election every few years—locked in dialogue with one another, struggling with principle and precedent against pressures and prejudices to hammer out the difficult decisions that help to keep our nation on a stable course along coordinates still basically those charted by the founders two centuries ago.

About the restorationist resort to history, one author has commented:

> The historical materials themselves will not settle anything. The task of the judge is not the task of the academic historian—the judge is not concerned with the loving recreation of the past in all its diversity. The job of a constitutional Court is precisely to choose *between* conflicting traditions. The Justices of the Supreme Court must decide whether *they* think the establishment clause should serve a peace-keeping purpose independent of . . . free exercise of religion. If they do so decide they should tell us why (as Justice Frankfurter so clearly did), then use the available historical materials to legitimize the choice. Mr. Justice Black may be properly faulted for hiding behind history and for failing to explain the policy choice involved in adopting the Madisonian theory in *Everson,* but the fault is only compounded by critics who then urge their own historical interpretations as dispositive.[7]

In reaching their conclusions, the Supreme Court's options are certainly far narrower than the legislature's. How narrow or wide they should be is a subject of endless—and rather fruitless—disputation, especially when justices who pride themselves on their strict-constructionist views sometimes come forth with a radically revisionist decision and their strict-constructionist adherents applaud because they like the result, however attained. Suffice it to say that no justices worthy of the office can—or should—disregard the results of their decisions.

The results are one of the factors in the complex equation they must solve. Of greater weight, of course, are the words of the Constitution, the intent of its authors, adopters, and ratifiers (to the limited degree that they can be reliably ascertained), and the interpretations of prior courts. These shape the main contours of precedent, which no court is suddenly going to throw over without the justification of extraordinary crisis.

Probably the most important factor is the justices' whole understanding of life: of what human beings are like, what can and should be expected of them, what sort of relations should be cultivated among them that will make for peace, prosperity, freedom, and justice, and how government and the Court can properly advance those kinds of relations. So turning from the questions of history and the founders' intent, let us ask ourselves what kinds of results we are seeking in the area of church and state that are consonant with the pertinent words of the Constitution (and with what little we may be able to ascertain of their original meaning), consonant with the accumulated wisdom of precedent, and consonant with our best understanding of the kind of nation we want this one to be, particularly with respect to freedom of religion. To that consideration I now turn, using some of the concerns and concepts that seem to be congenial to this forum.

Does Religion Need an Adam Smith?

The Vision of "Free Enterprise." Many of the religion-clause restorationists seem also to resonate to the vision of "free enterprise" in the realm of economics, a vision that for our purposes can be considered a telescoping of two concepts: *free* competition for private *enterprise.* Like most visions or systems, the capitalist arrangement is a complex bundle of interlocked ideas and relationships, two of which can be lifted up as implicating the rest.

First, the actors in the economic sphere are ideally to be private individuals or entities. They each decide for themselves how best to employ their abilities and resources; they each are free to enter on or depart from any enterprise that they deem to be in their interest (subject, of course, to the fulfillment or discharge of commitments made); and government is not to participate in the economic sphere in the role of entrepreneur, partner, competitor, manager, or proprietor.

Second, the private actors are to be free to compete as best they can in the common marketplace without restriction, regulation, or interference by government, which—however well intended—would inevitably disrupt the natural equilibrium of market forces.

The Actuality Falls Short of the Vision. Of course, the actual economic system today is a very imperfect reflection of this vision, and existing entrepreneurs might well be the first to object to greater actualization of the ideal vision. It would tend to eliminate or curtail the present pattern of governmental price supports, tariff barriers, import restrictions, corporate bail-outs, bankruptcy protections, and direct and indirect subsidies from which they benefit, as well as governmental strictures against "unfair competition," which actually reduce the rigors of an entirely free market. But these contradictions of the ideal vision do not seem to prevent its being proclaimed as the portrayal of the Golden Age to which the nation should return.

The Restorationist Vision for Religion. Likewise, a Golden Age to which the nation should return is envisioned for religion, one in which the government recognizes, accommodates, encourages, and aids the people in the attainment of their religious needs and aspirations, as it was (supposedly) expected to do by the founders back in the lost Golden Age. This restoration would include "permitting" children to pray in public schools, by which is meant the institution, under governmental auspices, of some kind of oral, collective, ritual prayer according to some particular form or forms, none of which could be truly voluntary or nonsectarian; tax credits and other forms of assistance to private religious schools; and governmental provision for public observance of religious holy days.

Why Is the Vision for Religion the Opposite of the Vision for Economics? It appears that the restorationist vision for religion is the opposite of the restorationist vision for economics. If the vision of free competition for private enterprise has been more nearly realized in one area of American life than in any other, it is in the area of religion, where it has produced a flourishing of religious vitality unrivaled anywhere else in the world. Yet—contrary to the adage If it ain't broke, don't fix it[8]—the advocates of free enterprise in economics seem to want to stamp out free enterprise in religion. Far from wanting to "get the government off our backs" in religion, they seem determined to give the government an ever greater role in sponsoring, regulating, subsidizing, and assisting the people's religious activities.

The First Amendment Seems Designed to Ensure Free Enterprise in Religion. "Free exercise of religion" is the perfect counterpart of the principle of "private enterprise." Each person is to be free to follow his or her own inclinations as to the most congenial form or expression of religion and to apply his or her abilities and resources in adherence to and furtherance of that faith as he or she sees fit without governmental leading, tutelage, or influence. Government is not to participate in the religious realm as sponsor, partner, competitor, manager, or proprietor.

"No establishment of religion" is the perfect counterpart of the principle of "free competition." The private parties in religion are to prosper or decline according to their own merits in the free marketplace of ultimate meanings without governmental "assistance," restriction, regulation, or interference.

One might expect that restorationists imbued with a healthy suspicion of governmental intervention in the economic sphere—whether as proprietor or regulator—might see the wisdom of a similar course in the religious sphere and strive to restore that meaning to the religion clauses of the First Amendment rather than one of antithetical effect. Perhaps what is needed today is an Adam Smith urging "free enterprise in religion."

Religion's Adam Smith. Fortunately, we *have* an Adam Smith for religion, who wrote more than a century before Smith's *Wealth of Nations* (1776) and not only wrote but put his preaching into practice on this continent beginning in 1636. His name is Roger Williams, and he categorically rejected the then generally accepted idea that the government has responsibility in the area of religion:

> The civil state of the nations, being merely and essentially civil, cannot (Christianly) be called Christian states. . . . The civil sword (therefore) cannot rightfully act either in restraining the souls of the people from worship, or in constraining them *to* worship, considering that there is not a title in the new Testament of Christ Jesus that commits the forming or reforming of His spouse and Church to the civil and worldly power. . . .
>
> Can the sword of steel or arm of flesh make men loyal or faithful to God? Or careth God for the *outward* loyalty or faithfulness, when the *inward* man is false and treacherous?[9]

Government, Roger Williams believed, cannot really aid religion; even when it tries to help, it only hinders by leading the people to rely on earthly powers rather than on God and their own faith.

> The unknowing zeal of Constantine and other (Christian) emperors did more hurt to Christ Jesus His crown and Kingdom than the raging fury of the most bloody Neros. . . . When Christians first began to be choked, it was not . . . in cold prisons, but in down-beds of ease.[10]

As for the supposition that the civil population should be expected to join in the worship offered to God by Christians, he said: "What a world of profanation of the holy Name and holy ordinances of the Lord in prostituting the holy things of God to profane, impenitent, and unregenerate persons!"[11] Without trying to evaluate the validity of laissez-faire ideology in the economic realm, we may point to several laudable—or at least lauded—aspects of the American economic experience (or its romanticized idealization) as suggesting claims of freedom that are even more compelling in the area of religion.

Free Enterprise in Religion

Hospitality to New Entrepreneurs. This country has always prided itself, at least in theory, on the possibility that anyone with imagination, thrift, perseverance, and application could start his or her own business and become in time a captain of industry. (The windrows of bankruptcies are thought to testify not to a flaw in the vision but to inadequacy of application, perseverance, thrift, or imagination.) Yet in a nation that claims to honor religious liberty, it should be even more a source of pride that anyone with inspiration, insight, charisma, and endurance could launch his or her own religious group and lead people to salvation, becoming in time a revered prophet, saint, or guru.

That does not seem to be the case. New religions do not have an easy time here (or anywhere else). They are even less welcome than new businesses, especially by their closest competitors, the existing, accepted religions. They are met by suspicion, animosity, ostracism, persecution. Atrocity tales are circulated about them (as they have been about the Jehovah's Witnesses, the Christian Scientists, the Mormons, the early Wesleyans, the first Christians). They are accused of being shysters or charlatans out to bilk the unsuspecting of their money or to use the gullible to gain power and influence. (Thus do economic and political imputations ever seek to displace or discredit religious ones.)

The American system of law has sometimes assisted persecution with prosecution (as in the Mormon cases of the nineteenth century and the conviction of Sun Myung Moon in the twentieth) and has sometimes resisted it (as in the Jehovah's Witnesses' cases of the 1940s). The frontier where new religions emerge is at once the zone of greatest threat to religious liberty and that of the expansion of religious rights. Today we see the hostility to new religions taking several forms, with the anticult movement (itself a kind of cult) leading the attack.

• Criminal prosecutions, as of Sun Myung Moon. Moon was sent to prison on the basis of a conviction secured by the abrogation of an ecclesiastical trust, contrary to the law of New York, the forum state, as pointed out by the dissenting appellate judge, and by denying him a bench trial because he had accused the government of prejudice.

• Forcible abductions, called deprogrammings, designed to reverse conversions unacceptable to the (adult) convert's family. Police, prosecutors, and judges have often assisted, condoned, or disregarded private violations of law on the basis that it is "all in the family" and the object is, after all, to "get the kid out of a cult."

• Tort suits against religious groups, charging fraud, outrageous conduct, kidnapping, even wrongful death, and sometimes obtaining fantastic damage awards (usually reduced or reversed on appeal). This is a growing and ugly area of litigation, even though usually unsuccessful.[12]

• Conservatorship statutes. Efforts have been made in many states to legalize deprogramming by permitting courts to grant conservatorship orders to families to take custody of an adult convert and subject him or her to "therapy" to restore the ability to make independent judgments—which therapy is deemed to be complete only when the patient is able to decide ("independently") *not* to go back to the "cult." Thus far, fortunately, no such statute has been adopted, although the New York legislature has passed one twice, only to have it vetoed by the governor at the urging of the churches, which felt that such a statute not only would violate individuals' rights but would be a threat to the validity of all conversions.

In these respects we are seeing today a more concerted, systematic, and sophisticated attack on new religions than ever before in our history. In my view this is the greatest stain on the nation's record for religious liberty in this century. It is matched only by the crusade against the Mormons in the 1800s, which enlisted the U.S. cavalry and the Supreme Court in opposition to a new religious movement that, despite the worst they could do, has survived and become one of the conservative bulwarks of the nation (especially in the area of free-enterprise economics).

The picture is somewhat complicated by the recent emergence of a number of ingenious economic entrepreneurships disguised as religions, what the Internal Revenue Service calls "mail-order ministries" or "tax protesters." These purport to be house churches maintained by a family and perhaps a few friends, to which they give all or most of their income as charitable contributions, receiving back generous stipends for living expenses, so that their standard of living is not diminished; they just do not have to pay taxes. Unfortunately for this kind of free enterprise, a number of these imaginative entrepreneurs (of the Basic Bible Church and others) have received prison sentences for tax evasion, and rightly so. This kind of put-on should not be confused with genuine new religions, which should not be tarred with its brush.

Government Shall Not Engage in Competitive Enterprises (Either as an Entrepreneur Itself or by Aiding Some Existing Entrepreneurs against Others). In the economic realm protests are often heard when the government engages in economic activity (unless it be in an area that is unprofitable to private enterprise), and the charters of some municipalities forbid their entry into any activity that would compete with existing businesses.[13] Whatever the merits of this principle in the economic realm, it applies a fortiori in the religious realm. Yet we see violations of this principle endorsed by restorationists and even upheld by the courts.

State proprietorships in religion. Public school prayers, which are advocated by some restorationists, would unavoidably involve agencies of the state in sponsoring, arranging, and prescribing (if only by delegation to teachers or pupils) the form and content of oral, collective, ritual prayers to be recited in a public institution. The supposition that excusal remedies any affront to pupils of minority faiths or none is itself a telltale indication that the activity is inappropriate (as we shall see below).

Municipal religious displays are likewise instances of governmental proprietorships in religion. They identify one or another particular sectarian symbolism with the instrumentalities of governance, which are supposed to be equally representative of, and responsible to, all the citizens, not just those of a particular religious persuasion.[14]

Legislative chaplains, designated and paid by the legislature from tax funds collected by force of law from all citizens, are another state proprietorship in religion. If it could be said—as it might be with respect to military personnel in isolated installations or inmates of prisons or long-term-care hospitals—that the government has removed some persons from their normal civilian environment and must therefore supply them with surrogates for their own normal religious ministrants to preserve a semblance of their free exercise of religion, there might be some justification for this arrangement. But legislators can hardly be said to be unable to repair to their normal civilian sources for the consolations of religion. And the Supreme Court's reasoning in upholding such an arrangement in Nebraska—that since the First Congress employed a chaplain shortly after endorsing the First Amendment, it must be all right—is vulnerable to the wry comment of Justice William J. Brennan in dissent:

> To treat any practice authorized by the First Congress as presumptively consistent with the Bill of Rights is . . . somewhat akin to treating any action of a party to a contract as presumptively consistent with the terms of the contract. The latter proposition, if it were accepted, would of course re-

solve many of the heretofore perplexing issues in contract law.[15]

Far from being welcomed as laudable accommodations to the religious needs of the people, these practices should be rejected as state proprietorships in religion—prima facie violations of the principle of free enterprise in the realm of religion.

State preferences for one religion over another. The Supreme Court has been rather vigilant to prevent the kind of establishment of religion that arises when the state prefers one religion over another,[16] but it has failed to deal with egregious examples of such preference.

1. The appointment of an ambassador to the Vatican. The president's appointment of a full ambassador to the Holy See—an appointment endorsed by the Senate and funded with appropriations initiated by the House—is a clear case of the U.S. government's showing special favor to one particular religious body and not to others. If some contend, as the State Department and the first ambassador, William Wilson, have, that the embassy is only to the civil entity of Vatican City, they would do well to be corrected by Wilson's counterpart, Pro-Nuncio Archbishop Pio Laghi, who, in an address at the Catholic University of America on April 6, 1984, explained the significance of the appointment from the viewpoint of the Vatican:

> Papal diplomacy has been referred to as *sui generis* because nowhere is it exactly paralleled. In fact, the Catholic Church is the only religious body that I know of that engages in direct relations with various states. You recall the confusion and controversy that arose in the media at the time it was announced that the United States and the Holy See intended to reestablish diplomatic ties. Some mistakenly tried to justify the American government's action by implying that it was entering into a diplomatic relationship not with the Roman Catholic Church as such, the Holy See, but rather with the sovereign Vatican City-State.
>
> "Papal Diplomacy rests essentially upon the spiritual sovereignty of the Holy See and not upon dominion over a few acres in the heart of Rome." (R. A. Graham, S.J., *Vatican Diplomacy*, p. 15)
>
> It is therefore the Pope's religious authority which confers upon him the classical right of legation, a diplomatic standing in the world. Those who interpret Papal Diplomacy as emanating from the Pope's temporal sovereignty are failing to understand the true nature of the mission of the Holy See.

Of course, sending ambassadors to all churches would not be feasible and would be objectionable for other reasons. But the salient vice of the present appointment is giving privileged access to one particular faith at the expense of others.

2. Aid to one particular mode of religious education. Proposals are repeatedly heard for various kinds of state aid to parochial schools. Whatever their merits, one thing is clear: they constitute state favoritism toward one particular mode of religious education. Several denominations—Roman Catholics, Lutherans, Seventh-Day Adventists, Orthodox Jews, and some independent Baptist churches—have chosen to impart their faith to their children by means of church-sponsored schools of general education. Other denominations rely on Sunday schools, daily vacation Bible schools, summer camps, and so on. Any state aid to the first-named kind of religious education would constitute a massive tilt toward that mode of inculcating the faith and would inevitably attract other denominations to opt for that favored mode. More and more parochial schools would be founded by otherwise disfavored denominations.

3. Prayer in public schools. If school prayer were to be instituted by constitutional amendment, it would also inevitably result in state favoritism toward the forms of prayer of the religious majority in every community, to the derogation of citizens of minority faiths or none. This kind of unfair governmental preference, objectionable enough in the economic realm, would be even more offensive in the realm of religion.

An Entrepreneur Should Be Able to Manage Internal Affairs without Government Interference. *Internal structure and the exercise of authority.* One of the prime requisites of freedom is the ability to manage one's own affairs. Of course, when those affairs impinge on other persons, that freedom must be accommodated to their rights as well. But when it affects only oneself and those who have voluntarily chosen to associate with one—and who can withdraw at will—the claim of autonomy seems strong. Yet we have recently seen some surprising impairments of that autonomy by law—and also some commendable tributes to it—from the courts.

One such impairment is the "congregationalizing" of hierarchical churches. One of the prime principles of autonomy is that a body should be able to determine for itself the locus of its internal decision making. If a corporation wishes to decide some policies at the branch level, others at the regional level, and still others at the national or international level, it is usually entitled to do so. Certainly that is the authority assumed by most organizations and especially by religious bodies. But in the arena of church property law we have seen a curious drama enacted.

Beginning in the Civil War era, the Supreme Court held—in *Watson* v. *Jones*—that when the highest ecclesiastical tribunal in a hierarchical religious body decided on the use of local church property, the civil courts were bound by that decision and could not second-guess the religious tribunal. That was generally the law of the land until recently.[17] As Justice Felix Frankfurter observed in *Kedroff,* what is at issue is not just property but the exercise of ecclesiastical authority.[18]

Beginning in 1970 with *Hull Church II* and *Sharpsburg Eldership,* however, a new note was heard.[19] No longer were civil courts obliged to defer to ecclesiastical tribunals in church property cases. If they saw fit, they might rely instead on "neutral principles of law" in deciding such cases. That is, they could examine the property deeds, contracts, and church charters or constitutions to see if a trust was impressed on local church property for the benefit of a higher body. That doctrine emerged full-blown in *Jones* v. *Wolf.*[20] Some courts—though not all—have taken that option, while others have remained with the venerable teaching of *Watson* v. *Jones.* The effect of *Jones* v. *Wolf* (as of *Hull Church II*) was to award the local church property to the local congregation, thus "congregationalizing" the Presbyterian church by taking two local church properties away from it.

Recently a federal judge published a law review article contending that civil courts should always rely on neutral principles of law rather than automatically according deference to hierarchical authority. He reasoned that such deference would restrict the right of local congregations to affiliate with the denomination of their choosing because they would then be signing over "their" property to the denomination.[21]

The only flaw in this reasoning is that in most instances local congregations of a hierarchical denomination are not independent contracting parties. In nine cases out of ten, local congregations are founded, financed, staffed, and sustained by the denomination. Hull Church happened to have preexisted its connection with the denomination, as did the Presbyterian church in the more recent case in Schenectady, New York, but they are rare exceptions. To contend that they should be able to pull out of the denomination and take the local church property with them is like saying that a local outlet, branch office, or assembly plant of General Motors could declare its independence, set up in business for itself, and take the property and inventory with it.

Another impairment of autonomy, of opposite effect, is the "hierarchicalizing" of connectional churches. This is seen in a recent decision involving the United Methodist church. When the Pacific Homes retirement facilities in California went bankrupt, some of the residents sued the Annual Conference with which the homes had been related, the General Council on Finance and Administration of the denomination, and the United Methodist church. The general council contended that there was no one to answer suit for "the United Methodist Church," since there is no suable entity corresponding to those words. The church has a national existence only during the two-week session of the General Conference every four years, and in between it has no interim body, officers, employees, assets, or decision-making mechanism.

The Annual Conference does have such attributes, as does the General Council on Finance and Administration, and they were answering suit, but the church has taken pains to be a decentralized, connectional body rather than a hierarchical one. The court ruled that it could still be sued because the homes had held themselves out to be related to the United Methodist church and no one had said nay. Whatever it was they claimed to be related to, therefore, might be found to share responsibility for the breach of contract entered into by the residents, in reliance on the proffer made in connection with "the United Methodist Church."

The case was eventually settled out of court, but this threshold decision,[22] in effect, defined the United Methodist church as having a structure other than it had chosen for itself. It was not a question of the church's trying to avoid liability, since several substantial church agencies did answer suit. It was solely a question of legal definition, one in which the autonomy of the church in defining its own structure should have been respected by the court but was not. In such instances of alleged "ascending liability," it is significant that churches may not be accorded the insulation that commercial corporations may enjoy from responsibility for the torts of wholly owned subsidiaries when there has been no "piercing of the corporate veil."

Supervision of employees. Another important aspect of autonomy is the supervision of employees. Of course, in this area autonomy is more restricted, since it impinges on the rights of the employees. And here churches may have somewhat greater autonomy than businesses.

In *NLRB* v. *Catholic Bishop of Chicago,* the Supreme Court held that in the National Labor Relations Act Congress had not intended to give the National Labor Relations Board jurisdiction over the election of union representation by lay teachers in Roman Catholic parochial schools, since such intervention by a government agency might lead to impairment of the church's ability to control the teaching of its faith.[23]

In *McClure* v. *Salvation Army*, a federal circuit court of appeals held that in the Equal Employment Opportunities Act Congress had not intended to intervene in the relationship between a church and its clergy. Therefore, Mrs. McClure could not appeal to that act to obtain redress for alleged discriminatory treatment of women members of its clergy by the Salvation Army.[24]

In *Southwestern Baptist Theological Seminary* v. *Equal Employment Opportunities Commission* (EEOC), a federal circuit court of appeals held that the seminary was an essential part of the church and was therefore outside the jurisdiction of the EEOC with respect to its teaching and administrative staff but would have to file with the EEOC the reports required by law with respect to its other, nonteaching employees.[25]

In *Bob Jones University* v. *U.S.* the U.S. Supreme Court upheld the revocation of tax exemption of this unique institution because of the alleged racial discrimination implicit in campus rules prohibiting interracial dating or marriage by students or faculty.[26] Despite a footnote purporting to confine this holding to educational institutions rather than extending it to churches as such (which Bob Jones University had claimed to be), the Court may have opened a door to loss of tax exemption of religious bodies that discriminate against women in the ordination of clergy, as some observers have warned, or that violate "public policy" in other respects.

Allocation of resources. A third important area of autonomy encompasses an organization's deployment of its financial and other resources. If the government can tell a church how to spend its money, its area of freedom is considerably circumscribed. A church operates mainly on the freewill offerings of its members and friends, and those funds are dedicated to the advancement of its mission. They are virtually impressed with a trust for the attainment of the church's purposes, and if the church is not able to determine freely what its purposes are and how they can best be served by the contributions designated therefor, an important area of freedom has been impaired. Yet that is exactly what has happened in several instances.

Under New York's landmarking statute, several religious structures in New York City have been "landmarked" against their will. The Lutheran Church of America was able to persuade a court to revoke the designation of its headquarters at 231 Madison Avenue— the former J. P. Morgan mansion—but others have not been as fortunate.[27] In the courts at this writing (1985) are the cases of St. Bartholomew's Episcopal Church on Park Avenue and the United

Methodist Church of St. Paul and St. Andrew at Eighty-sixth Street and West End Avenue. The vice of this law—from the churches' standpoint—is that the city, by designating a structure a landmark, can require the congregation to maintain the façade, at whatever cost, or suffer criminal penalties, whether the church has any money left to carry on its religious work inside or not. If that is not a clear-cut "taking" of private property without just compensation, it is hard to think what would be, but New York's highest court has said it is not.[28]

When the churches of New York asked the legislature to amend the statute so that no religious structure could be landmarked without its consent, a great hue and cry was raised, and borough presidents, preservationists, and Jacqueline Onassis appeared in Albany to oppose such an amendment. The mayor of New York City went on television to assure the populace that "we won't let them destroy your landmarks." *Your* landmarks? Do the churches now belong to the public, whether the public has or has not ever paid a penny to build or maintain them? Apparently so, at least according to the mayor, and the church members are to have the privilege and responsibility of patching up a crumbling edifice to gratify the artistic sensibilities of the passer-by. What would Roger Williams have said to that? "Abandon the old heap of stones; let them have it; and go out into the streets and carry on the work of the Lord!"

I have mentioned the conviction of Sun Myung Moon for tax fraud, but one aspect of *Moon v. U.S.* falls under this heading. The prosecution cited as evidence that the funds in question were Moon's and not the church's, that the money was held in his own name, that he had complete dominion and control over it, and that he used much of it for investment in commercial enterprises. (Of course, any trustee has dominion and control over trust funds.) The jury was asked to determine whether—in its lay view—the funds had been used for "religious" purposes, and the jury found they had not. No evidence was admitted as to the church's view of whether that use contributed to its religious mission, and of course no other churches ever invest surplus funds in commercial enterprises.

Seemingly lost sight of in the rush to put Moon behind bars was the consideration that the most natural, direct, and effective way to advance a religious cause is to give one's contributions to its founder and leader, since he will know better than any board or committee what needs to be done. This truth is succinctly expressed in what could be called Whitefield's principle, as found in the *Journal of John Wesley,* the founder of Methodism, in an entry for May 9, 1739, describing his efforts to build a meetinghouse in Bristol for two of the societies he had founded.

I had not at first the least apprehension or design of being personally engaged, either in the expense of this work or in the direction of it, having appointed eleven [trustees], on whom I supposed those burdens would fall. . . . But I quickly found my mistake; first with regard to the expense: for the whole undertaking must have stood still, had not I immediately taken upon myself the payment of all the workmen; so that before I knew where I was, I had contracted a debt of more than a hundred and fifty pounds. And this I was to discharge how I could; the subscription of both societies not amounting to one quarter of that sum. And as to the direction of the work, I presently received letters from my friends in London, Mr. Whitefield in particular, . . . that neither he nor they would have anything to do with the building, neither contribute anything towards it, unless I would instantly discharge [the trustees], and do everything in my own name. Many reasons they gave for this; but one was enough—viz., "that such [trustees] always would have it in their power to control me; and if I preached not as they liked, to turn me out of the room I had built." I accordingly yielded to their advice, and calling all the [trustees] together, cancelled (no man opposing) the instrument made before, and took the whole management into my own hands.[29]

It is ironic that the government should have claimed its supposed taxes and secured Moon's conviction by—in effect—taking the church's money and awarding it to Moon and his heirs forever, when no one in the church had accused Moon of misusing its funds or diverting them to his own use.

Problems of "Consumer Protection" and Quality Control. Some manufacturers and producers seem to have excellent quality control and rightful pride in their products, while others seem to be willing to maximize their profits at the expense of the consumer. The apostles of consumer protection have sought government intervention to require by law that certain standards of safety, purity, and merchantability be met, since the average consumer cannot know enough to be a wise purchaser of goods and services that are highly technical and whose originator may be far removed from the marketplace transaction. This rationale for consumer protection—whatever its merits in the economic realm—has been carried over into the religious realm, where its merits are less obvious and its results curiously contradictory. The government is apparently expected to punish religious entrepreneurs who "take advantage of" the consumer and at the same time also to punish those who try to exercise quality control in their operations.

131

Government inspection of religion? One may rightly wonder whether government—whatever its capacities with respect to pure food and drugs or automobile safety—is well suited to determining the truth or falsity of religious claims and beliefs. Is the government supposed to get into the business of inspecting, evaluating, grading, and certifying religion as it does meat? One would have thought this question had been settled by *U.S.* v. *Ballard* in the 1940s, but it still keeps cropping up.[30] In that case the Supreme Court held that a civil court could not undertake to determine the truth or falsity of religious beliefs but only the sincerity of those who promulgated them, and Justice Robert H. Jackson—with what is probably even more durable constitutional insight—would have forbidden them even to do that.

Yet in several recent cases, such as *Christofferson* v. *Church of Scientology, Van Schaick* v. *Church of Scientology,* and seven suits filed against the Church of Scientology in Boston alone, civil courts are being asked to determine whether religious fraud has been committed.[31] It is not just a question of fairly obvious secular defalcation, which even Justice Jackson admitted would be triable in civil courts—whether money given for building a church was actually used for the personal aggrandizement of the fund raiser—but of whether the religious claims of the religious organization are valid. The Church of Scientology has been treated as a legitimate religious organization by several courts (because the government prosecutors did not challenge its *bona fides*), and its purportedly religious teachings are not being challenged but only whether they were offered for religious or for secular purposes, such as obtaining money from inquirers.

Several disillusioned former members are now claiming that they were defrauded, that Scientology had promised to make better persons of them if they subscribed for advanced training courses and had failed to do so. If an automobile is defective, the manufacturer must make good on the warranty. It is usually relatively simple to determine whether the car is defective, but how does a court determine whether the religious product is defective?

The efficacy of religion depends to a significant degree on the fervor of the disciple and not solely on the charisma of the guru, and a common explanation for the failure of religious ministrations to produce miracles is that the believer's faith was not great enough. Is a civil court equipped to weigh the faith of the adherent against the acumen and sanctity of the purveyor? Can a jury determine whether the disciple has attained the standards set by the master sufficiently to be entitled to salvation? Apparently, several courts are willing to undertake this formidable task, for they have refused to dismiss these suits for religious fraud or to grant summary judgment for the defendant religious group. So a new religious movement seems to be letting itself in for some legal risk when it offers its teachings to the public. When it tries to discipline or winnow its membership, however, so that only the earnest and the faithful are retained, it can run into trouble too.

But don't be too strict! Recently members of religious groups who have been disciplined or expelled have been taking the religious groups to court, and the courts have been entertaining their suits.

In *Bear* v. *Mennonite Church* Robert Bear, a potato farmer in Pennsylvania, was put under the ban by his bishop for stirring up dissension in the church. He took the bishop to court for breaking up his home and his business, since none of the church members would associate or trade with him while he was banned. His suit was dismissed by the trial court, but an appellate court reversed and remanded it for trial. On trial so much damaging evidence about Bear's own faults in the affair came out that the court found against him, but the case should never have gone to trial.[32]

In a case we might call *"Squire"* v. *"Elders,"* the minister and two lay elders of a Reformed church in Iowa drew up an ecclesiastical admonition against the dominant member of the congregation, remonstrating with him for "unChristian behavior." They followed the procedure provided by the denomination in such cases and even hand-delivered the document to the squire's door to be sure that it did not fall into anyone else's hands. The squire was incensed. He showed the letter all around town and then sued the elders for libel. Instead of throwing the suit out as a matter of internal ecclesiastical discipline, the court (and original defense counsel) treated it as a run-of-the-mill libel case and granted discovery of church records to determine malice. The case was eventually settled out of court when the elders— afraid of losing their farms—capitulated to the squire and apologized for their effrontery.

Recently, in *Guinn* v. *Church of Christ*, a woman in Oklahoma sued the Church of Christ congregation to which she had belonged for defamation because of a formal denunciation of her, for "fornication," delivered from the pulpit.[33] She was awarded damages by the jury, but this case was different from the others described above because she had formally resigned in writing before the denunciation and was therefore no longer within the jurisdiction of the church. The castigation was therefore gratuitous and actionable.

Sometimes the church invokes the civil law in an effort to discipline its clergy. A Lutheran pastor, the Reverend Douglas Roth of Clairton, in the Mahoning Valley near Pittsburgh, defied his bishop.

The bishop, at the request of what is claimed to be a majority of the congregation, deposed the pastor because of his involvement in a protest movement against industrial firms and banks alleged to have caused wide unemployment among steelworkers. The pastor was jailed for contempt of court at one point because he defied a court order to vacate the church at the bishop's behest.[34]

Moving beyond Metaphors and Parallels

Less Freedom for Religion Than for Business? In some instances commercial enterprises seem to enjoy greater freedom from government interference than churches. One such circumstance was a remarkable theory of the attorney general of California, under which he viewed himself as the guardian of all charitable trusts in the state, including churches. In this capacity he obtained a court order placing the Worldwide Church of God in receivership—until the legislature amended the statute to make clear that the attorney general was not to be the overseer of churches. But during his brief heyday he contended that the beneficiary of all charitable trusts is the public and that the attorney general, as representative of the public, had the duty to make sure that contributions to such trusts were not diverted from the public benefit. To do that he claimed the right to examine all the books and activities of such trusts and to determine whether—in his view— they met the public interest. As one commentator observed, he would never have claimed such a prerogative with respect to commercial businesses, let alone private citizens.[35]

Another such instance is the claim by the Internal Revenue Service (IRS) of the right to examine not only the books of account but all the activities of tax-exempt organizations, to determine whether they continue to qualify for exemption. That is a much more sweeping degree of scrutiny than the IRS devotes to taxpayers, including commercial enterprises, where its audits are normally limited to the taxpayer's financial records. (The Church Audit Procedures Act of 1984 may somewhat restrict the service's intrusion into churches, although the scope of such audits still remains broader than those of taxpayers.)

Some may think it improper for government to be more intrusive into churches than into commercial firms; others may not, depending on their general outlook and values. How should legislatures and courts weigh the competing claims for freedom from government regulation?

Since the closing of the frontier, it might be contended, we all must get along together with an increasing population on a (socially) shrinking planet. Therefore, there may be less room for the exercise of *all* freedoms, religious as well as economic. If that is the case, then what room is left should be allotted by priority: first things first. And since economics pertains to the very essentials of existence—food, clothing, shelter, energy, medicine, transportation—it should take precedence, some might maintain, over mere luxuries, indulgences, and intangibles such as religion.

Religion Is Not Dispensable. In other places I have argued at some length that religion is one of the essential functions that every society needs to have performed if it is to survive.[36] Everyone in society has a strong *secular* interest in seeing that the religious function is fulfilled for those who need it, whether they themselves feel the need for it or not. It is not just a matter of a sentimental indulgence of the religiously inclined but a very utilitarian solicitude for the survival of society as a whole that gives religion its high place in the priorities of the nation, a place fittingly signaled by its rank at the head of the Bill of Rights.

The importance of ultimate meaning. Every society seems to need one or more ways for most of its members most of the time to find a system of ultimate meaning within which to locate their lives. Unless people can see beyond their own troubles, doldrums, and frustrations to a framework of higher purpose, broader value, and deeper significance, they are apt to succumb to various maladies of meaninglessness that are increasingly prevalent in our society: despair, boredom, anxiety, bitterness, anomie, despondency, rage, hopelessness. These can lead to various escapes, such as alcohol or drug addiction, derangement, and even some forms of crime and suicide.

The same form of religion does not do for all persons. The widest variety of religious formulations seems the best way of ensuring that everyone's religious needs can be met, not that everyone necessarily finds the kind best suited to his or her propensities or is willing to pay the price to appropriate it (since the main ingredient in the religious transaction is how much it costs to lay hold of it, and in that market money is relatively cheap). Religious freedom is the condition in which the widest variety of religious options is available and everyone can choose (or refuse) any offering or change from one to another.

Ensuring the availability of religion. Governments have long been aware of the importance of religion and have tried to ensure its availability, usually in the wrong ways and for the wrong reasons. The wrong reasons include using religion as a device for social control: to bolster the throne and to keep down dissidence. The wrong ways

135

include establishing a favored religion, which is invariably the least effective in meeting the religious needs of those who need it most (the poor and the oppressed), and persecuting disfavored religions, which are invariably the newer and more vigorous ones and therefore the most effective in meeting religious needs.

For government even to try to help religion is to hinder it, since the kind of "help" that government can give serves to take away much of the cost of religion and therefore much of its effectiveness.[37] By long and bitter experience, humankind may have begun to learn that the best way for government to ensure the fulfillment of the religious function is to leave it alone, neither "helping" nor hindering.

The solution of the First Amendment. Fortunately, that is precisely the solution provided by the religion clauses of the First Amendment: government is neither to sponsor nor to inhibit religion. Thus in the United States are found the ideal conditions for the flourishing of religion, with the not surprising result that religion in this country shows more variety and vitality than in most other parts of the globe—without any need for latter-day revisionisms.

Progressive Discovery of the Implications of the American Experiment in Religious Freedom. The First Amendment reflects the first broad effort to found a nation on the revolutionary notion of free enterprise in religion. The founders had a bold and broad idea of the kind of freedom that was needed and possible, but they could not foresee how its implications would work out in all future circumstances.

It is the function of the Supreme Court not only to apply the founders' broad principles to changing conditions through the centuries but to explore and plumb the fuller implications of those principles, which may not have been grasped by the founders themselves in the few years allotted to them. For instance, the founders may not have asked themselves whether appointing and paying a congressional chaplain was consonant with the no-establishment clause. If they had, they might not have done it.

The founders themselves, like all of us, were to some degree captives of their inherited and familiar habits of thought. They were accustomed to the old European arrangement in which the stability of the civil realm was predicated on all its members' subscribing to the same religious commitments—or pretending to do so. When the founders launched the outrageous new adventure on these shores, in which all citizens were to be fully and equally members of the civil commonwealth without also having to subscribe to the prevailing religious orthodoxy, they may not yet have glimpsed what that would mean for such things as public school prayers, to take one example. (Their prescience was probably inhibited as well by the fact that they did not yet have public schools.)

The furthest advance in the inherited European frame of reference at that time was religious toleration—a great advance over burnings at the stake, to be sure, but a far cry from religious freedom. Many of our forebears left Europe because they were not satisfied with the two options open to them under religious toleration: either to endure the civil homages to the favored or majority religion without protest or causing scandal to the faithful or to emigrate to another realm where their religion was in the majority (if they could find one).

Curiously, those are exactly the same two options that would be open to children of minority religions or no religion if a public-school-prayer amendment were to be adopted: go along without a fuss or ask to be excused (emigrate temporarily), thus evidencing that they are like guests in someone else's house. The public schools, which are as much theirs as anyone else's, are somehow less theirs if they have to endure or emigrate because of something going on there. They become for that time and that reason second-class citizens because of their religion.

Not until 1962–1963 did the Supreme Court have or take occasion to confront the question whether state-sponsored, collective oral prayer in public schools was consonant with true religious liberty or was a vestige of the European tradition of mere toleration. It decided for religious liberty. Some Americans, however, seem still to be living in the mind-set of King George III, believing that the sovereign (in a democracy, the majority) should rule in religion as in other matters, and want to amend the Constitution to restore the European principle of mere toleration that many of our forebears fled.

The true and enduring constitutional principle is that some things are placed by the Bill of Rights beyond the reach of majorities:

> The very purpose of a Bill of Rights was to withdraw certain subjects from the vicissitudes of political controversy, to place them beyond the reach of majorities and officials and to establish them as legal principles to be applied by the courts. One's right to life, liberty, and property, to free speech, a free press, freedom of worship and assembly, and other fundamental rights may not be submitted to vote; they depend on the outcome of no elections.[38]

In that statement breathes the spirit of free enterprise in religion, the one area of human life where it is more to be desired than all others.

Conclusion

It has been the burden of this essay to contend that every individual should enjoy the maximum freedom consonant with the common good and the noninjury of others, whether in economics or religion or other aspects of life, and that government regulation designed to advance the common good and to protect against injury can be and often is counterproductive and even pernicious when it overrestricts private initiative, preempts the responsibility proper to other spheres of life, or arrogates to itself decisions about the most immediate and intimate aspects of personhood.

The claims of freedom have been asserted in both the economic and the religious realms but not necessarily by the same claimants. Some who have urged that government intervention in the economic realm be minimized seem to offer a contrary prescription for the religious realm. It is true that the same rule need not run in both realms, but it is the contention of this essay that freedom from governmental regulation is even more urgent and essential in the religious realm than in the economic, both because religious commitments are more basic and central to a person's self-understanding and because they usually have less direct and material effect on others.

This essay seeks to draw parallels between the claims to freedom asserted in the economic realm under the rubric of free enterprise and those asserted in the religious realm to show that some of the same considerations might be seen to apply in both. It notes the irony that actual practices in the economic realm do not always match the preaching of free enterprise but does not attempt to judge whether that is justifiable, desirable, or necessary. Many of the champions of free enterprise may have deemed the aid of government in the economic realm desirable on the supposition that the resulting risk of government regulation would be manageable or that regulation would result even without aid: why not with the bitter take the sweet? Whatever the reason, the ideal of free enterprise has been extensively compromised in actuality.

That the proponents of free enterprise in economics have made their peace with the "realities" of a very different condition of government aid-and-regulation, however, does not mean that a similar compromise should be sought in the religious realm. As long as the rhetoric of free enterprise is still being offered in the economic realm, it is legitimate to appeal to the ideals it articulates—despite contrary practice—to argue for continued adherence to those ideals in the religious realm, where they are even more crucial. It is an a fortiori kind of argument: if freedom is desirable in the economic transactions of life, how much more is it to be desired in the affairs that lie even closer to the heart!

That is exactly the perspective in which the Constitution places these matters. The first clauses of the first article of the Bill of Rights provide uniquely for religion a status insulated from both governmental regulation and governmental aid, which inevitably invites and leads to regulation. That status is continually at risk of being modified to match the pervasive permeation by government of other areas of life. Whatever may be the case in those areas, the realm of religion is constitutionally sui generis, and free enterprise should prevail there forever whether it does anywhere else or not.

Notes

1. See Michael J. Malbin, *Religion and Politics: The Intentions of the Authors of the First Amendment* (Washington, D.C.: American Enterprise Institute, 1978); and Robert L. Cord, *Separation of Church and State: Historical Fact and Current Fiction* (New York: Lambeth Press, 1982).

2. E. S. Corwin, "The Supreme Court as National School Board," *Law and Contemporary Problems,* vol. 14, no. 3 (1949); E. N. Griswold, "Absolute Is in the Dark," *Utah Law Review,* vol. 8 (1963), p. 167; T. M. Cooley, *Principles of Constitutional Law* (Boston, 1898), pp. 224–25; and Joseph Story, *Commentaries on the Constitution* (Cambridge, Mass.: Hilliard, Gray, 1833), vol. 2, secs. 1870–79.

3. Malbin, *Religion and Politics,* p. 15.

4. Ibid., pp. 4, 12, 13.

5. Leonard W. Levy, "School Prayers and the Founding Fathers," *Commentary* (September 1962); emphasis in original. See his more recent work expanding on this theme, *The Establishment Clause* (New York: Macmillan, 1986).

6. Abington Township v. Schempp, 374 U.S. 203 (1963).

7. Richard E. Morgan, *The Supreme Court and Religion* (New York: Free Press, 1972), p. 186; emphasis in original.

8. See Walter Berns et al., *Religion and the Constitution* (Washington, D.C.: American Enterprise Institute, 1984), p. 23.

9. Perry Miller, *Roger Williams* (Indianapolis: Bobbs-Merrill, 1953), pp. 198, 133; cited in Dean M. Kelley, "Beyond Separation of Church and State," *Journal of Church and State,* vol. 5 (November 1963), p. 188.

10. Miller, *Roger Williams,* pp. 136–37.

11. Ibid., p. 152.

12. See Christofferson v. Church of Scientology, Oregon State Court of Appeals, May 3, 1982; and George v. ISKCON, Superior Court for County of Orange, Case No. 27-756S.

13. For example, the Charter of the City of New York.

14. Cf. Lynch v. Donnelly, 465 U.S. 668 (1984).

15. Marsh v. Chambers, 463 U.S. 783 (1983).

16. Cf. Larson v. Valente, 465 U.S. 228 (1982).

17. See Kedroff v. St. Nicholas Cathedral, 344 U.S. 94 (1952); Mary Elizabeth Blue Hull Memorial Presbyterian Church v. Presbyterian Church, 393 U.S. 440 (1969); and Serbian Eastern Orthodox Diocese vs. Milivojevich, 423 U.S. 696 (1976).

18. Kedroff v. St. Nicholas Cathedral.

19. Hull Church II, 396 U.S. 1041 (1970); and Sharpsburg Eldership, 396 U.S. 367 (1970).

20. Jones v. Wolf, 443 U.S. 595 (1979).

21. Arlin Adams and William R. Hanlon, "*Jones v. Wolf:* Church Autonomy and the Religion Clauses of the First Amendment," *University of Pennsylvania Law Review,* vol. 128 (June 1980), pp. 1291–1339.

22. Barr v. United Methodist Church, 90 Cal. App. 3d 259 (1973).

23. NLRB v. Catholic Bishop of Chicago, 440 U.S. 490 (1979).

24. McClure v. Salvation Army, 460 F.2d 553 (5th Cir. 1972).

25. EEOC v. SWBTS, 651 F.2d 277 (1981).

26. Bob Jones University v. U.S., 51 U.S.L.W. 4593 (1983).

27. Lutheran Church v. City of New York, 35 NY2d 121 (1974).

28. Ethical Culture v. Spatt, 51 NY2d 449 (1980).

29. John Wesley, *Journal of John Wesley,* May 9, 1739.

30. U.S. v. Ballard, 322 U.S. 78 (1944).

31. Christofferson v. Church of Scientology; and Van Schaick v. Church of Scientology, 535 F. Supp. 1125 (1982).

32. Bear v. Mennonite Church, 341 A.2d 105 (1975).

33. Guinn v. Church of Christ of Collinsville, CT-81-929, Okla. Dist. Ct., Tulsa County, Mar. 16, 1984.

34. *New York Times,* December 28, 1984.

35. Sharon Worthing, "The State Takes Over a Church," *Annals of the American Academy of Political and Social Science* (November 1979), p. 136.

36. Dean M. Kelley, *Why Conservative Churches Are Growing* (New York: Harper and Row, 1972, 1976), pp. 36ff.; and idem, *Why Churches Should Not Pay Taxes* (New York: Harper and Row, 1977), pp. 47ff.

37. See discussion of the reasons why establishment of religion is counterproductive in Kelley, *Why Churches Should Not Pay Taxes,* pp. 50–57.

38. West Virginia Board of Education v. Barnette, 319 U.S. 624 (1943).

7

The American Civil Religion and the American Constitution

Jeffrey James Poelvoorde

"Let us, if we must, debate the lessons learned at some other time. Today, we simply say with pride: Thank you, dear son, and may God cradle you in his arms." With this simple prayer, President Reagan spoke for the nation as the flag-draped casket of the Unknown Soldier of the Vietnam War lay before him. Before the young soldier's body was lowered into the ground, however, other prayers were uttered. Four military chaplains—a rabbi, a Greek Orthodox priest, a Roman Catholic priest, and a Protestant minister—pronounced prayers of final committal of their respective faiths.[1] While not shunting aside the critical issues raised in the bitter divisions that the war produced—in fact, he affirmed the necessity of continuing the debate over the meaning of the war—President Reagan nevertheless asked his fellow citizens to touch a stratum of sentiment more fundamental than the opinions contested in the preceding decade. Could the bitterness of the nation's divisions be reduced, perhaps, in the common hope that the young man who sacrificed his life might find eternal rest and in the common appreciation of his sacrifice?

Over a century before, President Lincoln addressed a nation rent by a fundamental political controversy become a bloody war as he assumed the burden of a second term of office. He traced the origins of the struggle up to its current developments but then shifted the tone of his address.[2] In this political sermon, Lincoln went beyond instructing his fellow citizens in their founding principles, especially the principle of a man's equal right to the fruit of his own labor; he taught them about God and His purposes, too. The American Civil

The author would like to acknowledge the editorial assistance and helpful suggestions in the preparation of this essay of his former colleague in the Department of Government at the College of William and Mary, David Dessler.

141

War was no mere political squabble but part of the providential rectification of the human condition. Moreover, the instrument of that rectification—the North—was also to feel the effects of the divine scourge. True, the South had sinned, against the Declaration of Independence and against God, but so had the North. It, too, had profited from the common nationhood erected upon the compromise with slavery and had participated in a national commerce that embraced the institution. Now, however, the restoration of the Union, purged of that grave defect, was the urgent task of the American people. Certainly Lincoln hoped to initiate that restoration by reminding Americans of their common sin, their common heritage, and their common destiny. What better way was there to do this than by placing the brutal struggle against the backdrop of divine justice—and forgiveness?

Almost a century before this, President Washington had sealed the period of the founding with his Farewell Address, offered on the occasion of his declining to present himself as a candidate for a third term in office. This compendium of political advice, distilled from his (and Alexander Hamilton's and James Madison's) experience and reflection,[3] nevertheless had the aspect of an invocation, for Washington added, near the beginning and the end:

> Profoundly penetrated with this idea, I shall carry it with me to the grave, as a strong incitement to unceasing vows that Heaven may continue to you the choicest tokens of its beneficence—that your union and brotherly affection may be perpetual—that the free Constitution, which is the work of your hands, may be sacredly maintained . . . to the applause, the affection, and the adoption of every nation which is yet a stranger to it.[4]

More personally:

> Whatever they may be, I fervently beseech the Almighty to avert or mitigate the evils to which they [my errors] may tend. I shall also carry with me the hope that my country will never cease to view them with indulgence.[5]

Of course, Washington's invocations were hardly innovations, for the nation's founding document, the Declaration of Independence, itself contained several references to divine justice and pleas for divine assistance: "the Laws of Nature and of Nature's God," "they are endowed by their Creator with certain unalienable rights," "appealing to the Supreme Judge of the World," "for the support of this Declaration, with a firm reliance on the Protection of Divine Providence, we mutually pledge to each other our Lives, our Fortunes and our sacred Honor."[6]

Does America possess a "civil religion"? Regardless of the difficulties inherent in the term, both in general and in reference to American political life, we may have to employ it in order to understand the phenomena discussed above. In addition to presidential speeches and the founding documents, we can observe Americans at a public function reciting the Pledge of Allegiance ("one nation under God") or bowing their heads during an invocation. There is something common in these examples and, indeed, in the country's myriad songs, hymns, mottoes, and anthems,[7] which can only be understood as "religious." America's civil religion is embedded in the presidential rhetoric spanning two centuries and in the habits and beliefs of the body of citizens to which the presidents were appealing. Yet public support of the religious character of the nation continues to be a subject of great controversy.

The civil religion exists in that area of our civil life best called the "constitution." We could call the same concept by a different name: the "regime," or even by its ancient Greek word, "polity." These three words refer to the same thing: a country's comprehensive ordering of its fundamental political principles, institutions, policies, and national customs—in short, they answer the question of what "constitutes" a nation's political existence. Although we can distinguish these four parts of a constitution (fundamental ideas, institutions, laws or policies, and customs or the character of the citizens as it shapes their behavior) for purposes of analysis, they are in reality inseparable and mutually affect each other.[8]

The most authoritative or governing part of the American constitution or regime is the second part, the fundamental institutions, but the civil religion is generated in, and forms the core of, the fourth part of the constitution, the realm of customs or citizen character. Against the tendency of contemporary observers of politics to lessen the importance of (if not ignore) this latter realm, therefore, I shall argue that it is as important to the maintenance and survival of the whole constitution as any of the other parts. Indeed, I shall argue that an identifiable American civil religion exists (although we must be clear about what we mean by the term), that its benefits outweigh its disadvantages, and that far from being unconstitutional, public support of America's civil religion may well be indispensable to the continual success of the American republic.

The Concept of a Civil Religion

Although Robert Bellah's 1966 essay, "Civil Religion in America," did not originate the controversy over the existence (and, if this is granted, the character) of an American civil religion, it certainly

143

crystallized the question and gave it focus.[9] At the least, it generated a flurry of comment and rejoinder that has endured for two decades. Bellah's claim to have turned to an issue as yet unarticulated in American scholarship therefore deserves some credence, insofar as he set the terms for the ensuing debate by coining the central concept in that debate.[10] His essay is an appropriate place to begin our examination of American civil religion.

In his central thesis Bellah held that "there exists alongside of and rather clearly differentiated from the churches an elaborate and well-institutionalized civil religion in America."[11] In spite of the formal separation of church and state, the political sphere possesses a "religious dimension . . . expressed in a set of beliefs, symbols, and rituals."[12] In addition to this formal definition of civil religion, he provided examples of its major rituals, such as the inauguration of a president (specifically, President Kennedy's) and public memorials. Besides rituals, the American religion contained all of the other hallmarks of other religious traditions: sacred texts (the Declaration of Independence, the Constitution, Washington's Farewell Address, Lincoln's Gettysburg Address and Second Inaugural, and Kennedy's Inaugural); a calendar (Memorial Day, Thanksgiving Day, Veterans' Day, the Fourth of July, and, we may add, Presidents' Day); "prophetic" figures or "saints" (Washington, Jefferson, Lincoln, perhaps Kennedy—and, certainly today, Martin Luther King, Jr.);[13] and even a fairly well-developed concept of God.[14] The major themes in the American civil religion have hovered around the special character and destiny of the American nation and its institutions. Democracy, fairness and the rule of law, personal liberty, and even, ironically, the separation of church and state have blended together with the belief that the standards that undergird our political life and guide our actions (under the best of conditions) are rooted in a nonhuman, nonarbitrary divine will. These constitute the basic "creed" of the American faith.[15]

Bellah acknowledges Jean-Jacques Rousseau's *Social Contract* as the source of the term "civil religion." Rousseau, in book IV, chapter VIII, entitled "Civil Religion," attributed to Thomas Hobbes the insight into how to reconcile the otherwordly claims of faith and the claims of political life: the "reunion of the two heads of the eagle, and the restoration throughout of political unity, without which no State or government will ever be rightly constituted."[16] The sovereign must fix an official set of religious beliefs, the limits of which are set by the political necessity of maintaining law-abidingness and social unity.[17]

While it is clear that we have attained in practice much of what Rousseau spoke of, the public religion in America is much more diffuse than what he described. It is not an authoritative theology, but is more the result of historical chance and blending (although to assert that no conscious deliberation has gone into its formation would be an exaggeration). While the American civil religion, then, is only a civil religion in the loosest, not the strictest, sense,[18] it nevertheless satisfies many of the purposes for which earlier thinkers advocated a civil religion and therefore deserves the title.

The Elements of the American Civil Religion

"Civil religion" sounds so strange to Americans because the term appears to them a self-contradiction. It *is* difficult, indeed, to speak analytically of the "public faith of a secular republic." The tensions inherent in the notion explain both Bellah's claim that the phenomenon had rested more or less unarticulated and unobserved and the range of subsequent reactions of historians and sociologists. It also explains the vagueness in the phenomenon itself and why it is so hard to speak of dogmas or tenets in the American civil religion.[19]

Bellah describes the civil religion in its own right, with "its own seriousness and integrity,"[20] but if he were correct about the integrity or wholeness of the American civil religion, we would have to characterize it as a synthesis. In fact, however, the elements of the American civil religion have not become something new by virtue of combining, even though they have been importantly affected, if not improved, by their existing in combination with each other.[21] Moreover, the American civil religion is ever dependent upon the health of its discrete, though combined, elements. Instead of a synthesis, the civil religion is a syncretism: it cannot stand on its own without the accompanying presence of its constituent elements in their original state. They, in turn, must retain their own health and integrity, for not only theirs but the health of the blending itself depends upon it.

Hence, the American civil religion does not possess the integrity of a revealed or founded religion. Because of this, it also cannot supply the ultimate satisfactions that the concrete religious traditions provide, for its content is too vague to shape the mind or console the heart to the degree that the historical religions do.[22] Nor does the civil religion supply an organizing principle of wholeness by which citizens can easily identify and understand it. Americans are, in fact, largely unaware of the civil religion as a concrete blending, although they can grasp some of the elements directly. They know, for instance, that they are Presbyterians or Catholics, they can see the Declaration of Independence and the Constitution, and they can listen to their presidents appealing to the principles of the founding.

It is, however, harder for them to see the more intangible blending itself that had no serviceable name before Bellah coined one.[23]

We can discern four components of the American civil religion: the Enlightenment tradition of secular constitutionalism with the doctrine of natural rights at its core, the particular Western scriptural religions of the original European settlers (and of most Americans today), the emergence of a multiplicity of religious sects before and since the founding of the Republic, and the unique historical condition of the United States as the first modern republic. The American civil religion is the result of all these four elements acting upon each other. More accurately, the first two are the substantive components of the civil religion and the last two the environmental components, but the combination would not exist without the presence of all four and their mutual influence.

The most authoritative component in the American political order, hence in the civil religion, is the concept of natural rights. This principle both justified the revolution and provides the end for which the Constitution is the means: the securing of the safety of the citizens and the preservation of their liberty, so far as the latter is consonant with the former. For this reason, the tradition of government that derives from the concept of rights is called "liberalism": it teaches that the task of government is limited to securing the conditions of liberty. So deeply embedded in our language and our minds is this concept that Americans (and all modern men and women) cannot even speak of justice without speaking of freedom and equality, the two conceptual poles that form the axis of the notion of rights.

The founding principles govern our lives, but they are not religious. They do not rest upon faith, require faith for their understanding, or point to faith as the activity that completes the human being.[24] One can argue, of course, that acceptance of natural rights does require an unquestioned horizon of belief as thoroughly as does Christianity or Buddhism. The Declaration's claims about the world and the human beings in it, however, rest neither upon a holy text nor upon an incarnation of divinity for their authority. They rest, at least self-consciously, upon what one can observe and understand by looking at and reasoning about real human beings.[25] In this sense they are fully secular. They are not mutually exclusive of religious faith, however. The truth is that the concept of natural rights can coexist and even blend with religious ideas and consciousness. As we shall see, it is this compatibility that explains in part the existence of an American civil religion.

The second major component of the American civil religion is the actual content of the Western biblical faiths, which formed the basis of society from the time of the first colonies up through the founding. These religions provided the theological language and habits of piety for the religious dimension of American public life. Even though the major sects in America were Protestant, it would be inaccurate to characterize their influence upon American life simply as such. No doubt the less hierarchical, sacramental, and legalistic beliefs and practices of Protestant Christianity helped to prepare the way, so to speak, for the democratic principles of modern republicanism. Nevertheless, the main contours of the religious sentiments present in the civil religion are biblical rather than specifically Protestant: a God who has created and governs the world, cares about human beings and history, shapes that history, and whose redemptive action rewards righteousness and punishes evil. Of course, the idea of a chosen people obligated to institute a just nation and to serve as example to the nations, transposed to the American context, straddles both the Jewish and Christian testaments. Even if it was particularly "Protestant" circumstances and dogmas that permitted the initial transposition of that idea to America—that is, that European Christianity had corrupted the Christian revelation and that recovery of the seed of the original faith required new soil—the notion of American chosenness easily spread to the subsequent immigrant faiths and became amplified once the nation assumed historical existence. It thus took its place as a principal element of the civil religion.

Distinct from the content of the biblical faiths as a factor in the development of the civil religion was their multiplicity. In his account of that moment in which the American civilization's main elements coalesced to set it in motion as a distinct society, Alexis de Tocqueville described the great irony of the initial New England settlements. Refugees from the persecution and corruption of Europe, the first colonists often turned toward dissident sects and opinions among themselves with a ferocity more intense than that of their former persecutors.[26] Yet, as the diversity of sects multiplied, the practical necessity of accommodation grew. By the time of the Revolution, when political necessity forced national cooperation among the numerous geographic and social factions, the practice of toleration had become so firmly rooted in American experience and dispositions that it was elevated to the level of principle.[27] This diversity, while less visible in some respects than the manifestations of the natural rights doctrine and the practice of the biblical faiths, was nevertheless as critical in the shaping of American religious consciousness. It is impossible, indeed, to decide whether the doctrine of natural rights or the diversity of religious sects was more influential in creating the important strand of tolerance in the civil religion.

Finally, the historical distinction of being the first nation to found itself in practice upon the natural rights doctrine (and the liberal republicanism that issues from it) contributed to the sentiments of uniqueness and mission in the American civil religion. Prepared, as we have suggested, by the preexisting Protestant imagery of the New World as a land chosen by God to renew the articles of the Christian faith, the American continent provided an equally accommodating home for the exuberant universalism of the Enlightenment. The sense of uniqueness and mission did not diminish in America as the incipient exuberance of the Enlightenment boiled into existence elsewhere, in France and subsequently throughout Europe and around the globe. Of the several factors that might explain this, one stands as preeminent: the uniqueness of American institutions and life is genuine. Even today, when fewer than 20 of the world's 170 nations are liberal republics, American republicanism remains the exception rather than the rule in political life.

Accepting, however, the description of the civil religion as a syncretic blending, one may still wonder what makes that blending possible. In particular, how can a nonreligious (even, perhaps, antireligious) concept such as natural rights combine with theistic piety? If these elements are antithetical, are not American citizens carrying contradictions around in their heads? There are actually two kinds of overlap regarding belief and moral teaching that bring the civil religion into being: the overlap among the particular religious sects in American society and the overlap between religious faith and the natural rights tradition.

Finding the common elements of belief in the various religious traditions neither reduces them to a lowest common denominator nor amounts to an implicit endorsement of ecumenism. But the Western sects that constitute American religious life, as well as Islam, do share many fundamental beliefs about God, self-avowedly so. What we have characterized as biblical extends to them all, and much is even transferable to the Eastern traditions.[28] Their doctrinal differences are sharp and real, a truth to which much of their history attests, their very commonality at times inciting their ire. There is also an overlap in morality. Even though in many instances, say on the issues of abortion or nuclear weapons, the various religions have different teachings, they do agree on broad areas of individual and social conduct. No Christian, no Moslem, no Jew, or no Buddhist wants to rear children given to thievery. Nor, most likely, do they desire to live in communities where thievery is not condemned and punished. In both instances, their faiths bid them to work toward the actualization of the moral ideal.

Between the theistic traditions and the Enlightenment doctrine of natural rights, the areas of overlap are more difficult to see. As to the overlap in moral teachings, even if the doctrine of natural rights is not, strictly speaking, a moral teaching,[29] neither Thomas Hobbes nor the Church Fathers had good things to say about murder, rape, or theft. The same actions, in other words, can be condemned for different reasons. Moreover, the moral universalism of the particular religions resonated with the universalism of the initial impulses of the Enlightenment.[30] The Enlightenment had its own image of the corruptness of the human condition and saw therein a need for rectification, even perhaps redemption. True, the modern philosophers began with different premises about the human condition and ended with different conclusions about its correction from those of their predecessors in faith and thought. But insofar as they understood themselves to speak principles that were for the good of humanity, they could become practical allies with the Church Fathers, their erstwhile antagonists in this world.[31]

While one could never argue that the purposes and teachings of the great faiths, even the most worldly ones, and those of the American nation are identical, they are harmonizable. To adopt the viewpoint of the religions for the moment, we can say that this world, a world only dimly illuminated—but not yet redeemed—by revelation or enlightenment, is not totally irredeemable. It is improvable and worth the effort. As long as human politics has not sunk into wickedness or tyranny, it can be a vehicle for improvement of the human condition, worthy of the serious attention of religious people. As long as the regime of the United States falls within that category, the American civil religion will be a possibility.

The Benefits and Disadvantages of the Civil Religion

We shall consider the benefits of the American civil religion in four categories: the political, the political-moral, the moral, and the religious. The first three concern what is good for America, or Americans as Americans, the last with what is good for the particular religions. In general, the benefits in the first three categories derive from the character of the civil religion as a kind of mean between two extremes. On the one extreme is the unmoderated natural rights tradition as the foundation for public and private life. On the other is religious faith as the sole ground of public and private life. I do not mean to suggest that either natural rights or pure faith is a "vice," but only that from the perspective of political life each possesses some problematic tendencies that their blending helps to correct.

By political benefits of the civil religion, I mean what Rousseau and other authors have generally recommended a civil religion for: a religious support for civil authority. Whatever strengthens the political authority's capacity to govern, fosters civic unity, or makes for good government has been viewed as good for a country. The most obvious good produced by the American civil religion is the bolstering of patriotic sentiment and love of country. Alexis de Tocqueville distinguishes between two forms of patriotism: one akin to a sentimental but powerful love of one's parents, the other a by-product of reason and calculation.[32] Tocqueville argues that the first derives from the experience of "homeland" and tends to be indifferent to the form of government or way of life fostered by the kind of regime or constitution of the country. Therefore, the civil religion does not *create* this kind of patriotism; it does, however, intensify the sentiment by infusing it with the content and experience of religious faith. Like all forms of love, this can degenerate into excess. But life, even political life, requires love. When those unavoidable moments come when a citizen must choose the public good over his private good, this sentiment may often be the push that guides his preference. The natural rights tradition tends to encourage citizens to view their country simply as a means to their private ends. But on the battlefield facing the maw of the cannon or in the living room filling out an honest tax return, a citizen may have to transcend this view of his nation. Moreover, as we saw by our first examples, the American civil religion can be a powerful goad to overcoming differences of political viewpoint in the direction of necessary civic unity. By strengthening their feelings of reverence for the nation's ideals and institutions, it helps citizens to recall the common ground beneath their differences, sometimes at critical junctures in the nation's life.

From the standpoint of political benefits as well, the civil religion acts as a religious culture affecting its individual religious components. Because it wraps the experience of religious affiliation in the language of rights and the experience of pluralism, it tempers religious fervor with a trace of worldly rationalism. Since the natural rights tradition supplies the basic vocabulary of individual and social self-definition, American citizens often understand their own religious experience within those categories. What Americans of one religion are willing to claim as a right for themselves, they are compelled by definition to extend to members of all other religions. Religious belief is forced to view itself as a human characteristic shared by other humans, which tames some of the factious energy unleashed by unquestioned fervor. The practical experience of religious pluralism strengthens the influence of natural rights. Since the public realm is constituted by more than one religious group, attempts to persuade fellow citizens on issues of public policy must find a basis of appeal wider than only the language and authority of one tradition. For example, on the issue of abortion, Catholics who wish to persuade other religious groups to join with them in the condemnation of abortion must explain why abortion is not simply a "Catholic" concern. And all of them must explain to nonreligious citizens why abortion is not simply a religious concern.

The last kind of political benefit we should consider is the civil religion's ability to offer a basis for healthy criticism of the American regime in general and of specific policies in particular. The civil religion can become the source of humility, self-restraint, and healthy self-criticism for the same reason, ironically, that it can become a source of strident crusading and national self-righteousness: the universalistic character of both the Enlightenment doctrine of natural rights and the religious strains of the civil religion. It is easy to see how a universalistic tradition easily becomes smug or aggressively missionary: contained therein is an alleged blueprint for mankind's perfection. Yet, no particular nation can claim to be the perfect embodiment of universalistic or transcendent principles. Indeed, there is no such thing. The unbridgeable distance between the ideal and the real enables us to make necessary criticisms of our national life and policies. This critical posture, too, can degenerate into a vice: moralistic and utopian self-hatred that has lost touch with political prudence.

There is, in addition to the political benefits, a range of considerations that straddles the distinction between politics and ethics or the public and private realms. President Washington touched upon it when he spoke in his Farewell Address of the impossibility of maintaining a republic without morality. Tocqueville, too, was concerned with the issue of what kind of character citizens must possess to support and maintain a decent democracy. In fact, it is *Democracy in America*'s most persistent theme.[33] Tocqueville argued that in a democratic regime the moral character of the people is even more important than in other political systems. In a monarchy or aristocracy, the essential direction of the country comes from above, so to speak, from one or a few. But in a country where the essential direction comes from the majority of the inhabitants, two conditions exist that make morality a critical political issue. First, since there is literally less government from above, society or individuals must maintain social order and harmony by making up for the lack of centralized authority. Second, since the spirit of the government itself is majority rule, the ruling majority must possess characters capable of self-rule. If an individual is incapable of governing himself, he will be incapable of participating in common rule over his fellows.[34] At the same time that democracies increase the need for stable and sensible self-governing characters, they render it more difficult to foster these characteristics among their citizens. Because of the general equality of conditions of social life and the prevalence of personal mobility, democracies unleash a certain restlessness and instability into society. Opinions and habits flash and vanish like fads, all opinions being of equal worth anyway.

How is it possible to remedy these tendencies of a liberal democratic political order? For Tocqueville, one aspect of the remedy is the maintenance of religious faith among the populace. Religious mores teach the American people how to combine the widest amount of personal freedom with the greatest amount of self-governance.[35] Religion, according to Tocqueville, helps to elevate the notion of freedom in the minds of Americans and connect it with the highest human purposes. In the midst of the tumult of American life, he found that a center of serenity, repose, and mature perspective on the priorities of life predominated in the broad masses of the American citizenry. The American civil religion, as the shorthand way of designating this combination of influences, stands as a bulwark of those characteristics without which a democratic citizenry cannot govern.

Insofar as we are concerned about the entire quality of American life, it is appropriate to consider the beneficial aspects of the civil religion in the realm of morality—the quest for human perfection or dignity—on its own merits. The doctrine of natural rights has moral overtones or implications, but instead of the practical moral question of how to act so as to enhance the perfection of our characters, the doctrine of natural rights transforms the question into, "How may I act so as to secure my interest?" Happiness itself comes to mean obtaining the objects of the passions. Except for the rational decision that we must restrain certain passions in order to gratify others, there is no internal criterion of self-restraint that would tell a person that he or she had consumed enough of a desired good, or even if a particular external good was worthy of being desired. If we consult the picture of human nature at the heart of the concept, we discover no principle that would indicate that one human being owes another anything. Relationships are constructed with others by an act of mutual contract to serve our use, and nothing bids us to take a serious interest in others beyond their instrumental usefulness. The market is the overall image that best describes the activity of incessantly calculating our profits and losses, consuming what and when we will, and using others when it serves our interests and leaving them alone when it does not.

The American civil religion helps to correct this somewhat bleak picture of human society by injecting into moral consciousness a principle other than self-interest and self-gratification. It tempers the radical individualism unleashed by the idea of rights and by the commercial society that has grown as its embodiment. Values such as charity and compassion, and personal qualities such as dignity and moderation, receive additional support that they might not receive in a purely rational, self-interested society. No doubt the specific religious traditions alone would have this effect upon their members anyway, probably with residual ripples in the wider society. But the civil religion cements the understanding that these are *American* qualities, to be cultivated and encouraged in American citizens as Americans.

Whether there could be a consistent and practical individual and communal morality based solely upon self-interest, or whether a society founded upon it would endure through the ages, is admittedly an open question. No human community has ever tried.[36] We do not know whether economic and political institutional arrangements alone can inculcate in people's characters the internal dispositions that enable them to develop and endure as individuals and as a nation. So far, we have never had to know in America; the civil religion, with its moderation of the rational selfishness of rights, has always been an element in the minds of American citizens and the political culture of the American nation.

The disadvantages of the American civil religion are as real as the benefits. Grounded in the transcendent principles of the Enlightenment and transcendent religious faith, the civil religion can inspire self-righteousness and crusading, as we have suggested. Bellah has chronicled this disease well, producing his harshest comments upon the subject.[37] We can say, though, that both nationalistic crusading and the opposite excess of moralistic self-criticism stem from a loss of political prudence. Between the self-contented religious apologists for slavery and the abolitionists who were prepared to tear down the fabric of the Constitution stood Abraham Lincoln, convinced that slavery was a sin but that the loss of the nation would be a greater one.

The closer that the content of the civil religion comes to recommending policy, especially national policy, the more likely it is to encourage factional strife in addition to moralism. Under these circumstances, the particular content or moral teachings of the various religious traditions (or nonreligious elements in the society) may

153

compete to become the basis of public policy, domestic or foreign. Abortion, nuclear weapons, economic redistribution, and family policy are all recent issues that have raised sharp differences, often along religious lines, among the American people. This is not an unmitigated evil, though. Part of the advantage of free, democratic government is the ability to air differences of opinion, even if some of the bases of those opinions are religious in origin. Nevertheless, A. James Reichley is correct in arguing that the civil religion exerts a more positive presence on American life the more diffuse it is and the more concerned it is with the broader aspects of citizen character and civic morality.[38]

We should not fail to mention intolerance and bigotry, even shading at times into persecution. This corruption of the civil religion depends, however, on one of the elements of the civil religion overwhelming the others. In particular, for religious intolerance to occur, the individual must almost forget the foundation of the political order itself in natural rights. One can never ensure that Americans will possess the most healthy understanding of the nation's political-religious culture, its constitution in the broadest sense. The same is true, of course, of any religion and any political order. Only through proper education and the shaping of character is it possible to tip the odds in favor of a balanced understanding.

Perhaps the greatest danger presented by the American civil religion is the dissolution of the specific religious traditions. Its blend of religious belief and toleration may in the long run do more than harmonize the particular faiths: it may homogenize them. Especially as the culture of the modern world progresses toward greater technology, secularism, and material comfort, the civil religion could serve as a self-defeating bridge to a nonreligious society. Safe and nondemanding in spiritual rigor, it may help people to shed the baggage of their traditional faiths without pain or guilt. The civil religion may gut the ancient faiths of content while preserving only their language and ritual.[39] This is a danger not only to the particular religions, but also to the civil religion itself. For, as we have said, like all syncretisms, its continued existence depends upon the internal health of its parts. If the particular religions should lose their vigor and identity, the civil religion will not be long behind.

Notwithstanding all the liabilities, the advantages of the civil religion outweigh them and recommend its maintenance. The general tendencies of the natural rights tradition establish the long-range currents of American political and social life. These principles are the life of the nation; the longer they are kept vibrant and high-toned, the greater the prospects for America's survival as a free and decent republic. While we should not minimize the excesses that the civil religion generates, we should recognize that they are occasional lapses in an otherwise healthy condition.

Civil Religion and the Constitution

If the civil religion is a social and political good, would a public policy designed to strengthen it succeed? Would it be desirable? Would it be constitutional? Many would answer no to these questions. Some maintain that the American civil religion was simply the result of chance; any attempt to generate it consciously would fail.[40] Others argue that the prior religious consensus in society that made the civil religion possible has disappeared. The idea seems to be that a civil religion could prove a force for social cohesion only when society itself was predominantly religious.[41] Today, we have "outgrown" the necessity and possibility of a publicly fostered religious culture.[42] Yet, the American civil religion was never truly the result of chance only. From the beginning of the republic, the public authorities of both the nation and the states consciously supported religious activity and affiliation. True, our society is more secular in orientation than it was a century or two ago. True, there is a somewhat greater diversity of religious traditions than that which existed at the country's birth. These do not, however, add up to the impossibility or undesirability of a public policy supporting religion.[43]

In thinking about this issue from the standpoint of both public policy and constitutional principle, we will find it prudent to keep our focus on the evils to be avoided and the goods to be secured by the separation of church and state. No one wants official persecution. No one wants religious civil war. No one, however, wants a society of individuals so disaffected or uninterested in their community or their self-governance that they are willing to retreat into atomistic shells of private life. No one wants a society where people do not care about each other. With Tocqueville, I have argued that these two considerations require the presence of a public dimension to religion. Yet, I certainly have no trouble agreeing with his broad argument that religion is strengthened and American government improved by the separation of church and state. Embracing the two arguments does not necessarily involve a contradiction. Even if, as appears to be clear from history, religion flourishes when primarily left alone and that political society is left in peace when political power is not used to resolve the question of the one true faith, the conclusion that there is no room for government shaping and support does not necessarily follow. While government cannot effectively or justifiably force citizens to be religious, it can foster a culture more hospitable to religion by suggesting that the experience of citizenship is fullest when it approximates religious experience or contains elements of religious experience.

One of the disadvantages of a public policy encouraging religion, many claim, is its manifest unconstitutionality. Yet, the Constitution, while clearly placing severe limitations regarding religion on the national government (and somewhat more flexible ones upon the state governments), is nevertheless quite open to a variety of answers as to how much religion is permissible in the public sphere. The civil religion exists as a part of the larger regime or constitution, in fact, because for two centuries the American people have viewed the Constitution as flexible enough to permit public religious support and expression. The question of the Constitution's disposition regarding religion resolves itself into two subsidiary questions. What is the policy contained in the religion clauses of the First Amendment, especially the "establishment" clause, regarding the national government? What policy does the Fourteenth Amendment require of the state governments regarding religious support and activity? Both of these issues have been ably debated elsewhere in this volume, but some remarks are appropriate here.

The supporters of the "high wall," or strict separation, approach to the First Amendment's religion clauses argue that the "accommodationists" make the mistake of reading their policy inclinations back into the Constitution, therefore blinding themselves to the essence of the principle of separation and even to the framers' intentions as a guide to that principle.[44] Even if there is truth to this accusation, the absolute separationists do the same, if not to a greater degree, preferring a public policy that recognizes no involvement of the public sphere with religion (or vice versa) on any level of government. One need not succumb to the temptation to regard the Constitution as a literary shell with a gelatinous core of no guiding or enduring principle in order to maintain that that core may be compatible with a range of policy glosses. The Constitution's principles do not settle all public questions, especially in the realm of the enumerated rights and limitations upon governmental power located in the amendments and throughout the original document. One may argue, to be sure, that the public policy of the nation or the states should be different from that of two centuries ago, but that is an issue to be debated and acted upon by the policy-generating institutions of the government. One cannot say, however, that the Constitution, then or now, mandates public noninvolvement with religion.

Regarding the states in the constitutional system, does the Fourteenth Amendment require them to abide by the First Amendment's ban on establishment in the same way as the national government? While the Fourteenth Amendment requires the states to extend to their citizens equal civil rights, it does not require them to be institutional duplicates of the national government. They must certainly be "republican governments."[45] But even a state with an established religion could be a "republican" government, as long as it operated along the lines of majority rule, drew its essential power from the body of the people, and maintained civil liberty.[46] In this sense, there is no internal necessity in either the Fourteenth Amendment or the incorporation doctrine to require the application of the establishment clause to the states. Somewhere between the cramped and inaccurate view of the Fourteenth Amendment in Justice Miller's seminal opinion in the *Slaughterhouse* cases[47] and the Fourteenth Amendment as blueprint for national reform—which it has become in the hands of the modern judiciary through the indiscriminate application of the incorporation doctrine—there is a reasonable middle ground that would provide the necessary protection for the practice of religion, which is the undeniable basis of free governments.

All the preceding discussion might nevertheless seem like so much lawyerly quibbling about specific clauses in the Constitution. Have we not lost sight, one could wonder, of the grand purposes of the constitutional order, of the "spirit" of the Constitution? It certainly would not be a misstatement of that spirit to suggest that it includes the aim of creating a national political order where one citizen is as free and feels as secure in his or her rights as the next and where every citizen feels equally a member of the public realm. Even if the civil religion were not, strictly speaking, an establishment of religion under the First Amendment, is it not a violation of the great goals of a secular republic? Public support for religion, either ceremonial, fiscal, or pedagogical, appears to force a citizen to support or even profess a religious belief that he may not hold. Even more, to the extent that the public sphere, state or national, possesses a religious content, nonreligious people will feel excluded from that realm. How may we respond to this argument?

The end of our system of government is the security, prosperity, and liberty of its citizens. The Constitution erects as a means to this end a republican government over a set of republican governments. In other words, the Constitution rests upon majority rule as the basis of public policy and institutional operation. We must see that the premise of the argument just articulated, if followed through, undermines majority rule. It would require that the public mind be unanimous before it could produce a policy, for the premise evidently stands upon the notion that a citizen has a right not to feel like a minority. True, one might respond that what is at stake here is not just a citizen's stance upon some question of public policy, but his vital identity and how that identity affects his membership in the political world around him. Religion, it might be reasonably maintained, is more like race or sex than party identification or ideology. But this is only partially true. Religion, as we have seen, unavoidably speaks to the issues of self-conduct, relationship with others, and the direction of common governance. It would be more accurate to say that religion occupies a middle position between the prepolitical factors in identity such as race and sex and the purely political factors such as party and ideology. While there must be unanimity on each person's equal right to formulate his or her own religious opinions and identity, unanimity is not required on the religious content of the public sphere. It is good to take extra precautions, as did the framers, to ensure that public policy, especially national public policy, stands at a comparative remove from religious sentiment, but the Constitution that they produced and that endures is not a catalog of absolutes. The American Constitution in this sense not only *permits* the existence of the American civil religion: when added to sound leadership and popular good sense, the Constitution is the *solution* to the problems of the American civil religion. In turn, the American civil religion supports and preserves the Constitution.

Conclusion

Let us close with a consideration of our original example of American civil religion, the Memorial Day service for the Unknown Soldier of the Vietnam War. Here the author must speak personally, yet, I think, relevantly to our topic. As a Jew, he could not help but be moved to reflect upon his people's condition as revealed by the solemn events of the day. For those who wish to penetrate to the character of religious liberty in America, indeed, to the character of the American regime as a whole, free of the occasionally distorting lens of abstractions, it is helpful to consider the fate of the Jews in the twentieth century.

Three of the most powerful nations the world has ever known have risen to global prominence in this century, each of them ironically pertinent to the welfare of the Jewish people, each a rival claimant to the title of vanguard of modern progress. The political constitution of Nazi Germany was devoted at its core to the murder of the Jews and accomplished its grisly end in the relentless churning of the crematoria. In the Soviet Union, where beneficent atheism is ostensibly the policy of the constitution, Jews to this day waste away in frozen prisons for the crime of studying their ancient language of prayer. In the United States of America, by contrast, during one of the highest public ceremonies commemorating the nation's war dead, a Jew spoke Hebrew words of mourning that rose aloft with those of the president—the country's highest officer. Member of the world's most despised and persecuted faith, the rabbi stood in that public arena not as a guest, welcomed grudgingly or even graciously, but as a fellow citizen and American.

Moreover, one could see in the event not only the great spectacle of a powerful nation having reversed centuries of Jewish persecution, for on the same dais as the rabbi stood ministers of three other religions. These men were representatives of faiths that in the past millennia have expended more hatred and blood in the effort to eradicate each other than tears and memory can measure. On that national stage could be seen one of the finest achievements of the American regime, a "consummation devoutly to be wished" of the aspirations of centuries of Western political experience and reflection. Must one personally have beheld the carnage, smelled the blood, heard the cumulative groans of the numberless victims of the martyr's pyre, the Crusades, the Inquisition, the jihad, and the pogrom to recognize the grandeur of the moment? Who among the slaughtered would not have uttered in their last agonies a prayer to their common Father to live to see such an event? This was no pallid symbolism, no mere political pageant. It was not tolerable as an "exception" to our principles because, like a religious motto on a coin, it was trivial.[48] If this was the civil religion at its best, it was also America at its best. In the *public* presence of these men, perhaps more than in their words, lay the most fitting memorial to the young soldier whom they mourned. Their *public* presence was the visible embodiment of the spirit of the republic for which he had yielded up his spirit. Indeed, the combination of their presence and his sacrifice was visible in a thousandfold magnification in the rows of crosses, stars of David, stars and crescents, barred crosses—and even blank marble—to be found upon the tombstones populating the final resting place of those men and women who fought and died for their country.

Yet, according to the understanding of those who insist upon the unbridgeable "high wall" version of the separation of church and state, this moment should not have existed, for it was profoundly un-American because profoundly unconstitutional. Yet it is their excessive, if well-intentioned, zeal that demands this irony, not constitutional principle. In public ceremonies such as this one, we remind ourselves of what we stand for as a nation. In particular, with respect to the issue of religious liberty, the display of the mix of religion and toleration of religion (and of irreligion) that we have attained in practice is rendered more secure when we see its benefits in the public view.

For the richness and significance of the Memorial Day service for the unknown soldier derive not only from its public display of toleration, but also from its religious character. It suggests that Americans, in their deepest and most somber moments, *as* Americans, may express their nationality publicly in prayer. They are allowed to speak and share the hope that the death encountered in war is not in vain— not only from the standpoint of attaining the end of a national policy, or even from the standpoint of attaining good and just purposes in the world. Indeed, to have the experience simply derive from these hopes would have embroiled us in the old controversies surrounding the war in Vietnam. Rather, the deepest level of experience touched by the ceremony is the very experience of death itself and its transcendence through community. Of course, public funerals of any sort, even those in the Soviet Union, touch upon this human wish to see the sting of death assuaged by communal grief. But the national *religious* funeral conducted by the president makes available to us as citizens the comfort and consolation that religion offers as we contemplate the grave: the longing for eternal life, for ourselves and those we love, beyond human power and reputation. This is an experience that is not available to a Soviet citizen. The confident atheism that rationalizes his nation's public order denies the possibility of life after death, hence denies the appropriateness of such sentiments, and therefore denies the opportunity to utter them. But for us, allowing ourselves to whisper along with the president's prayer that the young soldier's soul find eternal rest increases the awareness that his death is *our* loss, that it is both our national loss and our private loss, with our souls and his eternally bound together.

The diversity of the faiths represented in the memorial service serves as the visible and public embodiment of the principle of toleration. The religious content of that diversity, in the context of this most solemn national act of remembering our war dead, however, reminds us that what we tolerate is a diversity of opinions about the highest things. Present in the act as public ceremony is, therefore, the quiet encouragement to citizens to touch the high things. We must remember that religion is not just one more private pursuit, such as watching television. Religion gives people an experience of human life and consciousness according to which they are not full human beings unless they restrain their bodily desires, care for their fellows, guide themselves by the light of the eternally important, and seek their fulfillment in participation in a community of common purpose, purpose not simply reducible to the agglomeration of private desires or interests of its members. At the least, religion tends to shape human characters who feel the need to do these things. As we have seen, the principle of natural rights and the institutional and social life that flows from it are the most authoritative and fundamental layer of our national life, with many salutary effects upon citizen character. But might we not also appreciate the greater depth and complexity that public religion and the public encouragement of private religion add to human character?

True, we stand for the separation of church and state, which finally determines authoritatively the limits of public religion. The various expressions of civil religion point to liberty, to be sure, as the principled foundation of the regime, but to a view of liberty that is itself pointed toward a kind of perfection. "Pointed toward perfection" is perhaps the appropriate term to describe the resulting blend of influences that the American civil religion places at the core of American nationality. Our principles and our Constitution do indeed prevent us from enforcing the kind of transcendent perfection defining the religious traditions. But they do not prevent us from reinforcing a shadow of that perfection in the beliefs and habits of our citizens.

America is not the perfect political society, so much so as to be *the* "light unto the nations." Its imperfections at times cause the concerned spectator to groan with weariness, fume with indignation, or lapse into silent despair. We should remember, though, that our own civil religion, rightly understood, prevents us from possessing the pride requisite to that haughty self-designation. But it also encourages us to strive to be worthy of emulation, as Washington in his Farewell Address suggested we might be if we hold true to the promise of our national life. Surely on that Memorial Day we were *a* "light unto the nations," for quietly the message shone forth: We are the nation that does not imprison the Jew or Moslem, burn the Protestant or Orthodox, disenfranchise the Catholic, execute the Bahai, expel the Buddhist, or banish the unbeliever. We are the nation that beckons them all to join hands to mourn a common loss. Yet we are also the nation that, as part of our nationality, allows our citizens to compose their hearts before Eternity. This fitting blend of freedom and dignity—call it by its simple name: nobility—is the promise of America's civil religion and of the constitutional republic of which it is a part.

Notes

1. *New York Times*, May 29, 1984.
2. Both read the same Bible and pray to the same God, and each

invokes His aid against the other. It may seem strange that any men should dare to ask a just God's assistance in wringing their bread from the sweat of other men's faces, but let us judge not, that we not be judged. The prayers of both could not be answered. That of neither has been answered fully. The Almighty has His own purposes. "Woe unto the world because of offenses; for it must needs be that offenses come, but woe to that man by whom the offense cometh." If we shall suppose that American slavery is one of those offenses which, in the providence of God, must needs come, but which, having continued through His appointed time, He now wills to remove, and that He gives to both North and South this terrible war as the woe due to those by whom the offense came, shall we discern therein any departure from those divine attributes which the believers in a living God always ascribe to Him? Fondly do we hope, fervently do we pray, that this mighty scourge of war may speedily pass away. Yet, if God wills that it continue until all the wealth piled by the bondsman's two hundred and fifty years of unrequited toil shall be sunk, and until every drop of blood drawn with the lash shall be paid by another drawn by the sword, as was said three thousand years ago, so still it must be said, 'The judgments of the Lord are true and righteous altogether." (*Documents in American History,* ed. Henry Steele Commager [New York: F. S. Crofts & Sons, 1943], pp. 442–43)

3. For a thorough discussion of the multiple sources of the Farewell Address, see Felix Gilbert, *To the Farewell Address: Ideas of Early American Foreign Policy* (Princeton, N.J.: Princeton University Press, 1961), pp. 120–22, 124–26.

4. John Marshall, *The Life of George Washington* (Fredericksburg, Va.: Citizens' Guild, 1929), p. 282.

5. Ibid., p. 305. Washington's First Inaugural address even more explicitly wore the cast of an invocation: see also Commager, *Documents in American History,* pp. 151–53. He was also quite open in his Farewell Address about the necessity of religious sentiment to preserve the nation:

And let us with caution indulge the supposition, that morality can be maintained without religion. Whatever may be conceded to the influence of refined education upon minds of peculiar structure— reason and experience both forbid us to expect that national morality can prevail in exclusion of religious principle. It is substantially true that virtue or morality is a necessary spring of popular government. The rule indeed extends with more or less force to every species of Free Government. Who that is a sincere friend to it, can look with indifference upon attempts to shake the foundation of the fabric? (Marshall, *Life of Washington,* pp. 295–96)

6. "The Declaration of Independence," in Commager, *Documents in American History,* pp. 100–102.

7. The fourth verse of the "Star-Spangled Banner":
And thus be it ever when free men shall stand
Betwixt their loved homes and the war's desolation;
Blessed with victory and peace, may the Heav'n rescued Land
Praise the Power that hath made and preserved them a nation.
Then conquer we must, when our cause it is just,
And this be our motto: "In God is Our Trust."

And the Star-Spangled Banner in triumph shall wave
O'er the Land of the Free, and the Home of the Brave.

8. For extended discussions of the idea of the constitution or regime applied to the United States, see Robert A. Goldwin, "Of Men and Angels," and Joseph Cropsey, "The United States as Regime," in Robert Horwitz, ed., *The Moral Foundations of the American Republic* (Charlottesville: University Press of Virginia, 1977). The latter has also been reprinted in Joseph Cropsey, *Political Philosophy and the Issues of Politics* (Chicago: University of Chicago Press, 1977).

9. Bellah, "Civil Religion in America," reprinted in Russell E. Richey and Donald G. Jones, eds., *American Civil Religion* (New York: Harper and Row, 1974).

10. See the comments on Bellah's originality by Jones and Richey in their introductory chapter, "The Civil Religion Debate," in *American Civil Religion*, especially pp. 3–5; see also John F. Wilson, "The Status of Civil Religion in America," pp. 3–10, in Elwyn A. Smith, ed., *The Religion of the Republic* (Philadelphia: Fortress Press, 1971). Bellah himself acknowledged that others had dealt previously with the issue, although somewhat "semiconsciously" and polemically, *American Civil Religion*, pp. 33–34.

11. Bellah, "Civil Religion in America," p. 21.

12. Ibid., p. 24.

13. Compare Will Herberg's essentially corroborative essay in the same volume, "America's Civil Religion: What It Is and Whence It Came," pp. 76–87:

> It is an organic structure of ideas, values, and beliefs that constitutes a faith common to Americans as Americans, and is genuinely operative in their lives; a faith that markedly influences, and is influenced by, the professed religions of Americans. Sociologically, anthropologically, it is *the* American religion, undergirding American national life and overarching American society, despite all indubitable differences of ethnicity, religion, section, culture, and class. And it is a civil religion in the strictest sense of the term. (pp. 77–78, especially note pp. 80, 82)

14. "The God of the civil religion is not only rather 'unitarian,' he is also on the austere side, much more related to order, law, and right than to salvation and love. Even though he is somewhat deist in cast, he is by no means simply a watchmaker God. He is actively interested and involved in history, with a special concern for America." Bellah, ibid., p. 28.

15. In American political theory, sovereignty rests, of course, with the people, but implicitly, and often explicitly, the ultimate sovereignty has been attributed to God. This is the meaning of the motto, "In God we trust," as well as the inclusion of the phrase "under God" in the pledge to the flag. . . . The will of the people is not itself the criterion of right and wrong. There is a higher criterion in terms of which this will can be judged right and wrong; it is possible that the people may be wrong. The president's obligation extends to the higher criterion. . . . When Kennedy says that "the rights of man come not from the generosity of the state but from the hand of God," he is stressing this point again. (Ibid., pp. 24–25)

16. Jean-Jacques Rousseau, *The Social Contract and the Discourses*, trans. G. D. H. Cole (London: Everyman, 1973), p. 271.

17. There is therefore a purely civil profession of faith of which the Sovereign should fix the articles, not exactly as religious dogmas, but as social sentiments without which a man cannot be a good citizen or a faithful subject. While it can compel no one to believe them, it can banish from the State whoever does not believe them—it can banish him, not for impiety, but as an anti-social being. . . .

The dogmas of civil religion ought to be few, simple, and exactly worded, without explanation or commentary. The existence of a mighty, intelligent, and beneficent Divinity, possessed of foresight and providence, the life to come, the happiness of the just, the punishment of the wicked, the sanctity of the social contract and the laws: these are its positive dogmas. Its negative dogmas I confine to one, intolerance, which is a part of the cults we have rejected. (Ibid., p. 276)

For an account tracing the origin of the concept to more ancient sources, see Michael P. Zuckert, *Locke and the Problem of Civil Religion*, Bicentennial Essay no. 6 (Claremont, Calif.: Claremont Institute for the Study of Statesmanship and Political Philosophy, 1984), pp. 3–4. Zuckert attributes the notion, through the reports and interpretation of St. Augustine, to Marcus Terentius Varro, a Roman thinker who drew a distinction between "natural" theology and "civil" theology.

18. Compare Herberg's comment, note 13 above.

19. "What makes civil religion different is that at this stage it . . . remains chiefly the product of the scholar's world; the man on the street would be surprised to learn of its existence or to know that he is one of its professors." Martin E. Marty, "Two Kinds of Civil Religion," in Richey and Jones, *American Civil Religion*, p. 141.

20. Bellah, "Civil Religion in America," p. 21.

21. Thinking analogically to the natural sciences, we may say that a synthesis stands in relationship to a syncretism as a molecular combination stands to a solution. The French sociologist Emile Durkheim attempted to apply a version of this distinction to social phenomena. Certain kinds of social and political arrangements create properties that did not exist before in the isolated individuals that compose the arrangement. The new properties are not simply reducible to a congeries of specific characteristics that existed in the individuals beforehand; they are new kinds of behavior with their own integrity, a new layer of reality. *The Rules of Sociological Method* (Glencoe: Free Press, 1938), pp. xlvii–xlix. Likewise, in the *Politics*, Aristotle distinguishes between the city, an association that introduces a new level of human reality, and an alliance or commercial market, which does not. *Politics*, Book I, 1252a, 1–20; Book II, 1261a, 23–30.

22. Bellah has intimated this in his description of the American civil religion as nonsalvational: "The God of the civil religion is . . . much more related to order, law, and right than to salvation and love." ("Civil Religion in

America," p. 28). It cannot offer what it does not possess; also, "There is no formal creed in the civil religion." (Ibid., p. 37)

23. This is not to say that the resulting blend of the civil religion does not exist in their consciousness or influence their characters and actions. The civil religion is not simply a scholarly construct imposed upon an amorphous reality; see also Marty, "Two Kinds of Civil Religion."

24. Walter Berns, *The First Amendment and the Future of American Democracy* (Chicago: Gateway Editions, 1985), pp. 15–21.

25. Compare Hobbes's own distinction between "knowledge" and "belief": *Leviathan*, ed. C. B. Macpherson (New York: Penguin Books, 1968), chap. 7, pp. 132–34; chap. 11, pp. 166–68.

26. Alexis de Tocqueville, *Democracy in America*, ed. J. P. Mayer (Garden City, N.Y.: Anchor Books, 1969), pp. 42–43.

27. Berns, *First Amendment*, pp. 2–3.

28. The concept of "religion-in-general" employed by many sociologists is useful for characterizing the common aspects of religious traditions; see, for example, the comments of Richey and Jones in their introduction to *American Civil Religion*.

29. See, for example, Tocqueville's discussion of the differences and similarities between the idea of rights and the idea of virtue, *Democracy in America*, pp. 237–40.

30. One may detect continued resonances between the biblical faiths and subsequent (and more radical) impulses of the Enlightenment in today's "liberation" theologies or in the way some religions have absorbed the derivative teachings of existentialism.

31. Tocqueville, *Democracy in America*, p. 295.

32. Ibid., p. 235.

33. For a clear discussion of the meaning of the "republican virtue" tradition and its contemporary relevance, see Richard John Neuhaus, *The Naked Public Square: Religion and Democracy in America*, 2d ed. (Grand Rapids, Mich.: William B. Eerdmans Publishing Co., 1984), pp. 136–43.

34. Tocqueville, *Democracy in America*, pp. 301–15, especially 313–14.

35. Ibid., pp. 290–301; "Religion, which never intervenes directly in the government of American society, should therefore be considered as the first of their political institutions, for although it did not give them the taste for liberty, it singularly facilitates their use thereof." (p. 292)

36. Even Tocqueville is ambiguous on this point, either because he has enveloped his political doctrine in a salutary public teaching about the necessity of religious faith, or because he genuinely never pushes the issue to theoretical consistency within *Democracy in America*. Initially, he argues that republican government cannot survive without a vibrant religious core to the political culture. At other times, he seems to suggest that "self-interest, rightly understood" *could* carry both an individual and a democratic nation. By "self-interest, rightly understood," Tocqueville means a wider or more sophisticated grasp of the web of consequences that flow out from one's actions. Well-constructed institutions could perhaps teach people to feel the

results of their behavior sufficiently, he intimates, to compel them to impose civilized behavior upon themselves. Ibid., pp. 525–28.

37. Bellah was much more sober in his evaluation of civil religion in the epilogue to the Richey and Jones anthology, printed in 1973, as he turned to an analysis of Richard Nixon's second inaugural address. Part of that sobriety derived from his judgment about the character of the Vietnam War:

> Better indeed it would be for us if President Nixon were not congratulating himself on peace with honor but were telling his people that this was America's most criminal war, for which we have already paid a terrible price and for which we will continue to pay the wages of sin for decades and generations to come. (p. 261)

Indeed, he was much more explicit about the militant strain of American civil religion:

> From that seed [of John Winthrop's words of 1630] would grow the terrible sense of righteousness in the face of our enemies that would allow Americans with a clean conscience to use the most dreadful weapons and tactics of the day—from the massacre of Indians to the lynching of Negroes to the atom-bombing of Japanese to the napalming of Vietnamese children. (p. 269)

Nevertheless, he did not fundamentally change his assessment of the existence and essentially positive role of the civil religion—as long as it did not lose its "transcendent" character. See also his extended development of this theme in *The Broken Covenant: American Civil Religion in Time of Trial* (New York: Seabury Press, 1975).

38. A. James Reichley, "Religion and the Future of American Politics," *Political Science Quarterly*, vol. 101, no. 1 (1986), pp. 23–48, especially pp. 47–48:

> But in their pluralism, the main threads of our religious tradition have fostered shared commitment to the sanctity of each human life, the individual's responsibility and need to establish caring relationships with other human beings, and the presence in the universe of transcendent moral authority and purpose. . . . The most important *social* function of the churches . . . is to breed and nurture the values out of which democracy grows.

39. Will Herberg, *Protestant, Catholic, Jew: An Essay in American Religious Sociology* (Garden City, N.Y.: Doubleday and Co., 1955), p. 260.

40. Attempting to fit the civil religion in the same government program with various sectarian goals risks breakdown of the national religious consensus, since the values of right and wrong are the essence of sectarian factionalism on issues from divorce to dancing and playing cards; from women's rights to drinking coffee and serving in the armed services; from abortion to transubstantiation. . . . To put these questions into a political realm makes for intractable disputes since matters of faith cannot be compromised, while compromise is the essence of politics. (Keith B. Richburg, "America Already Has a Civil Religion," *Washington Post*, September 8, 1985)

41. See, for example, N. J. Demerauth III and Rhys H. Williams, "Civil Religion in an Uncivil Society," *Annals of the American Academy of Political and Social Science* (July 1985), pp. 154–66.

42. Leonard W. Levy, "The Establishment Clause," chap. 4 of this vol.

43. It is certainly an interesting question whether religious differences on other matters of public policy have sharpened over the past thirty years. The explanation may have less to do with a fundamental transformation in American society than with the forced expression of certain moral and religious concerns on the level of national policy, given the tendency of the Supreme Court to invite the centralization of such concerns. Of course, the nationalization of the media and increased national mobility would have an influence on this issue.

44. Levy, "Establishment Clause."

45. U.S. Constitution, Art. IV, sec. 4.

46. On the potential breadth of the definition of republican government, see *Federalist* 39, *The Federalist*, ed. Clinton Rossiter (New York: New American Library, 1961), pp. 240–41.

47. The Butchers' Benevolent Association of New Orleans v. Crescent City Live-Stock Landing and Slaughter-House Co., 16 Wallace 36 (1873). Miller's trivialization of "privileges or immunities" to procedural access to the organs of the national government severed it from a tradition of interpretation stretching back to the Articles of Confederation and the original Constitution; see Raoul Berger, *Government by Judiciary: The Transformation of the Fourteenth Amendment* (Cambridge: Harvard University Press, 1977), pp. 37–49. In the major case in which the "privileges and immunities" clause of Article IV received attention, Corfield v. Coryell, 6 F. Cas. (no. 3230) 546 (C.C.E.D. Pa. 1823), Justice Washington interpreted the clause to oblige states to extend to citizens of other states the same "privileges and immunities" that it granted to its own citizens. Which ones? The "fundamental" ones. The overall effect of the clause in the constitutional system was to create a national floor of citizenship with attendant rights, which remained, nevertheless, somewhat implicit. As long as states retained the power to determine legal personhood, a national jurisdiction over the states' treatment of their own citizens stood in tension with the constitutional system, as evidenced by Chief Justice Taney's opinion in the *Dred Scott* decision (Dred Scott v. Sanford, 19 Howard 393). Accordingly, the Fourteenth Amendment corrected this situation by rendering state citizenship derivative of national citizenship, the latter determined by birth, the former by residence.

48. Levy, "Establishment Clause."

Appendix:
A Memorial and Remonstrance
(1785)

James Madison

To the Honorable the General Assembly
of
the Commonwealth of Virginia.

We, the subscribers, citizens of the said Commonwealth, having taken into serious consideration, a Bill printed by order of the last Session of General Assembly, entitled "A Bill establishing a provision for Teachers of the Christian Religion," and conceiving that the same, if finally armed with the sanctions of a law, will be a dangerous abuse of power, are bound as faithful members of a free State, to remonstrate against it, and to declare the reasons by which we are determined. We remonstrate against the said Bill,

    1. Because we hold it for a fundamental and undeniable truth, "that Religion or the duty which we owe to our Creator and the Manner of discharging it, can be directed only by reason and conviction, not by force or violence."[1] The Religion then of every man must be left to the conviction and conscience of every man; and it is the right of every man to exercise it as these may dictate. This right is in its nature an unalienable right. It is unalienable; because the opinions of men, depending only on the evidence contemplated by their own minds, cannot follow the dictates of other men: It is unalienable also, because what is here a right towards men, is a duty towards the Creator. It is the duty of every man to render to the Creator such homage, and such only, as he believes to be acceptable to him. This duty is precedent both in order of time and degree of obligation, to the claims of Civil Society. Before any man can be considered as a

member of Civil Society, he must be considered as a subject of the Governor of the Universe: And if a member of Civil Society, who enters into any subordinate Association, must always do it with a reservation of his duty to the general authority; much more must every man who becomes a member of any particular Civil Society, do it with a saving of his allegiance to the Universal Sovereign. We maintain therefore that in matters of Religion, no man's right is abridged by the institution of Civil Society, and that Religion is wholly exempt from its cognizance. True it is, that no other rule exists, by which any question which may divide a Society, can be ultimately determined, but the will of the majority; but it is also true, that the majority may trespass on the rights of the minority.

2. Because if religion be exempt from the authority of the Society at large, still less can it be subject to that of the Legislative Body. The latter are but the creatures and vicegerents of the former. Their jurisdiction is both derivative and limited: it is limited with regard to the co-ordinate departments, more necessarily is it limited with regard to the constituents. The preservation of a free government requires not merely, that the metes and bounds which separate each department of power may be invariably maintained; but more especially, that neither of them be suffered to overleap the great Barrier which defends the rights of the people. The Rulers who are guilty of such an encroachment, exceed the commission from which they derive their authority, and are Tyrants. The People who submit to it are governed by laws made neither by themselves, nor by an authority derived from them, and are slaves.

3. Because, it is proper to take alarm at the first experiment on our liberties. We hold this prudent jealousy to be the first duty of citizens, and one of [the] noblest characteristics of the late Revolution. The freemen of America did not wait till usurped power had strengthened itself by exercise, and entangled the question in precedents. They saw all the consequences in the principle, and they avoided the consequences by denying the principle. We revere this lesson too much, soon to forget it. Who does not see that the same authority which can establish Christianity, in exclusion of all other Religions, may establish with the same ease any particular sect of Christians, in exclusion of all other Sects? That the same authority which can force a citizen to contribute three pence only of his property for the support of any one establishment, may force him to conform to any other establishment in all cases whatsoever?

4. Because, the bill violates that equality which ought to be the basis of every law, and which is more indispensable, in proportion as the validity or expediency of any law is more liable to be impeached. If

"all men are by nature equally free and independent,"[2] all men are to be considered as entering into Society on equal conditions; as relinquishing no more, and therefore retaining no less, one than another, of their natural rights. Above all are they to be considered as retaining an "*equal* title to the free exercise of Religion according to the dictates of conscience."[3] Whilst we assert for ourselves a freedom to embrace, to profess and to observe the Religion which we believe to be of divine origin, we cannot deny an equal freedom to those whose minds have not yet yielded to the evidence which has convinced us. If this freedom be abused, it is an offence against God, not against man: To God, therefore, not to men, must an account of it be rendered. As the Bill violates equality by subjecting some to peculiar burdens; so it violates the same principle, by granting to others peculiar exemptions. Are the Quakers and Menonists the only sects who think a compulsive support of their religions unnecessary and unwarantable? Can their piety alone be intrusted with the care of public worship? Ought their Religions to be endowed above all others, with extraordinary privileges, by which proselytes may be enticed from all others? We think too favorably of the justice and good sense of these denominations, to believe that they either covet pre-eminencies over their fellow citizens, or that they will be seduced by them, from the common opposition to the measure.

5. Because the bill implies either that the Civil Magistrate is a competent Judge of Religious truth; or that he may employ Religion as an engine of Civil policy. The first is an arrogant pretension falsified by the contradictory opinions of Rulers in all ages, and throughout the world: The second an unhallowed perversion of the means of salvation.

6. Because the establishment proposed by the Bill is not requisite for the support of the Christian Religion. To say that it is, is a contradiction to the Christian Religion itself; for every page of it disavows a dependence on the powers of this world: it is a contradiction to fact; for it is known that this Religion both existed and flourished, not only without the support of human laws, but in spite of every opposition from them; and not only during the period of miraculous aid, but long after it had been left to its own evidence, and the ordinary care of Providence: Nay, it is a contradiction in terms; for a Religion not invented by human policy, must have pre-existed and been supported, before it was established by human policy. It is moreover to weaken in those who profess this Religion a pious confidence in its innate excellence, and the patronage of its Author; and to foster in those who still reject it, a suspicion that its friends are too conscious of its fallacies, to trust it to its own merits.

7. Because experience witnesseth that ecclesiastical establishments, instead of maintaining the purity and efficacy of Religion, have had a contrary operation. During almost fifteen centuries, has the legal establishment of Christianity been on trial. What have been its fruits? More or less in all places, pride and indolence in the Clergy; ignorance and servility in the laity; in both, superstition, bigotry and persecution. Enquire of the Teachers of Christianity for the ages in which it appeared in its greatest lustre; those of every sect, point to the ages prior to its incorporation with Civil policy. Propose a restoration of this primitive state in which its Teachers depended on the voluntary rewards of their flocks; many of them predict its downfall. On which side ought their testimony to have greatest weight, when for or when against their interest?

8. Because the establishment in question is not necessary for the support of Civil Government. If it be urged as necessary for the support of Civil Government only as it is a means of supporting Religion, and it be not necessary for the latter purpose, it cannot be necessary for the former. If Religion be not within [the] cognizance of Civil Government, how can its legal establishment be said to be necessary to civil Government? What influence in fact have ecclesiastical establishments had on Civil Society? In some instances they have been seen to erect a spiritual tyranny on the ruins of Civil authority; in many instances they have been seen upholding the thrones of political tyranny; in no instance have they been seen the guardians of the liberties of the people. Rulers who wished to subvert the public liberty, may have found an established clergy convenient auxiliaries. A just government, instituted to secure & perpetuate it, needs them not. Such a government will be best supported by protecting every citizen in the enjoyment of his Religion with the same equal hand which protects his person and his property; by neither invading the equal rights of any Sect, nor suffering any Sect to invade those of another.

9. Because the proposed establishment is a departure from that generous policy, which, offering an asylum to the persecuted and oppressed of every Nation and Religion, promised a lustre to our country, and an accession to the number of its citizens. What a melancholy mark is the Bill of sudden degeneracy? Instead of holding forth an asylum to the persecuted, it is itself a signal of persecution. It degrades from the equal rank of Citizens all those whose opinions in Religion do not bend to those of the Legislative authority. Distant as it may be, in its present form, from the Inquisition it differs from it only in degree. The one is the first step, the other the last in the career of intolerance. The magnanimous sufferer under this cruel scourge in

foreign Regions, must view the Bill as a Beacon on our Coast, warning him to seek some other haven, where liberty and philanthropy in their due extent may offer a more certain repose from his troubles.

10. Because, it will have a like tendency to banish our Citizens. The allurements presented by other situations are every day thinning their number. To superadd a fresh motive to emigration, by revoking the liberty which they now enjoy, would be the same species of folly which has dishonoured and depopulated flourishing kingdoms.

11. Because, it will destroy that moderation and harmony which the forbearance of our laws to intermeddle with Religion, has produced amongst its several sects. Torrents of blood have been spilt in the old world, by vain attempts of the secular arm to extinguish Religious discord, by proscribing all difference in Religious opinions. Time has at length revealed the true remedy. Every relaxation of narrow and rigorous policy, wherever it has been tried, has been found to assuage the disease. The American Theatre has exhibited proofs, that equal and compleat liberty, if it does not wholly eradicate it, sufficiently destroys its malignant influence on the health and prosperity of the State. If with the salutary effects of this system under our own eyes, we begin to contract the bonds of Religious freedom, we know no name that will too severely reproach our folly. At least let warning be taken at the first fruits of the threatened innovation. The very appearance of the Bill has transformed that "Christian forbearance,[4] love and charity," which of late mutually prevailed, into animosities and jealousies, which may not soon be appeased. What mischiefs may not be dreaded should this enemy to the public quiet be armed with the force of a law?

12. Because, the policy of the bill is adverse to the diffusion of the light of Christianity. The first wish of those who enjoy this precious gift, ought to be that it may be imparted to the whole race of mankind. Compare the number of those who have as yet received it with the number still remaining under the dominion of false Religions; and how small is the former! Does the policy of the Bill tend to lessen the disproportion? No; it at once discourages those who are strangers to the light of [revelation] from coming into the Region of it; and countenances, by example the nations who continue in darkness, in shutting out those who might convey it to them. Instead of levelling as far as possible, every obstacle to the victorious progress of truth, the Bill with an ignoble and unchristian timidity would circumscribe it, with a wall of defence, against the encroachments of error.

13. Because attempts to enforce by legal sanctions, acts obnoxious to so great a proportion of Citizens, tend to enervate the laws in general, and to slacken the bands of Society. If it be difficult to execute

any law which is not generally deemed necessary or salutary, what must be the case where it is deemed invalid and dangerous? and what may be the effect of so striking an example of impotency in the Government, on its general authority.

14. Because a measure of such singular magnitude and delicacy ought not to be imposed, without the clearest evidence that it is called for by a majority of citizens: and no satisfactory method is yet proposed by which the voice of the majority in this case may be determined, or its influence secured. "The people of the respective counties are indeed requested to signify their opinion respecting the adoption of the Bill to the next Session of Assembly." But the representation must be made equal, before the voice either of the Representatives or of the Counties, will be that of the people. Our hope is that neither of the former will, after due consideration, espouse the dangerous principle of the Bill. Should the event disappoint us, it will still leave us in full confidence, that a fair appeal to the latter will reverse the sentence against our liberties.

15. Because, finally, "the equal right of every citizen to the free exercise of his Religion according to the dictates of conscience" is held by the same tenure with all our other rights. If we recur to its origin, it is equally the gift of nature; if we weigh its importance, it cannot be less dear to us; if we consult the Declaration of those rights which pertain to the good people of Virginia, as the "basis and foundation of Government,"[5] it is enumerated with equal solemnity, or rather studied emphasis. Either then, we must say, that the will of the Legislature is the only measure of their authority; and that in the plentitude of this authority, they may sweep away all our fundamental rights; or, that they are bound to leave this particular right untouched and sacred: Either we must say, that they may controul the freedom of the press, may abolish the trial by jury, may swallow up the Executive and Judiciary Powers of the State; nay that they may despoil us of our very right of suffrage, and erect themselves into an independant and hereditary assembly: or we must say, that they have no authority to enact into law the Bill under consideration. We the subscribers say, that the General Assembly of this Commonwealth have no such authority: And that no effort may be omitted on our part against so dangerous an usurpation, we oppose to it, this remonstrance; earnestly praying, as we are in duty bound, that the Supreme Lawgiver of the Universe, by illuminating those to whom it is addressed, may on the one hand, turn their councils from every act which would affront his holy prerogative, or violate the trust committed to them: and on the other, guide them into every measure which may be worthy of his [blessing, may re]dound to their own praise, and may